THINKING,
REASONING,
and WRITING

LONGMAN SERIES IN
COLLEGE COMPOSITION AND COMMUNICATION

Harvey S. Wiener, Series Editor

THINKING, REASONING, and WRITING

Elaine P. Maimon

Barbara F. Nodine

Finbarr W. O'Connor

Longman
New York & London

Thinking, Reasoning, and Writing *808.042*
T348
89-0600

Longman Inc., 95 Church Street, White Plains, N.Y. 10601

Associated companies:
Longman Group Ltd., London
Longman Cheshire Pty., Melbourne
Longman Paul Pty., Auckland
Copp Clark Pitman, Toronto
Pitman Publishing Inc., New York

Executive editor: Gordon T.R. Anderson
Production editor: Marie-Josée A. Schorp
Cover design: Kevin C. Kall
Text art: Hal Keith
Production supervisor: Kathleen M. Ryan

Library of Congress Cataloging-in-Publication Data

Thinking, reasoning, and writing.

(Longman series in college composition and communication)
Bibliography: p.
Includes index.
1. English language—Rhetoric—Study and teaching. 2. Critical thinking—Study and
teaching. 3. Reasoning—Study and teaching. I. Maimon, Elaine P. II. Nodine,
Barbara F. III. O'Connor, Finbarr W. IV. Series.
PE1404.T48 1988 808'.042'07 88-9261
ISBN 0-582-28604-2

89 90 91 92 93 94 9 8 7 6 5 4 3 2 1

Contents

Preface

Thinking, Reasoning, and Writing brings together essays on the teaching of thinking from the perspectives of three fields: cognitive psychology, logic, and composition. Each of the three volume editors represents one of the fields in question: Barbara Nodine, psychology; Finbarr O'Connor, philosophy; Elaine Maimon, composition. We found in our own conversation the first impetus for this volume. From 1981 to 1984, a grant from the Fund for the Improvement of Post Secondary Education (FIPSE) allowed us to extend this conversation to include colleagues nationally who were trying to rethink thinking. In addition, the 11 conferences on writing and thinking sponsored by the University of Chicago further confirmed our impression of widespread interest in ways to teach thinking.

We decided that our primary audience for this volume would be composition instructors, since we had sufficient evidence that they were hungriest for insight into the process of thinking—composition instructors have constituted the largest group, by far, in attendance at the University of Chicago conferences. But we also determined to make this collection readable to the non-composition specialist, as well as to the non-specialist in psychology and applied logic. We tested general readability by holding a conference for the authors (sponsored by FIPSE) to read and discuss drafts of each essay. This conference also allowed us to identify intersections among the fields in question. At this meeting, the composition specialists and psychologists discovered that a quiet revolution, analogous to the one in composition studies, had been proceeding simultaneously among the logicians. Both revolutions, in composition and in logic, brought us closer to the psychologists' concern with applications to the classroom.

Bringing the people and perspectives from various disciplines together has involved complicated planning, in which we have had much help. We are grateful to FIPSE for the funds that made cross-disciplinary conversations possible. With limited resources—severely limited in the 1980s— FIPSE has purchased much with its federal dollars.

Joseph Williams, Professor of English at the University of Chicago, and Carol Schneider, now Vice President of the American Association of Colleges and for several years Deputy Director of Continuing Education at the University of Chicago, deserve thanks from the several thousand participants in the University of Chicago conferences on critical thinking. They provided a meeting ground on the shores of Lake Michigan for many of the authors included in this volume. More important, they helped set the agenda for the 1980s in many colleges and universities in the United States.

A timely advance from Longman allowed several of the authors to meet in Philadelphia to review early drafts. Special thanks to T. Gordon Anderson, our editor and friend, for his imagination, flexibility, confidence, and patience.

Thanks, too, to Donald McQuade, Professor of English at the University of California/Berkeley, and to Carol Waldman, Senior Project Director at the Strategic Marketing Corporation, for joining the authors and sharing their responses with us. Jenny Hnatuk and Marie Lawrence kept track of complicated logistics, typed, retyped, and encouraged.

We thank our families, who did without us during precious weekend moments, especially during the time when one of us was commuting from Providence, so that we could devote time to this volume. Finally, we thank each other for the capacity to work together in this decade after our first partnership. Such sustained colleagueship lights our middle years.

About the Contributors

Michael Basseches is a psychologist specializing in cognitive and personality development in adolescence and adulthood. He received his Ph.D. from Harvard in 1978, and subsequent clinical training at Tufts Counseling Center, Clark University, and the South Shore Mental Health Center. His work has been devoted to both researching and facilitating processes of human development in the contexts of higher education, the workplace, and psychotherapy. He is the author of *Dialectical Thinking and Adult Development* (Ablex, 1984), as well as of numerous published articles dealing with these three contexts. He has served on the faculties of Swarthmore College, Cornell University, and the Massachusetts School of Professional Psychology. Currently he is on the staff of the Bureau of Study Counsel at Harvard University, where he provides academic and personal counseling for students, consults to faculty and teaching fellows on the teaching and learning process, and conducts research on student development. He also co-directs the Extern Program at the Clinical-Developmental Institute in Belmont, MA, and maintains a private practice in psychotherapy, supervision of psychotherapy, and developmental consultation to colleges and workplaces.

J. Anthony Blair is Professor of Philosophy at the University of Windsor, Ontario, Canada. He is co-editor of the journal, *Informal Logic*, co-author of the textbook, *Logical Self-Defense* (2nd ed., McGraw-Hill Ryerson, 1983), and co-editor of the proceedings of the 1978 International Symposium on Informal Logic (Edgepress, 1980) and of the three-volume proceedings of the 1986 Amsterdam Conference on Argumentation (Foris,

1987). He has published numerous articles on the theory and the teaching of informal logic, critical thinking, and argumentation, and presented numerous workshops on their teaching and application. He teaches informal logic, ethics, political philosophy, and the philosophy of education. His current research is on the normative theory of argument cogency.

Kenneth A. Bruffee is Professor of English and Director of the Honors Program at Brooklyn College. His publications include *Elegaic Romance: Cultural Change and Loss of the Hero in Modern Fiction* (Cornell UP, 1983), *A Short Course in Writing* 3rd ed. (Little, Brown, 1985), and a series of articles in *Liberal Education* and *College English* on collaborative learning, liberal education, and the authority of knowledge. He has led colloquia on those subjects at Bard College, Brown University , Bucknell University, New York University, University of Minnesota, University of Pennsylvania, and Yale University, and at the Woodrow Wilson Foundation Workshop on Interpreting the Humanities at Princeton University.

Jerry B. Cederblom is Associate Professor at the University of Nebraska at Omaha. In 1974, he helped design a course in critical reasoning which he has taught regularly for the Goodrich Scholarship Program as a part of its innovative core curriculum. He also teaches courses in ethical theory and epistemology for the Department of Philosophy. He is co-author and co-editor of *Justice and Punishment* (Ballinger, 1977), and is co-author of *Critical Reasoning* (Wadsworth, 1982, 2d ed. 1986). He is completing a new book, *Ethics at Work*. He has been active in consulting, lecturing, and conducting workshops on critical thinking across the curriculum.

Linda Flower is Professor of Rhetoric at Carnegie Mellon. As Co-Director of the Center for the Study of Writing at Berkeley and Carnegie Mellon, she is conducting research which will appear in *Reading-to-Write: Studying a Cognitive and Social Process* on the way strategic knowledge in writing affects students' transition into academic discourse. As director of the Making Thinking Visible project with Pittsburgh schools and colleges, she is working with a group of teacher-research teams to teach strategies for collaborative planning and engage students and teachers in exploring their own planning processes. Author of *Problem Solving Strategies for Writing* (Harcourt, Brace, Jovanovich, 1987), she has published numerous papers on cognition, writing, and reading, including "Detection, Diagnosis and the Strategies of Revision," which won the 1987 Braddock Award.

Bridget A. Franks is a doctoral candidate in developmental psychology at the University of Nebraska-Lincoln and a certified school psychologist. Her research interests include cognitive development, reading comprehension, and logical inferences in reading and writing. She is currently involved in a developmental study of the ability to make various types of deductive inferences based on premises in prose passages. She is also interested in exploring ways in which our knowledge of developmental processes can be of use in affecting social and educational policies.

Janice Haney-Peritz is Associate Professor of English at Beaver College, where she teaches undergraduate and graduate courses in academic writing, the principles of written communication, contemporary critical discourse, and 19th century literature. As chairperson of Beaver's English department, she instituted a M.A. in English program designed to bridge the gap between advanced literary study and composition theory, and practice. Besides conducting college-level workshops on writing to learn, she has participated in two major projects to improve literacy education in Philadelphia area public and parochial schools. Her publications include articles on rhetorical politics, romantic irony, allegorical indeterminacy, feminist criticism, and the sexual politics of novelistic discourse. Currently she is working on two projects: the MLA sponsored *Romantic Movement Bibliography* edited by David Erdman and a study of the sexual politics of 18th and 19th century literary discourse in England.

Ralph H. Johnson is Professor of Philosophy and Head of the Department of Philosophy at the University of Windsor, Ontario, Canada. He is co-editor of the journal, *Informal Logic*, co-author of the textbook, *Logical Self-Defense* (2nd ed., McGraw-Hill Ryerson, 1983), and co-editor of the proceedings of the 1978 International Symposium on Informal Logic (Edgepress, 1980). He has published numerous articles on informal logic, and presented workshops and seminars on the teaching of critical thinking and informal logic. His current research is on the relationship of cognitive psychology and informal logic, and he is currently at work on a theory of reasoning.

James L. Kinneavy is Jane and Roland Blumberg Centennial Professor of English at The University of Texas at Austin. He is author of nine books, including *A Study of Three Contemporary Theories of the Lyric* (Catholic University of America, 1956), *A Theory of Discourse* (Prentice-Hall, 1971; Norton, 1980), *Writing in the Liberal Arts Tradition (Harper, 1985), and Greek Rhetorical Origins of Christian Faith: An Inquiry* (Oxford, 1988). He has also published numerous articles and chapters of books on contemporary rhetoric, the history of rhetoric, and the history of composition.

Elaine P. Maimon is Professor of English and Dean of Experimental Programs at Queens College, City University of New York. Before going to Queens she was Associate Dean of the College at Brown University, where she taught graduate courses in composition theory and practice. Formerly Associate Vice President and Professor of English at Beaver College, she initiated and directed one of the nation's first programs in writing across the curriculum. An active consultant, she planned and implemented the Writing Across the University program at the University of Pennsylvania, her alma mater for the B.A., M.A., and Ph.D. degrees in English. Widely published in numerous scholarly journals, she is also a co-author of *Writing in the Arts and Sciences* (Little, Brown, 1982) and co-editor of *Readings in the Arts and Sciences* (Little, Brown, 1984).

David Moshman received his Ph.D. in developmental psychology from Rutgers University in 1977 and is currently Associate Professor of Educational Psychology at the University of Nebraska-Lincoln. Co-author of *Developmental Psychology* (Little, Brown, 1987), Moshman teaches an introduction to developmental psychology and graduate courses in adolescent psychology and cognitive development. He has published numerous articles and chapters on the development of reasoning, especially during adolescence and beyond, and on the nature and development of rationality. Also interested in the role of the First Amendment in promoting rationality, Moshman is the editor of *Children's Intellectual Rights* (Jossey-Bass, 1986), author of *Children, Education, and the First Amendment: A Psycholegal Analysis* (University of Nebraska Press, forthcoming), and President of the Nebraska Civil Liberties Union.

Edith D. Neimark is Professor of Psychology at Rutgers University. She is the author of *Adventures in Thinking* (Harcourt Brace Jovanovich, 1987) and an editor of *Moderators of Competence* (Erlbaum, 1985). She has served as a member of the Board of Trustees of the Jean Piaget Society. She is currently teaching a course in effective thinking that tries to put into practice some of the recommendations proposed in her chapter in this volume and, more extensively, in *Adventures in Thinking*. Her current research examines the development of evaluative criteria.

Barbara F. Nodine is Professor of Psychology at Beaver College. She is co-author of *Writing in the Arts and Sciences* (Little, Brown, 1982) and co-editor of *Readings in the Arts and Sciences* (Little, Brown, 1984). She is guest editor of a special issue, "Written Language" *Topics in Learning and Learning Disabilities* (October 1983). A Fellow of the American Psychological Association and past president of its Division on Teaching, she has served as an external evaluator of psychology departments and as a member of several committees on undergraduate education, and has conducted workshops on writing across the curriculum at dozens of universities. Her current research is on children's oral and written composition.

Finbarr W. O'Connor is Associate Professor of Philosophy at Beaver College. He is co-author of *Writing in the Arts and Sciences* (Little, Brown, 1982) and co-editor of *Deviance and Decency: The Ethics of Research with Human Subjects* (Sage, 1979), *Readings in the Arts and Sciences* (Little, Brown, 1984), and *Morality, Philosophy, and Practice: Historical and Contemporary Readings and Studies* (Random House, 1988). He has written articles in ethics, political philosophy, and problem solving. His current research is on William Ockham's role in the development of the concept of natural rights.

James F. Voss is Professor of Psychology at the University of Pittsburgh and also Associate Director of the Learning Research and Development Center of that institution. In recent years Dr. Voss has published a number of papers on expert and novice differences, with emphasis being placed upon the nature of such differences as found in problem solving and reasoning in social sciences.

Joseph Williams is Professor of English at the University of Chicago. He received his B.A. and M.A. in English from Miami University, Oxford, Ohio, and his Ph.D. in English and Linguistics from the University of Wisconsin-Madison. He is currently Professor of English and Linguistics at the University of Chicago, and Director of University Writing Programs. For the last four years, he has been Co-Director of the series of bi-annual Institutes held at the University of Chicago on higher order thinking, writing, cognitive development, and other educational issues. He is author of *Origins of the English Language*, *Style*, and co-editor with Timothy Shopen of *Standards and Dialects* and *Style and Variables*. He has published numerous articles on stylistics, discourse anlaysis, history of the English language, and on other language-related topics.

Introduction

After worrying in the 1960s and 1970s that Johnny and Janey can't read or write, educators in the 1980s concluded that the real problem is that students can't think. Upon reaching that conclusion, some educators have decided to reclose the golden door of open access to education and to emphasize "excellence." Others, more committed perhaps to Jeffersonian educational principles, have wondered whether it might not be possible to reimagine education itself in the hope of finding ways to teach students to think. If thinking itself, can be taught, then the conflict between excellence and access becomes moot. Every young citizen, regardless of family background or socioeconomic class, could find in the schools opportunities to learn the rituals and processes associated with educated behavior. Students would be no more defined and confined by initial I.Q. scores than by other accidents of birth.

Such goals of educational reform have led us to the following fundamental questions: What *is* thinking? Can we *teach* students to think, and if so, how do we do it? What experts should we consult? What fields of scholarship illuminate the workings of the human mind and shed light on appropriate ways for educators to intervene? How will the teaching of writing be influenced by scholarship in these areas?

We have concluded that three fields stand out in their systematic investigations of thinking: cognitive psychology, informal logic, and composition. The object of this volume is to bring together essays on thinking from these three fields and to point out, where appropriate, the agreements and conflicts among scholars who have, for the most part, been reading different bibliographies, doing different kinds of research, and publishing in different journals.

Why would teachers of composition be interested in this research? There are two reasons: first, composition studies in the last 20 years have been revolutionized from a preoccupation with surfaces to an examination of the connections between writing and thinking; second, writing teachers who can no longer escape to the surface of students' prose discover that their work concerns itself ineluctably with thinking made visible. Instructors who do not assign writing can play "Let's Pretend," as Richard Lanham, Professor of English at UCLA, calls the belief that students are thinking when they appear marginally attentive at lectures. Writing teachers see their students' writing on the morning after the brilliant lecture. Writing teachers, to the general detriment of their sanity, cannot play "Let's Pretend."

We have selected the tripartite title *Thinking, Reasoning, and Writing* with the idea that each term approximates the general approach to cognition taken by one of the three major disciplines represented in this text. We assign the most general and undifferentiated term, *thinking,* to the psychologists because their concern is with intellectual activity in all its manifestations. For the hundred years or so that psychology has been a separate area of study, parents and teachers have consulted psychologists on questions about how students learn. Psychologists have responded with systematic studies of memory, perception, and intellectual development— all components of what the layperson might call thinking. The field of cognitive psychology, which has developed its own bibliography in the last 30 years, has looked more particularly at the complex interactions of mental processes, some observable and some not.

Reasoning is the term we have selected to represent the approach of the logicians because of the long association of reasoning with the systematic expression of thought that we identify as rational explanation, good sense, and judgment. Logicians, whether their work is in symbolic, informal, or applied logic, are concerned with structured thinking. Although logic is older than psychology, it is only since the late 1960s, with the emergence of informal logic, that logicians have returned to concern themselves with the pedagogical implications of their study. Non-specialists may always have harbored the hope that the ability to decipher the mysteries of p's and q's would lead somehow to improved thought processes, but logicians themselves have until quite recently disclaimed any such utility. The logicians in this book openly seek ways to apply instruction in the structured thinking that we call reasoning to useful capacities in the world beyond the syllogism.

Writing, the title of the third part, does not designate merely what thinking and reasoning are to be applied to. We join contemporary composition theorists in denying the division between thought and its expression, although *Thought and Expression* was until recently one of the most popular titles for the college freshman composition course on numerous campuses. We are convinced that writing is epistemic, and we see the composition classroom fundamentally as a workshop in the teaching of thinking. We are likewise committed to the teaching of writing across the curriculum because we see such instruction as teaching thinking across the curriculum.

We are also aware that the three fields represented in the three parts of this book are neither unified within themselves nor entirely distinct one from another. In fact, cognitive psychology, logic, and composition have been silently borrowing from each other for a long time. In the 1970s, the interactions between cognitive psychology and composition theory have been overt. In this text, Linda Flower's essay would fit just as comfortably in the *Thinking* section as it does in *Writing*. Collaboration between logic and psychology or between logic and composition has been less frequent. Yet most composition texts still refer to induction and deduction, and those texts that are more up-to-date give a nod toward Steven Toulmin and other contemporary logicians.

We represent the collaboration—actual and potential—among the three disciplines by adding to each part's introduction commentary from the perspective of the other two disciplines. Thus, after we introduce the material written by the psychologists in *Thinking*, we propose ways that logicians and composition theorists would respond. In *Reasoning*, we propose ways that psychologists and composition scholars would respond. And in *Writing*, we propose the applications, connections, and demurs of the psychologists and logicians. In each case, the commentaries, written by the editors, are based on conversations among the authors of the essays. We hope that readers will find additional intersections and continue the conversation.

As you read these dozen papers from three disciplines, you will find differences in approach, in terminology, and in presentation. But each of the disciplines contends with issues that transcend its section of the book. Among these, we select for your attention three that we see as fundamental.

One issue is whether thinking or reasoning is a unitary subject or multiple. Is the problem sloganized as "Johnny and Janey can't think" to be diagnosed as a lack in Johnny and Janey of some one fundamental capacity or of some one skill, or is it due to a multiple incapacity? For some educators, of course, the diagnosis is lack of information. But it is probably more common these days to deny that one teaches thinking *tout court*. Instead, the prevailing view in education seems to prefer a "thinking as" approach: thinking *as* a historian, *as* a scientist, *as* a literary critic. Law schools like to say lawyers think differently from the rest of us—at least while they are practicing law.

It is evident that how this issue is settled has immediate implications for how a curriculum is structured—if historians *qua* historians think differently from scientists, a complete curriculum should include both subjects; if biologists *qua* biologists think differently from chemists, again, both biology and chemistry should be included. Indeed, so evident are the implications that a cynic will be tempted to interpret thinking-as claims as mere rhetorical counters in political battles over curricular turf.[1]

In fact, however, there is more to it. This issue has bedeviled epistemology from its beginning. James Kinneavy's essay finds in the classical tradition a strong preference for the thinking-as thesis. Yet even Plato himself did not speak in one voice on this issue. Whereas Kinneavy looks to some of the other dialogues to place Plato on the side of multiplicity of kinds of thinking (and writing), in the *Republic* Plato seems to have taken the unitary view, at least in his claim that knowledge is hierarchical, all forms of it being ultimately dependent on the ruling dialectic. By contrast, Aristotle thought there were autonomous structures of knowledge.[2] Thus mathematics has its own axioms and theorems, different from those of physics or biology. It is, says Aristotle, a gross error to expect from political science the same degree of precision appropriate to mathematics. But as Kinneavy shows, Aristotle failed to put the issue to rest. And, indeed, he bequeathed to us the question whether the autonomy of disciplines implies autonomous kinds of thinking.[3]

Where philosophers tend to debate the issue in terms of knowledge structure, and rhetoricians, language structure, psychologists have entered the debate with their own terminology and approach. On the one hand, expert-novice research (discussed here by James Voss) offers a way to study how "thinking as X" differs from "thinking as Y." On the other hand, Edith Neimark's conception of the "mature thinker" seeks a characterization, albeit multidimensional, that will transcend disciplinary differences. Neimark's view takes in personality differences, expectations, style of learning, and developmental capacities. Clearly, the debate has moved far from the consideration of merely the structure of knowledge.

A second issue involves a distinction between two kinds of knowledge. Two versions of such a distinction appear in this volume. Janice Haney-Peritz distinguishes between what she calls knowledge and knowing "how to." This is reminiscent of Gilbert Ryle's philosophical distinction of "knowing that" and "knowing how," and of the psychologist's distinction between, on the one hand, conceptual or factual knowledge, and on the other, procedural knowledge.

A second distinction involves distinct *levels* of knowledge and is associated with the term *metacognition* as used by developmental psychologists. The capacity to use a cognitive strategy without knowing how or when to invoke it constitutes the lower, or merely cognitive, level. The metacognitive level involves the ability to monitor and manipulate those intellectual strategies for thinking, remembering, and problem solving. Conscious deployment of strategies is a theme you will find in Neimark's identification of the mature thinker as "detached," in Jerry Cederblom's "willingness to reason," Voss's and Flower's discussions of expert strategies, and Finbarr O'Connor's definition of logical thinking as methodical.

When considering the educational consequences of such distinctions it may be illuminating to think of them as providing contemporary versions of the classic content versus method controversy. When so framed, we may expect arguments couched in terms of "sacrifice," as when curriculum debates took the form of inquiring how much content should be sacrificed for more method. Readers from composition should find in this an echo of the familiar objection, "How can I teach writing when I have so much content to cover?" Although the authors in this volume may differ on what is being contrasted to "content"—whether it is termed "know-how" or "metacognition" or just "strategies"—all seem to agree that we do not have the option of "just" teaching content.

A third issue raises the question of the degree to which we should consider knowledge and learning (and therefore thinking and reasoning) a social, rather than individual, phenomenon. No one will deny that knowledge is social in the sense that its sources are social (we learn from others), in the sense that we learn by language and language is social. What is controversial is whether what counts as knowledge is dependent on some community agreement or acknowledgment. The point at issue might be made, again, through Aristotle. He distinguishes the "demonstrative" syllogism and the "dialectical" syllogism. The former represents the kind of reasoning deployed in formulating the structure and conclusions of a scientific discipline. Its premises, he says, must be certain. By contrast, the dialectical syllogism is based on premises that are less than certain—Aristotle's word is *endoxon*. Conclusions reached dialectically do represent knowledge, but not scientific knowledge. Now, *endoxon* is capable of two interpretations. First, it could mean "probable." And "probable" need not have any connection to community agreement—the probability of winning a lottery is independent of what people think it is. On the other hand, *endoxon* could also be translated as "reputable," that is, what others will find reasonable relative to the state of opinion on the subject at the moment.[4] Now, an important component of contemporary informal logic is the question of credibility of premises (see J. Anthony Blair and Ralph H. Johnson). To the extent that credibility is determined by the state of opinion on the subject, and not by the state of "reality," informal logic can find a place to acknowledge social aspects of knowledge.

In this volume, Kenneth Bruffee takes a strong social constructionist view, as does Haney-Peritz. Similarly Michael Basseches is critical of standard developmentalist psychology for its inadequate consideration of the interplay between individual and society.

The idea that knowledge is dependent in any way on community agreement has, of course, political as well as epistemological dimensions. But then what constitutes a community? This volume suggests that the lines between psychologists and logicians, logicians and composition specialists are blurred. When we concern ourselves with the teaching of thinking, we cannot limit ourselves to a mere searching for the distinct patterns of thought engaged in by a psychologist, a logician, or a writer. What we want to teach and learn is how to think as a citizen of this complex planet.

As Cifford Geertz reminds us, we live in an age of "blurred genres," leading, or so he thinks, to the "refiguration of social thought." We hope that this text contributes to better ways of seeing this new refiguration. "Blurring" is not muddling, which implies the confusion of a junkyard. "Blurring," in its panoramic sense, implies a rainbow of colors—signaling connection and a bright future. We hope that *Thinking, Reasoning, and Writing* will help us see the disciplinary spectrum as a rainbow.

NOTES

1. That such arguments can be quite explicitly political can be observed in a famous confrontation in 17th-century England, when Edward Coke countered King James's assertion of royal authority over the law with the thinking-as claim that only lawyers are competent to interpret the law. In Coke's version of their confrontation, the king argued that "the law was founded upon reason, and that he and others had reason as well as the judge." To which Coke responded that the law is not a matter of "natural reason" but "artificicial reason," which "is an art which requires long study and experience, before that a man can attain to the cognizance of it." Historians see in this appeal by Coke a pivotal moment for the development of parliamentary power against the king. (Quoted in Pound 187).
2. For some scholars, this marks a profound difference between Plato and Aristotle. "One of Aristotle's most important contributions to human thought was the idea that demarcation lines can be drawn between different departments of expertise and that nothing is thereby lessened in the expertise of each distinct expert. In this his opposition to Plato is fundamental. For Plato believed that to know anything in the fullest sense it is necessary to know everything" (Evans 7).
3. In 20th-century philosophy, one might see Dewey as taking something like the Platonic position—in his view of *inquiry* as *the* method of intelligence. The most strikingly contrasting view—roughly parallel to Aristotle's—is the "forms of knowledge" school in philosophy of education (see Hirst).
4. Weil objects to the "probability interpretation" of *endoxon* and argues for "ac-

cepted" or "current theses." "Aristotle is concerned with the state of human knowledge at a given point in history—the point at which new investigations are being embarked upon.... Such a thesis is probable or plausible by virtue of its position in the intellectual life of the community" (97).

WORKS CITED

Evans, J.D.G. *Aristotle's Concept of Dialectic*. New York: Cambridge University Press, 1977.

Geertz, Clifford. *Local Knowledge*. New York: Basic Books, 1983.

Hirst, Paul H. *Knowledge and the Curriculum*. Boston: Routledge & Kegan Paul, 1974.

Pound, Roscoe, and Theodore Plucknett, eds. *Readings on the History and System of the Common Law*, 3rd ed. Rochester, NY: Lawyers Co-operative, 1927.

Ryle, Gilbert. "Knowing How and Knowing That." *Proceedings of the Aristotelian Society* 46 (1946): 1–16.

Weil, E. "The Place of Logic in Aristotle's Thought." *Science*. Vol. 1 of *Articles on Aristotle*. Ed. Jonathan Barnes, Malcolm Schofield, and Richard Sorabji. London: Duckworth, 1975. 88–112.

PART 1

Thinking

FROM THE PERSPECTIVE OF PSYCHOLOGISTS

In the period from about 1955 to 1970 American psychology underwent a profound transformation. The prevailing theoretical view had been *behaviorism,* an approach that focused on observable behavior and dismissed the study of mental processes as inherently unscientific. Although behaviorism continues to have some important practical applications, psychological theory and research are now highly *cognitive*; the direct study of thinking is widely viewed as important and scientifically feasible.

There are currently two major approaches to cognitive psychology. One, the information-processing approach, focuses on relatively specific skills, strategies, or abilities, with particular emphasis on how experts and novices process information in various domains of knowledge. The other approach, often labeled *developmental* or *Piagetian*, emphasizes the successive emergence of general stages of intellectual development.

The first two chapters of this part represent the developmental tradition, with particular emphasis on later stages of development. David Moshman and Bridget Franks describe Piaget's general theory of cognitive development, his postulation of the formal operations stage of development, and equilibration, the mechanism that Piaget postulated as the source of change from one stage to another. They also discuss more recent theories of how students develop in their conceptions about the nature of knowledge. In the second chapter Basseches postulates a stage of dialectical operations that develops later than Piaget's final stage. Although controversial, the notion of dialectical thinking is an enrichment of more traditional developmental models.

Chapter 3, by James Voss, considers problem solving from the perspective of information processing, including detailed analysis of expert and novice strategies. Voss's research is distinctive by the attention he devotes to "ill-structured" problems. Most of the work in cognitive psychology has concentrated on how well-structured problems are solved in areas such as physics—defining the methods used by and the differences between experts and novices at work in these areas. A "well-structured" problem is one for which all components are provided and a single clear answer can be obtained. By contrast, "ill-structured" problems are ones in which one or more of the components are left undefined—for example, the goal of the problem might be left unstated, or the goal might be stated but no information provided on how to reach that goal. Voss also discusses "strong" and "weak" methods of solving a problem, a weak method being a general method capable of being used to solve a wide variety of problems. Though the terminology "ill-structured" problems and "weak" methods might appear pejorative, in fact the domains of Voss's research are exactly the areas of most concern to educators in the social sciences and the humanities. A good example of an ill-structured problem is the task of writing a job application. It has no unique solution path and we are confined to weak methods (e.g., break the problem up into subproblems). Voss explores the role of knowledge or expertise in solving these problems and the complex relationship of this knowledge to the methods use by persons of varying levels of expertise.

Chapter 4 is more sweeping. Most psychologists would probably agree that although there are major theoretical differences between the developmental and information-processing perspectives, in many ways they are complementary. If we consider the thinker from both points of view, we are in a better position to understand his or her thinking or writing. Neimark draws on both developmental and information-processing considerations as well as on studies of cognitive style to posit a model of the mature thinker.

The above paragraphs situate the four chapters of this part by their orientations within the field of psychology. But since the discipline of psychology attaches such importance to empirical observations it is worth distinguishing them also with respect to the empirical base on which they rest. The Piagetian approach has a wealth of empirical research associated with it, although the results are not entirely consistent. Perry's theory, and that of Kitchener and King, do not have the same level of empirical support.The same is true of Basseches's dialectical theory. Voss's chapter describes his own empirical research contrasting novices and experts, but he can also draw for support on a large body of such research on thinking strategies. Neimark's chapter synthesizes a massive body of empirical data.

FROM THE PERSPECTIVE
OF COMPOSITION SCHOLARS

Teachers of composition reading these essays will be struck by how they verify what we have always felt: writing creates situations in which students can learn to think. In the terminology of Moshman and Franks, the writing task creates the challenging disequilibrium that fuels the process of development of ideas. The discomfort students feel when confronted with a writing assignment is, as we always suspected, the discomfort of growth. When writers confront their initially recorded thoughts, inadequately expressed two-dimensionally on the page, they see before them an objective correlative of the world of experience—inadequately perceived but existent, subject to revision by the action of the mind.

Intellectual development, like writing, is an active construction, the mind acting on the world, the mind of the writer acting on the page. Revision is the key. The 17-year-olds whom we teach may not have achieved the stage of formal operations before they come to college, but they are ready for our instruction, as they have never been ready before. We can teach them to manipulate abstractions—to operate formally—by teaching them to rethink what they write at first. As Moshman and Franks say, teaching revision means teaching the inversion of reality and possibility. Students who enter our classes thinking that revision means tinkering with minor corrections can complete our courses with some experience in reimagining what has been initially written. Writing taught as an active process of revision can likewise help students to detach themselves from the object of their thinking and to transform the content of thinking in order to show that they have become Neimark's mature thinker.

Writing teachers can create the favorable circumstances that Moshman and Franks suggest are necessary to develop formal reasoning abilities. Classroom techniques also draw from Basseches's emphasis on the importance of the dialectical and multiple frames of reference. Peer review in the classroom is a productive way to help students see interpretations different from their own readings of what they have written. Role-playing can also help students put themselves in the place of someone in opposition to their ideas.

Flower applies the same type of analysis used by Voss to the study of writing, as she characterizes writers as novices or experts. This analysis is especially useful in the college classroom because instead of considering students as more or less adequate writers, we can more productively see them as functioning at different levels of mastery. They may or may not have mastered the strategies for manipulating the conventions of a particular genre or the expectations of an audience.

FROM THE PERSPECTIVE OF LOGICIANS

Time was when philosophers, inoculated by the view that a sharp distinction could be made between the descriptive and the prescriptive, would have said psychology had little to say relevant to logic, the latter being prescriptive, while psychology was descriptive. The distinction, however, has met the fate of the other famous distinctions that have fallen on hard times—fact and value, theoretical and observational, conceptual and empirical. On a variety of philosophical topics philosophers and psychologists appear once again to be conversing with one another in a way one would not have expected 20 years ago. This is not to say controversy does not rage on what the limits of relevance are, but certainly the atmosphere has changed.

Still, it is with a sense of uneasy foreboding that we approach the literature on developmental psychology. On the one hand, we believe any college student can be taught logic and philosophy. On the other hand, we have all had students who appear to sit in a philosophy class with not the slightest idea of what is going on, and many teachers of formal logic believe that students can learn how to manipulate symbols successfully and appropriately without exhibiting any good understanding of what the validity of arguments is all about. Developmental psychology seems to offer an explanation of why we are unsuccessful with such students—that they have simply not yet reached the stage necessary to comprehend the subject matter we teach. Most of us have some sense of Piaget's theory and recognize in his description of the stage of formal operations the capacity necessary for engaging in formal logic. Many of us have heard or read the folklore that 50 percent or more of college freshmen have yet to achieve formal operations. This would certainly account for our failures. Aristotle once observed that not every topic should be dealt with by argument: "For people who are puzzled to know whether one ought to honor the gods and love one's parents or not need punishment, while those who are puzzled to know whether snow is white need perception" (105a). Thus one might say some students need reason before they can be taught logic. Some might find this a welcome removal of responsibility from the teacher; others find it a discouraging and even socially irresponsible conclusion.

Even more discomfiting to those of us who teach philosophy are theories such as Perry's and Kitchener and King's. If fundamental philosophical positions such as relativism or skepticism are matters of development, it appears unfair to expect of freshman a competence in philosophy. Plato (in the *Republic*) warned against exposing young people to philosophy—but his concern was not their inability to understand it but their tendency to abuse the skills it imparted.

If the formal operations stage were equivalent to the capacity to engage in formal reasoning as such, philosophers should wait for psychologists to develop reliable measures by which to filter out of our classrooms those who have not yet reached the requisite stage. It is therefore with some sense of relief that we learn from Moshman and Franks that we are not to understand formal operations as an all-or-nothing stage, that its onset is less clear-cut and rather more messy than the folklore leads us to believe.

Voss's essay raises several questions of interest to the logician. One is how the distinction he makes between well-structured and ill-structured problems (or their domains) matches the distinction between formal and informal logic. Voss seems to take it that formal reasoning (exemplified in the research on syllogisms, propositional calculus, and decision making) is problem solving of well-structured problems. This implies that the problems of formal logic are a subclass of well-structured problems and that problems of informal logic are a subclass of ill-structured problems. If this is so, then the shift of research interest from well-structured to ill-structured problems, as Voss reports it, marks a parallel to the shift in logic from formal to informal logic. Certainly Voss's observation that in the case of well-structured problem solving the solution requires no further justification (whereas in ill-structured problem solving, the solver needs to "build a case" for the solution) is readily illustrated from formal logic. A standard "problem" in formal logic is to prove that a given proposition follows from another proposition or propositions. One "solves" it by giving a "proof"—a sequence of propositions so arranged that it can be "seen" that each follows from the preceding, the proposition to be proven coming last. Here, nothing else need be said.

Voss's essay, however, can bear another interpretation, namely that the distinction of formal and informal reasoning is theoretically independent of the taxonomy of problems, so that both kinds of reasoning are employed in both kinds of problem-situations, though, perhaps, as he suggests, the kind of reasoning found in ill-structured problem solving is dominantly informal. One wants, in that case, to press the question of how he is distinguishing between formal and informal reasoning, and in turn, how "weak" and "strong" reasoning methods are related to formal and informal reasoning.

It is noteworthy that in explicating what he means by the formal/informal reasoning distinction Voss appeals to the notion of "dialectic." Basseches also speaks of "dialectical reasoning." An unwary reader might be led to believe Voss's informal reasoning is Basseches's dialectical reasoning. Of course, this is not so. "Dialectic" is one of those notoriously multifaceted words, capable of multiple meanings, each carrying distinct implications. Roland Hall identifies eight distinct meanings—and he traces its history only as far as Hegel. Without canvassing all meanings, it should be observed that Voss means it as Aristotle meant it, while Basseches means it in its Hegelian sense. Both usages call for a brief comment.

Aristotle seems to have used "dialectic" both to mark out what we would now call logic (as opposed to rhetoric) and to mark out inside logic a particular kind of argument. In the latter sense, a dialectical argument is one whose premises are generally agreed upon, whereas a demonstrative argument is one whose premises are necessarily true. But the different status of the premises of the two arguments does not affect the logical relationship between premises and conclusion, so that the conditions of validity of a dialectical and a demonstrative argument should be the same: both are syllogisms. In these terms, an enthymeme (which Voss identifies with informal reasoning) is simply a syllogism with pieces missing, which suggests that we are dealing here not with a special kind of reasoning but with a special way of getting premises.

The inspiration of Basseches's use of "dialectic" is Hegelian rather than Aristotelian, and it suggests an approach to teaching reasoning not represented by the logic essays in this volume. There is a celebrated tradition in philosophy—illustrated first in the Socratic conversations—that reasoning develops through conflict. Thus Socrates taught by uncovering contradictions in the positions held by his interlocutors. Similarly, the most celebrated teacher of the Middle Ages, Abelard, taught by forcing students to confront contradictions in the authors they accepted as authorities. Here logic is used by the teacher to force the student to face inadequacies of a position. And the implication of this for a logic classroom might be that we should find ways to place students in situations of internal cognitive conflict, out of which we hope to encourage growth. (This approach would be consistent with Dewey's view [154–156] that reasoning can take place only in response to *actual* problems students have.)

In the above, dialectic is taken as a method of teaching. Basseches, however, regards dialectical reasoning more as a full-blown philosophical position, stressing change, wholeness, and interconnectedness. Thus in his example of the three mothers (p. 25), it is not that the third mother has grown into her position from the other two; it is rather that her position is more correct, more mature, than the others. Now, whether Basseches is correct or not in his philosophical position, the thrust of his view is toward growing capacities of the *person* rather than the acquisition of separable cognitive skills. Thus his model becomes one of the growth in epistemological capacity rather than in logical skills.

Neimark, too, sees reasoning skill as just one of a variety of capacities characteristic of the mature thinker. Yet, for the most part logic teachers not only would be ready to acknowledge as desirable the four characteristics she identifies (although there may be some philosophical opposition to taking detachment as a value) but would be willing to include them among the aims of a logic course. Most of us would like to believe that students at the end of a logic course will be more mature along each of Neimark's dimensions. True, logic teachers are not alone in hoping their courses promote these qualities; but there does seem to be some special relationship between the content of a logic course and these qualities. Indeed, Neimark's characteristics might well be used as a marker to differentiate among types of logic courses. Thus, judging by the likely content of the course, one would expect formal logic courses to result in a higher index of transformative abilities, while informal logic courses should yield a higher evaluative capacity.

One would like to know how one might "push" students toward maturity. Perhaps some hints of this can be read into Neimark's discussion of the "skills" approach. The issue here is the old problem of transfer, and although Neimark is not sanguine on the possibility of transfer, she does suggest that if we wish to bring about transfer, it should be directly a matter of instruction: we should not leave it to happenstance. Ordinarily, the transfer question involves taking skills learned in one domain or content area and using them in another. In this sense of transfer, the lesson of Neimark's analysis is that logic teachers should make a special effort to *show* how the skills they teach have application in a variety of domains. But Neimark's model of maturity raises a different kind of transfer problem, namely, whether learning the skills of logic can be "transferred" or transformed into a personal characteristic, quality, or habit of mind. It is a puzzle how one might go about encouraging this. Ordinarily, one might encourage transfer across domains by showing, for example, how a particular form of reasoning shows up in different domains. It does not seem the same, however, to discuss a form of reasoning and then to show how it relates to detachment, or to transformation, or to evaluation. On the other hand, the component of maturity that logic courses may do least well, or least explicitly, is the metacognitive component. And to discuss explicitly detachment or evaluation may at least move in the direction of metacognition.

WORKS CITED

Aristotle. *Topics*. Trans. W.A. Pickard-Cambridge. *The Complete Works of Aristotle: The Revised Oxford Translation*. Ed. Jonathan Barnes. 2 vols. Princeton: Princeton University Press, 1984. Vol. 1.

Dewey, John. *Democracy and Education*. 1916. New York: Macmillan, 1954.

Hall, Roland. "Dialectic." *Encyclopedia of Philosophy*. 8 Vols. Ed. Paul Edwards. New York: Macmillan, 1967. 2: 385–389.

CHAPTER 1

Intellectual Development: Formal Operations and Reflective Judgment

David Moshman and Bridget A. Franks

Thinking and writing are closely interrelated. How we think influences our writing, and the process of writing, in turn, changes our thinking. Teachers of writing, accordingly, have two reasons to be concerned about students' thinking. First, they can use information about students' thinking to better understand why students write the way they do and to effectively improve student writing. Second, they can work on students' writing in such a way as to positively influence student thinking. In other words, we should not limit ourselves to either focusing on thinking as a means of improving writing, or focusing on writing as a means of improving thinking. Rather, we should see both good thinking and good writing as valuable— and closely interrelated—ends in themselves and should see our role as teachers as facilitating both.

Obviously, not all people think the same way. Some differences in thinking reflect enduring personal styles (see Neimark, Chapter 3), some reflect different degrees of expertise in a given field (see Voss, Chapter 4), and some reflect differences in more general sorts of intellectual ability. Any piece of writing will reflect all three aspects of thinking: the writer's personal style of thinking, his or her expertise in the specific topic, and his or her general intellectual abilities.

This chapter focuses on the development of general intellectual abilities, The overall approach reflects the perspective of the Swiss psychologist Jean Piaget (1896–1980), the preeminent theorist of cognitive development. In the first section, we present Piaget's highly influential analysis of the nature of intelligence and development. Then we turn to his specific theory of formal operations, seen by him as the highest stage of intellectual development. Finally, we consider some more recent work on aspects of mature knowing outside the scope of orthodox Piagetian theory.

PIAGET'S THEORY OF INTELLECTUAL DEVELOPMENT

The Nature of Intelligence

How smart is Suzy? Is Suzy smarter than Robert? These are the kinds of questions we immediately think of when we come across the word *intelligence*. They are questions about individual differences: How intelligent is a given person compared to someone else or to people in general?

Piaget did not deny that some people are brighter than others. But this is not what interested him. Even the least intelligent individual, as he saw it, has intelligence. Everyone has knowledge about the world, makes sense of the environment in terms of that knowledge, and improves that knowledge by better organizing it and better adapting it to reality. Instead of emphasizing individual differences, Piaget's focus was more general questions. What is knowledge? How is it organized? How do we use it? How does it change?

To understand Piaget's answers to these sorts of questions, consider the following description:

> Laurent (age 10 months) is lying on his back but nevertheless resumes his experiments of the day before. He grasps in succession a celluloid swan, a box, etc., stretches out his arms and lets them fall. Sometimes he stretches out his arm vertically, sometimes he holds it obliquely, in front of or behind his eyes, etc. When the object falls in a new position (for example on his pillow), he lets it fell two or three times more on the same place, as though to study the spatial relation; then he modifies the situation. (Piaget 269)

In Piaget's view, Laurent was understanding his environment (the swan, box, etc.) by acting upon it (grasping, dropping, etc.). Piaget referred to the actions that Laurent was capable of as *schemes* and the process of using these schemes to make sense of the world as *assimilation*. For example, he assimilated the swan to his grasping scheme. But one cannot grasp a swan and a box in quite the same way. Thus, Laurent had to *accommodate* his grasping scheme to the unique characteristics of the swan. Moreover, Laurent *organized* his schemes of grasping and dropping for purposes of his systematic exploration of objects: he grasped and then dropped. And finally, we see that Laurent's schemes of grasping and dropping were well suited for dealing with toy swans and boxes—that is, they were *adapted* to the environment. In just a few seconds of infant behavior, we see what Piaget considered some of the major properties of intelligence: it is an *organization* of *schemes* that are *adapted* to the person's environment, meaning that the schemes can *assimilate* the environment and simultaneously *accommodate* to its unique features.

Consider now an example of a much older individual also exploring the physical world: Dei (age 16 years) is exploring the flexibility of a set of rods. Bärbel Inhelder, Piaget's major collaborator, asks Dei what factors are at work. The following conversation ensues:

DEI: "Weight, materials, the length of the rod, perhaps the form."

INHELDER: "Can you prove your hypothesis?"
             Dei compares the 200 gram and 300 gram weights on the same steel rod. "You see, the role of weight is demonstrated. For the material, I don't know."

INHELDER: "Take these steel ones and these copper ones."

DEI: "I think I have to take the two rods with the same form. Then to demonstrate the role of the metal I compare these two (steel and brass, identical in form, length, and cross-sectional area, with 300 grams on each). To demonstrate the role of the form, I can compare these two (round and square, identical in material, length, and cross-sectional area)."

INHELDER: "Can the same thing be proved with these two?" (rods varying in cross-sectional area as well as form)

DEI: "No, because that one is much narrower." (Adapted from Inhelder and Piaget 60.)

Although Dei is showing a much more sophisticated level of intelligence, her systematic isolation of variables (for example, studying the difference between steel and brass rods of the same form and length) can be thought of as a scheme. As Dei assimilates rods to her isolation-of-variables scheme and accommodates to the unique features of each rod, her behavior again shows the organized and adaptive nature of intelligence, this time at a higher stage of development.

Each stage, according to Piaget, is a unique way of knowing, qualitatively different from both earlier and later stages. At any stage, however, intelligence lies neither in assimilation alone (construing new information in terms of current schemes) nor in accommodation alone (adjusting current schemes to new information). Rather, intelligence lies in a balance of assimilation and accommodation, a state of *equilibrium*.

The Process of Intellectual Development

Although Laurent and Dei have much in common, there are also obvious differences. Both show intelligence, but Dei clearly shows a much more sophisticated way of dealing with the world. How can we explain the dramatic changes in intellectual ability as children get older?

Piaget considered and rejected two obvious possibilities. The first possibility is that new intellectual abilities are learned from the environment. For example, Dei might have been taught a strategy for isolating variables that Laurent has not yet been exposed to. The second possibility is that all intellectual abilities are programmed in the genes and emerge during the course of maturation. There might, for example, be an age at which the ability to isolate variables simply appears in all normal children, regardless of their environments.

Rejecting both of these alternatives, Piaget proposed a middle-ground position that he called *constructivism*. The central tenet of constructivism is that individuals construct their own knowledge during the course of interaction with the environment. Each new scheme is constructed through the coordination of earlier schemes. Such coordinations take place when the environment presents challenges that cannot be resolved using available schemes.

For example, a student who fails to isolate variables in exploring the flexibility of rods will get contradictory results. Situations like this produce *disequilibrium*, a discomfort that can be resolved only by constructing more adequate schemes. This construction of better-organized and better-adapted new schemes out of earlier ones returns the individual to *equilibrium* and is thus known in Piagetian theory as *equilibration*. By constructing and using an isolation-of-variables scheme, for example, the above student is now able to get consistent and useful information in studying a variety of situations. Equilibrium is now restored.

It is important to emphasize that equilibration is not a process of *learning* in the sense of acquiring new information from one's environment. Rather, it is a very gradual, internally directed construction, a process of *development*. One can facilitate this process by providing appropriate challenges—experiences just beyond the individual's current structures that will induce some disequilibrium. However, according to Piaget, one must recognize that resolution of such disequilibrium is never quick and simple. Equilibration or, more broadly, development—is an inherently gradual process.

Writing is an excellent example of a context in which incoherence in one's ideas is likely to become apparent and thus yield disequilibrium. The good writer assimilates and accommodates ideas to each other, organizes them effectively into higher-order structures, and actively constructs new ideas and general frameworks. And the excellent writer, like the self-conscious thinker, knows that even when equilibrium is achieved it is only temporary. Disequilibrium is always just around the corner; every essay, like every cognition, is always subject to revision.

In sum, new knowledge is a product not of genes or environment alone but rather of the active mind interacting with complex and changing world. Students (and writers) are constantly coming into contact with circumstances for which their current schemes are inadequate. They respond to such challenges by gradually constructing new schemes, new modes of understanding. Contradiction and disequilibrium, then, are not aberrations to be avoided but a normal part of development, the impetus for achieving higher levels of equilibrium.

Current Evaluation

Piaget's theory has been the basis for thousands of empirical studies all over the world. Although many specifics of the theory are open to serious question, the essential features of Piaget's perspective on intelligence and intellectual development are widely accepted. Piaget proposed that knowledge is highly organized, that learning involves assimilation of new experience to one's previous knowledge, and that intellectual development is not a passive incorporation of information but an active construction on the part of the knower (Furth; Ginsburg and Opper; Gruber and Vonèche). Although these ideas were considered radical at the time Piaget proposed them, they are now almost universally accepted by researchers and theorists.

PIAGET'S THEORY OF FORMAL OPERATIONS

In addition to his general conceptions about the nature of intelligence and about how intellectual development proceeds, Piaget studied a wide variety of cognitive abilities and distinguished four overall stages of development. During the first of these, the *sensorimotor stage*, the infant relates to the environment via his or her senses and physical activities, beginning with simple reflexes and gradually constructing sophisticated problem-solving and exploratory schemes and action-based concepts of time, space, causality, and objects. During the *preoperational stage*, beginning about age 18 months, the capacity for mental representation, language, and genuine thinking develops rapidly. This is followed by the stage of *concrete operations*, beginning about age 7 years, when the mental schemes of the preoperational period become increasingly organized to yield logical operations such as systematic classification and seriation.

  Concrete operational thinking, though highly sophisticated compared to what came before, is still limited to representations of known realities. Only with the emergence of *formal operations*, beginning about age 11, is this systematic logic applied to possibilities and hypotheses. Piaget proposed that formal operations is a single, integrated structure with a number of interrelated facets (Inhelder and Piaget). Three of the most important facets of formal reasoning are the inversion of reality and possibility, hypothetico-deductive reasoning, and second-order operations.

Of these, it is the first—the inversion of reality and possibility—that Piaget saw as most fundamental.

> There is no doubt that the most distinctive feature of formal thought stems from the role played by statements about possibility relative to statements about empirical reality. (Inhelder and Piaget 245)

Needless to say, Piaget was not suggesting that young children do not consider possibilities. He did propose, however, that the possibilities considered by young children are merely extensions of, or alternatives to, reality. Only at the formal level does the individual systematically construct sets of possibilities and think about realities within the context of these possibilities. For example, the formal thinker can figure out how many license plates could be produced by putting the letters A, B, C, and D in every possible order and understands that any given license plate (e.g., B A D C) is one of those possibilities.

To take a less mathematical example, all children learn about moral values from the people around them. According to Piaget's theory, preformal thinkers who are exposed to different values are likely to compare them to their own moral realities and conclude that the alternative values are deviant. The reality is taken as the standard for comparison. A formal thinker, on the other hand, is able to construct a variety of possible moral systems, perhaps even including some no society has ever used, and then reevaluate her own ideas from this broader standpoint. Her own reality is no longer the ultimate standard for comparison but merely one of many possibilities. At the level of formal operations there is thus a radical reversal of perspectives: Rather than considering possibilities with respect to reality, reality is considered with respect to possibilities. The central difference between the preformal and formal thinker, then, lies in the ability to spontaneously and systematically generate possibilities and, even more important, to rethink realities in light of these possibilities.

Differences among students in the ability to substantially revise something they have written can be seen as reflecting this aspect of formal thinking. The preformal thinker probably sees a piece of writing as a concrete reality and thus, if pressed to revise, is likely to think only in terms of relatively minor corrections. The formal thinker is much more likely to think in terms of the many possible ways a set of ideas could have been expressed. The actual first draft can thus be viewed as a particular realization within a broad set of possibilities, making it possible to seriously consider genuinely radical revisions.

Closely related to the new use of possibilities is *hypothetico-deductive reasoning*, the ability to pursue a line of reasoning that begins with a purely hypothetical (or even contrary-to-fact) assertion. Consider, for example, the following two arguments (adapted from Moshman and Franks):

1. Elephants are bigger than mice.
   Dogs are bigger than mice.
   Therefore, elephants are bigger than dogs.
2. Mice are bigger than dogs.
   Dogs are bigger than elephants.
   Therefore, mice are bigger than elephants.

A preformal thinker would consider the first to be most logical in that each of the three propositions within it is empirically true. A formal thinker, by contrast, would consider the second argument more logical in that the conclusion follows from the premises. Recognizing the validity of the second argument requires hypothetico-deductive reasoning—making a logical deduction from premises that are purely hypothetical or even patently false.

Consider a more complex example. What would happen if nobody owned things? For the preformal reasoner, the question itself is absurd since it asks one to reason from a false premise: People *do* own things. The formal thinker, on the other hand, though recognizing that the premise is false, can systematically deduce its consequences. This may lead to questions that would never occur to the concrete thinker. If nobody owned anything, would there be such a thing as stealing? Would people be less materialistic? Would they become *more* materialistic? Would society break down? Would it require a different form of government? A formal operational essay might explore such issues and provide sustained arguments that a preformal thinker would have trouble even following, much less producing. Hypothetic-deductive reasoning plays a central role in the exploration of possibilities, and that, in turn, deepens our understanding of the realities around us.

One additional characteristic of formal operations is that they are operations on operations, or *second-order operations*. To take a simple example, what does it mean to understand a proportion? When we say 6 is to 3 as 4 is to 2 we are indicating that the relation between 6 and 3 is the same as the relation between 4 and 2 (first number twice as great in each case). But in asserting that the two relations are equal, we are considering a relation between relations—that is, a second-order relation. Similarly, the formal thinker is capable not only of classifying objects but of classifying and seriating the classes themselves to achieve a more systematic understanding.

Piaget argued that the ability to operate on operations is directly related to hypothetico-deductive reasoning and the systematic elaboration of possibilities. Formal operations, like any other Piagetian stage, is not a collection of skills but a general structure of reasoning. Inhelder and Piaget proposed that this new cognitive structure begins to develop about age 11 and is essentially mature by age 15 or so in most normal individuals.

Extensive research on formal operations since 1958 has supported the view that genuine formal operational reasoning does not begin until at least age 11 but shows that, contrary to the original findings, older adolescents and even college students are highly inconsistent in whether or not they apply formal reasoning (Moshman and Neimark). Thus it seems that formal reasoning develops much more gradually than Piaget suggested; it is not clear that formal operations constitutes a single, tightly integrated structure. It may be more useful to construe formal operations as a set of interrelated abilities developing over a long period of time (beginning about age 11) than as a stage one moves into during early adolescence.

Evidence of nonformal reasoning in college students has led a number of researchers to assert that as many as 50 percent of all college students have not reached the stage of formal operations. A more detailed look at the literature, however, suggests that nearly all college students are capable of formal reasoning under favorable circumstances. Differences among college students appear to be a matter of how widely and efficiently they apply their formal competence rather than whether they have that competence (O'Brien). It is thus a dangerous oversimplification for college instructors to think in terms of turning concrete thinkers into formal thinkers over the course of a semester. A more useful perspective is to focus on helping students develop and apply a variety of formal reasoning abilities.

The above discussion assumes that a student capable of applying the whole range of formal reasoning abilities in a wide range of circumstances would be a fully mature thinker. There are, however, a number of reasons to question this. For one thing, formal operations as conceived by Piaget is very much rooted in traditional, formal logic (Braine and Rumain), though we have deemphasized his formal logical models in the present chapter. As we will see in later chapters, there is much more to mature thinking than formal logic. In addition, Piagetian research has focused on tasks involving various sorts of scientific thinking. As we will see in the next section of this chapter, tasks assessing students' philosophical conceptions reveal another dimension of development.

DEVELOPMENT OF PHILOSOPHICAL UNDERSTANDING

On January 27, 1985, the Sunday *Doonesbury* (Figure 1.1) showed a college professor lecturing at a podium:

"And in my view," he says, "Jefferson's defense of these basic rights lacked conviction. Okay, any discussion of what I've covered so far?" The students are busily taking notes. *Of course not,* he thinks, as they look up at him for the next gem of wisdom. *You're too busy getting it all down.*

"Let me just add," he continues, "that personally I believe the Bill of Rights to be a silly, inconsequential recapitulation of truths already found in the Constitution. Any comment?"

The students continue taking notes.

"No, *scratch* that!" he exclaims. "The Constitution *itself* should never have been ratified! It's a dangerous document! All power should rest with the *executive!* What do you think of *that?*"

The students continue taking notes.

"Jefferson was the ANTICHRIST!" he screams. "Democracy is FASCISM! BLACK IS WHITE! NIGHT IS DAY!"

The students continue taking notes. The professor collapses on the podium. "Teaching is dead," he moans to himself.

"Boy," says one student, still taking notes. "This course is really getting interesting."

"You said it," replies another. "I didn't know half this stuff."

Something about this situation rings true to anyone who has taught college students. Obviously, the placid students and the frustrated instructor have very different ideas about what is—and what should be—going on in the classroom. The professor is trying to elicit discussion by getting more and more controversial, while the students are viewing him as an unquestionable source of true facts to be written down in their notebooks. The students appear to differ from their professor in their conceptions about the nature of knowledge and the purpose of education.

After detailed study of college students at Harvard University, William Perry concluded that students differ not only from their professors but from each other in their level of philosophical understanding and that many make progress toward more sophisticated philosophical reasoning during their college years. Perry viewed this progress as a gradual, developmental transition. Increasing philosophical sophistication might be due at least partially to the broad intellectual experience of a college education but was not a matter of simply taking philosophy courses or learning techniques of reasoning.

Research expanding on Perry's work has indicated that concepts about the nature of knowledge, truth, reality, and the justification of ideas show a regular pattern of development over a long period of time, beginning in early childhood and extending well into adulthood (Broughton). Karen Kitchener and Patricia King, for example, extending the work of Perry, Broughton, and others, postulated seven stages of what they call *reflective judgment.* Each stage is characterized by a view about reality, a view about knowledge, and a concept of justification (see Table 1.1).

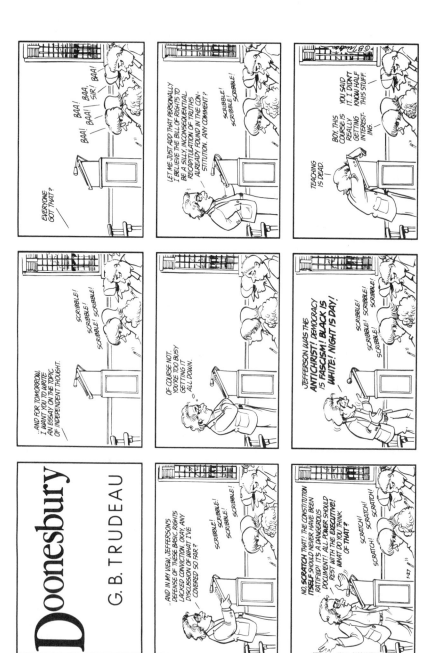

Figure 1.1

18

Although various theories about the development of philosophical conceptions differ on many details, there is substantial agreement about the general direction of development. There seems to be a trend from absolutism to relativism to rationality. At the level of *absolutism* (including Kitchener and King's stages 1 and 2 and the *Doonesbury* students), the student believes that reality and knowledge are absolute. The truth is either inherently known or learnable from the proper authorities (e.g., "but the professor told us. . . ."; "it says right here in the text that. . . ."). Recognition that some things are not known even by the authorities (stage 3) leads ultimately to the level of *relativism* (stages 4 and 5), at which knowledge is viewed as personal and subjective. Truth is relative: It depends on one's point of view, and anyone's point of view is as good as anyone else's. But is $2 + 2 = 5$ no more justifiable than $2 + 2 = 4$? Increasing recognition that some views really *are* better than others lead to the level of *rationality* (stages 6 and 7 and the *Doonesbury* professor). At this level, the individual believes that, even though we cannot obtain an absolute and final knowledge of reality, we can nevertheless improve our knowledge through evidence, reasoning, and discussion. Thus, even if none of our knowledge is absolutely the last word, some ideas are indeed better justified than others on the basis of rational standards.

To test their theory, Kitchener and King interviewed 20 high school students, 20 college students, and 20 graduate students about each of four dilemmas. Each dilemma involved a set of conflicting opinions (e.g., chemical additives to food are/are not safe) and was followed by questions designed to probe students' justifications for their views. Kitchener and King found that it was possible reliably to classify different levels of philosophical reasoning by using their seven stages. For most students, reasoning spanned two or three adjacent stages, indicating that people usually have a range of typical reasoning rather than fitting neatly into a single stage. As expected, the average level of reasoning was lowest for the high school students and highest for the graduate students, suggesting that philosophical development continues well beyond adolescence, at least for some people. College student reasoning ranged from stage 2 through stage 6. suggesting that there are substantial individual differences in the rate of development.

It seems likely that advances in philosophical conceptions would be accompanied by changes in the sophistication of one's writing. Although there is indeed some evidence in support of this view (Ryan), research on this question is sparse. In Table 1.1 we offer some speculations about what one might expect to see in the writing of students at each of Kitchener and King's seven levels.

TABLE 1.1. KITCHENER AND KING, STAGES OF REFLECTIVE JUDGMENT

	Concept of Reality	Concept of Knowledge	Concept of Justification	Concept of Writing
STAGE 1	There is an objective reality. Reality is precisely what I see.	Knowledge is absolute. My views exactly match the views of authorities and the true nature of reality. I gain true knowledge through direct perception and learning from authorities.	Beliefs simply exist. There are no differences of opinion and thus there is no need for beliefs to be explained or justified.	Communication is direct. What I write is what you read. We both know how things are. No need is seen to take the reader's point of view, to define terms, to express ideas clearly, or to justify assertions.
STAGE 2	There is an objective reality, though it may not be precisely what I see.	Absolute knowledge exists. It may not be immediately available to me, but the truth is known by the proper authorities.	True beliefs are based on the absolute knowledge of a legitimate of a authority.	A good paper identifies the proper authority on the topic and presents his or her views. Legitimate experts cannot differ. No need is seen to seek different sources and/or to evaluate sources critically.
STAGE 3	There is an objective reality but it is not completely known, even by the authorities.	Absolute knowledge exists in some areas. For other topics, however, knowledge is still incomplete and even the authorities are uncertain. We can get more and more evidence, however, and eventually reach the final truth.	True beliefs are based on an accumulation of evidence. For issues where sufficient evidence is not yet available, one can temporarily believe whatever one chooses.	The more sources you have the better. The more evidence you can present, the closer you are to the truth.
STAGE 4	There is an objective reality, but it can never be known with complete certainty.	Absolute truth can never be attained. There are many possible answers to every question, and there is no way to decide which is correct. No answer is better than any other. Knowledge is an individual matter.	My beliefs are personal and can be justified by personal evidence. I am the ultimate judge of my own truth. What is true for me may not be true for you, and what is true for you may not be true for me.	My writing is my personal statement. I don't judge your work, and you have no right to evaluate my ideas or my style of expressing them.

20

STAGE 5	There is no objective reality. Reality is a subjective, personal thing.	Absolute knowledge is impossible since there is no objective reality to be known. Knowledge is subjective and personal. What is true from one perspective may not be true from another.	Beliefs can be justified in terms of decision rules appropriate for a particular perspective or context (e.g., a simpler scientific theory is better than a more complex one.)	There is value in arguing a point of view or telling a story from more than one perspective. Different rhetorical strategies are appropriate for different writing tasks.
STAGE 6	An objective understanding of reality is not possible.	Objective knowledge is impossible since knowledge is constructed by a subjective perceiver and interpreter. One can, however, construct knowledge using general principles of reasoning and looking across different perspectives.	Particular judgments may be evaluated as more rational than others on the basis of relevant evidence and reasoning.	Good writing involves integration and rational evaluation of diverse sources. The inevitability of subjectivity does not place the writer beyond legitimate criticism.
STAGE 7	There is an objective reality against which our knowledge can and should be tested.	There are rational processes of inquiry, involving evidence and reasoning, through which beliefs can approach— though never actually reach— truth. Discussion among people with different perspectives is important in this process.	There are rational criteria for judging that some ideas— though not absolute and final truths— are more reasonable than others. Specific criteria may be a function of domain (e.g., religion, literature science, etc.)	Quality of distinct types of writing (e.g., poetry, essays, scientific reports) can be rationally evaluated and improved through the use of defensible criteria and through feedback from diverse sources.

CONCLUSIONS

Research on cognitive development shows important changes during adolescence and early adulthood. It seems likely that students' writing reflects these changes and, in turn, can be an important influence in facilitating them. Later chapters will explore other aspects of intellectual development and provide more detailed suggestions for teachers of writing.

WORKS CITED

Braine, M.D.S., and B. Rumain. "Logical Reasoning." *Cognitive Development.* Vol. 3 of *Handbook of Child Psychology.* Ed. P.H. Mussen. New York: Wiley, 1983. 263–340.

Broughton, J. "Development of Concepts of Self, Mind, Reality and Knowledge." *Social Cognition.* Ed. W. Damon. San Francisco: Jossey-Bass, 1978. 75–100.

Furth, H.G. *Piaget and Knowledge: Theoretical Foundations.* 2nd ed. Chicago: University of Chicago Press, 1981.

Ginsburg, H.S., and S. Opper. *Piaget's Theory of Intellectual Development.* 2nd ed. Englewood Cliffs, NJ: Prentice-Hall, 1979.

Gruber, H.E., and J.J. Vonèche. *The Essential Piaget: An Interpretive Reference and Guide.* New York: Basic Books, 1977.

Inhelder, B., and J . Piaget. *The Growth of Logical Thinking: From Childhood to Adolescence.* New York: Basic Books, 1958.

Kitchener, K.S., and P.M. King. "Reflective Judgment: Concepts of Justification and Their Relationship to Age and Education." *Journal of Applied Developmental Psychology* 2 (1981): 89–116.

Moshman, D., and B.A. Franks. "Development of the Concept of Inferential Validity." *Child Development* 57 (1986): 153–165.

Moshman, D., and E. Neimark. "Four Aspects of Adolescent Cognitive Development." *Review of Human Development.* Ed. T.M. Field, A. Huston, H.C. Quay, L. Troll, and G.E. Finley. New York: Wiley, 1982. 343–355.

O'Brien, D.P. "The Development of Conditional Reasoning: An Iffy Proposition." *Advances in Child Development and Behavior.* Ed. H.W. Reese. New York: Academic Press, 1987. Vol. 20. 61–90.

Perry, W.G. *Forms of Intellectual and Ethical Development in the College Years.* New York: Holt, Rinehart, and Winston, 1970.

Piaget, J. *The Origins of Intelligence in Children.* New York: Norton, 1963.

Ryan, M.P. "Conceptions of Prose Coherence: Individual Differences in Epistemological Standards." *Journal of Educational Psychology* 76 (1984): 1226–1238.

CHAPTER 2

Intellectual Development: The Development of Dialectical Thinking

Michael Basseches

I have argued elsewhere (1984) that theories of intellectual development in adulthood must be understood as making philosophical claims about the relative adequacy of "equilibrium" or some forms of thought vis-à-vis others. The mere empirical documentation of ontogenetic changes in the direction of a supposedly more mature form of thought is not sufficient to justify calling that form of thought more developed. However, in the context of a convincing argument that the later form of thought is more adequate than the former, such empirical findings can be interpreted as reflecting a process of equilibration (see Moshman and Franks, Chapter 1), in which inadequacies of earlier forms of reasoning are encountered and overcome by the construction of more adequate forms. Thus, in some-what circular fashion, a philosophical argument may support the interpretation of the documented changes in thinking as equilibration, while data on change in individuals' thought may reinforce the philosophical argument for the superiority of a later form of thinking. As an illustration of this point, imagine being presented with empirical findings that the thinking of prisoners of war changes over time in such a way that it appears to resemble more and more closely that of their captors. Most of us would be likely to assume that a process of "indoctrination," rather than development, is being documented. Now, should we interpret in a similar way findings

Sections of this essay have been adapted from Michael Basseches, *Dialectical Thinking and Adult Development* Norwood, NJ: Ablex, 1984. By permission of Ablex Publishing Corporation.

(e.g., Basseches 1980, 1984) that the thinking of college and university students, over the course of their education, comes to resemble more and more closely the thinking of their professors? 1 am suggesting that this depends on whether or not we are presented with a convincing philosophical argument showing that the change represents movement toward a more adequate form of organization of thought.

Moshman and Franks (Chapter 1) describe the type of adolescent thought that Piaget conceptualized as "organized by the structure of formal operations." They also describe development in the area of metaphysical and epistemological assumptions that occurs subsequent to the development of formal operations. However, they appear to accept the view that there are no fundamental organizational changes in the logic of the thinking process subsequent to the development of formal operations.

In contrast, I have argued (1984) that the development of thinking that is dialectically organized represents a cognitive transformation as fundamental as the transformation from concrete operational thought to formal operational thought that Moshman and Franks describe. Furthermore, I have suggested that the transformation to dialectically organized thought can be understood as growing out of encounters with the limitations of formal operational thought, just as the development of each of Piaget's stages is understood as growing out of encounters with the limits of the previous stage. While the transformations described by Piaget, for most individuals, occur largely during childhood and early adolescence, it appears from my research that it is during the late adolescent and adult years that the potential for the development of dialectically organized thinking may be found.

In this chapter, my principal goal is to describe what I have been calling dialectical thinking in a way that suggests its power, adequacy, and significance for adult intellectual development, especially in contrast to formal thought. I refer the reader to my other work (Basseches, 1978, 1980, 1984) for a full exposition of both the philosophical argument and the empirical findings supporting my claim that dialectical thinking reflects intellectual *development*. Pending examination of that work, I invite the reader to critically evaluate the philosophical position reflected in this chapter. If the reader cannot embrace this philosophical position, it may be more appropriate for him/her to use my description as a diagnostic tool for recognizing dialectical thinking in students' writing than as defining a goal to pursue in the teaching of writing. However, this chapter is offered to all educators who espouse the goal of teaching late adolescents and adults to think better, as a plausible account of the sort of intellectual development that higher education ought to promote.

Let me begin by offering a couple of scenarios of situations in adult life in which dialectical cognitive organization would make a difference in how phenomena are analyzed. I hope these examples will provide an initial feel for what I include within the scope of dialectical thinking, as well as its implications. In each example, I will start with two non-dialectical, but not unusual, ways of thinking about the problem at hand, and then contrast them with a third, dialectical alternative.

Mary, Helen, and Judy are all mothers of daughters. Each mother has held a set of values that have guided her efforts to raise her daughter. Now, the daughters have grown up and each of them is rejecting many of her mother's values.

Mary is very troubled. She sees only two possible interpretations. If her values are right, she has failed as a parent in not having successfully transmitted those values to her daughter. On the other hand, if her daughter's values are right, the whole foundation of the way Mary has lived her life is wrong, and Mary neither deserves nor is likely to receive her daugther's respect.

Helen, however, is shrugging the matter off. She reasons that values are totally arbitrary and irrational anyway. All people have their own values and live their lives by them, and who's to say which ones are right and which ones are wrong. The important thing is to respect others, even if they have different values. Helen respects her daughter in spite of their differences.

Judy begins to think about the matter by looking at the evolution of values in historical perspective. She reasons that human values change over the course of history as old values interact with changing environmental circumstances. People need values in order to decide how to act, but in acting according to their values they change the world, and the changed world in turn leads to the development of new values. Judy understands her daughter's values as resulting from the interaction of the values Judy tried to share with her and the experiences of the world that her daughter has had but Judy herself never had. Judy says to herself,

> Instead of assuming either that I am wrong or that my daugher is wrong, I can try to see what I can learn for my future life from her values borne of her experience. I can also see how she has learned from my values and transformed them to keep up with the times.

Mark, Howard, and George are college juniors. They are feeling very frustrated about three years of the routine of tests, paper assignments, and grades. They worry that going through this process has taken its toll, undermining their love of learning.

Mark is confused. Based on his own experience, it seems to him that students would learn much more if they were given more freedom to pursue their own intellectual interests, rather than being required to take

standardized tests and complete standardized assignments. On the other
hand, he assumes that the college is run by experienced educators, who
must have determined that the use of tests and assigned papers to measure
and grades to motivate is the soundest educational method.

Howard is angry. He locates the cause of his own demoralization and
that of his fellow students in teachers' illegitimate presumption that they
can pass judgment on students' ideas. He believes that much of grading is
subjective and that teachers use their power to impose their own personal
tastes on what students think and how students write. Although Howard
doesn't accept it as educationally legitimate for teachers to dictate what
students should learn and then to evaluate them by subjective standards,
he does accept that that's the way the system works. He has decided that
he wants to make it through the system, and has cynically dedicated
himself to cultivating the art of giving teachers what they want.

George begins to analyze the problem by locating the college within
the larger society of which it is a part. The college is expected to perform a
certification function for that society, providing transcripts that other social
institutions can use in their selection processes. But the college is also
expected to provide students with a good education. The problem that he
and Howard and Mark are experiencing reflects a contradiction between
the certificational and educational functions of the college. The need to
provide certification (grades) to the outside leads the college and its
faculty to employ practices that may not be educationally optimal (i.e.,
standardized assignments). Similarly, the concerns with providing a good
education leads to practices that may not be certificationally optimal (i.e.,
grading students on subject matter where completely objective evaluation
is impossible). George reasons that this contradiction will only really be
resolved when the basic relationship of the colleges and universities to
society is transformed. He decides that he will devote his time at college
to trying to learn all he can that might help him contribute to that kind
of transformation of educational institutions. He accepts that in the mean-
time he will be given standardized assignments and grades and will have to
make compromises just as his teachers do between what is educationally
and certificationally optimal. But he is resolved not to lose sight of his own
educational goals.

My understanding of dialectical thinking as a psychological phenomenon is derived from a conception of a dialectical philosophical perspective. I will now describe this philosophical perspective in a way
that indicates its underlying unity. In doing so, I will take the liberty
of casting a net that in some ways may be broader and in other ways
narrower than those nets intellectual historians might cast. My net may
be broader in that I am grouping ideas and ways of thinking under the

heading "the dialectical philosophical perspective" based merely on their philosophical and psychological similarities rather than establishing a "tradition" by demonstrating actual historical connections among ideas and thinkers. My net may be narrower in that I do not try to hold within it the various pre-Hegelian forms of thought that were called dialectical, whereas intellectual historians might advance accounts of the continuity between pre-Hegelian and post-Hegelian uses of the term.

THE DIALECTICAL PHILOSOPHICAL PERSPECTIVE

I view the dialectical perspective as comprising a family of world outlooks, or views of the nature of existence (ontology) and knowledge (epistemology). These world outlooks, while differing from each other in many respects, share a family resemblance based on three features: common emphases on change, on wholeness, and on internal relations.

Dialectical ontologies emphasize (1) that what is most fundamental in reality are some ongoing processes of change; (2) that in the course of these ongoing processes of change within existence as a whole, forms of organization emerge that have a coherence that cannot simply be accounted for by the nature of the parts that are organized within these forms (the forms are temporary and may disintegrate or give way to more complex forms of organization); (3) that everything that exists is in relationship to other things and that these relationships are internal to the nature of the things themselves—they are part of what makes the things what they are (and as a thing's internal relations change, its nature changes).

Similarly, dialectical epistemologies emphasize (1) that both individual and collective knowledge are essentially active processes of organizing and reorganizing understandings of phenomena; (2) that in these knowing processes there emerge individual and collective conceptual systems that give the knowledge a coherence that cannot simply be accounted for by the specific concepts, ideas, and facts organized within them; (3) that concepts, ideas, and facts exists in relationships not only to other concepts, ideas, and facts but also to the lives of the knowers who employ them. These relationships determine the meaning of the concepts, ideas, and facts, and as these relationships change, the meanings of concepts, ideas, and facts change also.

What ties together the emphases on change, wholeness, and internal relations in dialectical world outlooks is the concept of dialectic. This concept underlies both dialectical world outlooks and the particular approaches to analysis that constitute dialectical thinking.

The Idea of Dialectic

Dialectic is *developmental transformation (i.e., developmental movement through forms) that occurs via constitutive and interactive relationships.* The phrase "movement through forms" is meant to distinguish such movement from movement within forms. To illustrate this distinction, consider what happens when a road is built from one city to another. The road has a certain form to it, and the form of that road regulates the movement of the vehicles traveling between those cities. Thus, we may take this movement of the vehicles as movement within forms. On the other hand, the movement or change associated with the decay of the road, the emergence of trouble spots in terms of accidents or traffic jams, and the process of building a new and better road with a different form to replace or supplement the old road can be seen as a movement through forms. Through the notion of movement through forms, or transformation, the definition of dialectic relies upon and presupposes both the notion of movement and the notion of form and focuses on a particular relationship between them. Describing this movement through forms or transformation as developmental implies that there is a certain direction to it. This direction is usually associated with increasing inclusiveness, differentiation, and integration.

The definition relates this developmental transformational movement to constitutive and interactive relationships. A relationship may be understood as a connection. Although a relationship is often thought of as a connection between things, where the things are taken to exist prior to the relationship, the phrase "constitutive relationship" is meant to indicate the opposite—the relationship has a role in making the parties to the relationship what they are (cf., "internal relations," above). The adjective "interactive" implies that a relationship is not static but is characterized by motion or action of the parties upon each other.

Our example of the road will also serve to illustrate the concepts of constitutive and interactive relationships. Constitutive and interactive relationships can be identified among the builders of the road, the road itself, and the users of the road and their vehicles. The road is constituted not only by its interaction with road-builders (who build it) but also by its relationship with the vehicles that travel on it. For if no vehicles were permitted to travel on it, it would no longer be a road. It would perhaps be a road that had been converted to a mall. Or if only airplanes traveled on it, it would be a runway rather than a road. Thus, its being a road depends on its particular relationship to vehicles. Likewise, it is clearly relationships with roads that make road-builders road-builders. It is also, though perhaps less obviously, relationships with roads that make vehicles vehicles. Vehicles are vehicles because they have the capacity to transport one someplace, and the extent to which they have this capacity is dependent on the extent to which suitable thoroughfares exist.

The relationship between the vehicles and the road is interactive, as well as constitutive, in that the vehicles change the road and the road changes the vehicles. This should be clear from the previous discussion of road decay or wear (vehicles changing the road) and of developing trouble spots on the road that cause accidents to the vehicles (the road thus changing vehicles).

Once again, as was mentioned earlier, this interaction between road and vehicles leads to the transformation of the whole situation described earlier in terms of the building of a *new* road. This is the sense in which the transformation occurs via constitutive and interactive relationships. Thus the movement whereby a new road is built as a result of the interactive and constitutive relationships among the previous road, the road-users and their vehicles, and the road-builders, may be seen as an instance of dialectic.

Dialectical Thinking and Dialectical Analyses

Dialectical ontologies view existence as fundamentally a process of dialectic. Dialectical epistemologies view knowledge as a process of dialectic. Because dialectical thinking derives from a general world outlook, individual dialectical thinkers are likely to view both existence and knowledge dialectically. But it is possible to hold a dialectical veiw of one realm and not the other or to view neither realm as a whole in a fundamentally dialectical way but to think dialectically about particular phenomena. Most generally, we can say that dialectical thinking is any thinking that looks for and recognizes instances of dialectic and that reflects this orientation in the way in which it engages inquiry. Orienting toward dialectic leads the thinker to describe changes as dialectical movement (i.e., as movement that is developmental movement through forms occurring via constitutive and interactive relationships) and to describe relationships as dialectical relationships (i.e., as relationships that are constitutive, interactive, and that lead to or involve developmental transformation).

Formal operational thinking as described by Piaget can be understood as efforts at comprehension that rely on the application of a model of a closed system of lawful relationships to the phenomenal world. In contrast, dialectical thinking can be understood as consisting of efforts at comprehension relying on the application of a model of dialectic to the phenomenal world. These latter efforts may be termed dialectical analyses, in contrast to formal analyses. I am suggesting that dialectical thinking is an organized approach to analyzing and making sense of the world one experiences that differs fundamentally from formal analysis. Whereas the latter involves the effort to find fundamental fixed realities—basic elements and immutable laws—the former attempts to describe fundamental processes of change and the dynamic relationships through which this change occurs.

Dialectical analyses can be found in the history of a wide range of intellectual disciplines, representing the natural sciences (Provine; Feyerabend; Horz et al.), social sciences (Jay; Kilminster; Mandel) and humanities (Jameson; Adorno and Horkheimer). They have been used to support political stances ranging from the very conservative (Hegel) to the revolutionary (Marx and Engels). To illustrate the role of such analyses in intellectual history, I will consider briefly aspects of the dialectical analyses found in the work of Karl Marx and Thomas Kuhn. Then I will discuss dialectical analyses in day-to-day life.

Marx (1967) started with the observation that people collectively interact with nature so as to produce what they need to perpetuate themselves. He referred to this process as labor. In any particular society, this productive and reproductive activity takes a particular form (mode of production) and is characterized by a particular structure of social relations (relations of production) among the participants. Marx analyzed the history of production as a dialectical process in which many aspects of economic, social, technical, and intellectual life are all interrelated within a form of organization inherent in the existing mode and social relations of production. Tensions develop within these interrelationships as the form of productive life continues over time until eventually these tensions lead to the creation of a whole new mode of production that replaces the previous one. Marx described the replacement of feudal society with capitalist society as an instance of this kind of dialectical transformation and predicted the replacement of capitalism with communism.

Kuhn's book, *The Structure of Scientific Revolution*, provided a dialectical analysis of the history of science. He argued that within a scientific discipline, research is shaped by what he called a *paradigm*. A paradigm binds together implicit assumptions about the phenomena being studied with assumptions about the methodology appropriate for studying those phenomena and with methods of defining problems and recognizing solutions. However, a paradigm at its root is a particular piece of research yielding a particular insight, which serves as a model for other researchers. According to Kuhn, research following a paradigm tends to produce anomalies—findings that are not easily reconciled with other knowledge in the field. When enough such anomalies are produced to make scientists within the field uncomfortable, new alternative paradigms are advanced that compete with the dominant paradigm for followers. A scientific revolution has occurred when a new more comprehensive paradigm, with a new set of assumptions, a new methodology, and a new way of defining what constitutes a research problem and what constitutes a solution attracts enough followers to become dominant and to define the nature of the field.

In the cases of Marx and Kuhn, dialectical analyses were presented as alternatives to formal analyses in classical economic theory and philosophy of science, respectively. These formal analyses assumed that a single set of fundamental laws of economic behavior in one case and fundamental rules of evidence for scientific hypotheses in the other case were universally applicable. Neither the constitution of the economic laws by the existing social relations of production nor the possibility of transformation to new modes of production in which economic behavior was different was recognized by classical economic theory (Smith). Similarly, neither the constitution of rules of evidence by paradigms currently popular within scientific communities nor the possibility of reorientation of sciences to paradigms with new rules of evidence was recognized by confirmationist (Reichenbach) or falsificationist (Popper) philosophies of science.

We can find many examples of problems of adult life that, like scientific problems, may be approached in relatively formalistic or relatively dialectical ways, with differing outcomes. Consider, for example, the choice of a marriage partner. If I were to adopt a formalistic approach to analysis I might start with the assumptions that I am who I am and that there are one or more people out there who are "right" for me. I might proceed to analyze my personality traits and to try to logically deduce the traits a partner should have to be compatible. Courtship would then consist of evaluating potential partners to see if they have the desired traits and testing my hypotheses about the traits required for compatibility. Notice that the formalistic approach begins with the assumption that people have fixed traits and that the goodness of a relationship is systematically determined by a matching of traits.

A dialectical approach might begin with the assumption that my traits are not fixed and that the relationships I enter will shape who I become as much as they are shaped by who I am and who my partner is. Here, courtship would involve entering relationships with potential partners, being open to being changed by relationships. We would then need to evaluate whether the relationship is evolving in ways that allow both of us to develop as individuals while it continues to develop as a relationship.

The alternatives of formal analysis and dialectical analysis may also be applied when a relationship breaks up. If I adopt a formal approach, I might try to explain to myself why the relationship ended by choosing among the following three interpretations.

a. I was inadequate as a partner.
b. My partner was inadequate as a partner.
c. We weren't really right for each other, and we made a big mistake in choosing each other.

It I adopt explanation (a), the result is likely to be an increase in pain resulting from lowered self-esteem. If I adopt explanation (b), the result is likely to be a great deal of anger at my partner, which, among other things, will make it much harder for us to get back together in any sense. If I adopt explanation (c), the result is likely to be my devaluing a great deal of what was beautiful and valuable in our relationship for as long as it lasted, as well as possible hesitancy to make future commitments. I may say, "If I thought this person was right for me and I was wrong, it means I can't trust my own judgment."

In contrast, if I take a dialectical approach to analyzing the break-up, I am likely to look for how experience both within and outside of the relationship has led us to grow in different directions, so much so that we would be hampered by remaining so tied to each other. The assumption is that a relationship can reach a point where it tends to interfere with the development of one or both of the partners rather than helping them to grow further and growing with them. This kind of analysis is likely to make it easier, rather than harder, to deal emotionally with the break-up. It also is likely to facilitate our working together to strengthen or rebuild the relationship. If we don't blame each other and don't treat the relationship as a mistake, but instead treat the occurrence as a natural function of human development, we are more likely to ask, "How does the relationship need to change in response to the changes it has brought about in us in order for it to continue?" If we do this, a developmental transformation of the relationship rather than its continued disintegration is more likely to occur.

Another example of the difference between formalistic and dialectical approaches may be found in the analysis of value differences between parents and their children with which I introduced this paper. There a formal analysis (Mary's) led to a choice between viewing oneself as having failed as a parent or as unworthy of one's daughter's respect. The dialectical analysis (Judy's) viewed the problem in the context of a dynamic approach to the evolution of values. Similarly, in the example of frustrated college students, the formal analysis (Mark's) assumed that problems in the college's procedures derived from an educational theory. This analysis led to the two choices of either rejecting the wisdom of one's teachers or discounting one's own perceptions as incorrect. The dialectical analysis (George's) interpreted the problems as reflecting tensions in the interrelationahip of various aspects of the institution's functions and led to a recognition of problems facing teachers and students alike, as well as of potentials for the institution to be transformed.

In each case, a dialectial analysis does not preclude a formal analysis. We may believe that relationships change and that people change and still ask questions about what makes partners compatible and how individuals can learn to be better partners. We may believe that values change over time and still ask ourselves if our daughter's view or our own view is more adequate on any particular value disagreement. We may trace problematic procedures at a college to fundamental contradictions among its functions and still inquire as to the educational impact of those procedures.

However, the capacity for dialectical analysis makes it possible both to see the limits and to see beyond the limits of the context in which we apply fomal analysis. For example, in the matter of finding a marriage partner, I may hypothesize that I am a serious person and would have trouble getting along with someone who was not equally serious. But a dialectical perspective would prepare me for the possibility that in getting to know a very playful new friend I may reverse my thinking about compatibility and find I get along better with someone who can help me to laugh and play. I may even transform my prior assumptions about myself and find that I am a fun-loving person. I might then either (1) look back at my prior seriousness as simply an emotional defense and understand the interpretation of myself as serious as itself a useful product of the historical moment, or I might say (2) "No, I really was a serious person then and now I am a fun-loving one." While (1) reflects a dialectical *epistemological* perspective on the evolution of self-knowledge over time through interaction, (2) reflects a dialectical *ontological* perspective on the evolution of personality through interaction.

In *each* of the cases discussed above, I think the dialectical analysis has a power that is absent in the formal analysis. At the same time, the dialectical analysis can make use of the power provided by the formal analysis. Marxian economic theory may make use of the classical economic theory's clarification of the laws of human economic behavior under capitalism but also analyze the potential and actual transformations of those laws. Kuhnian analysis can make use of philosophical clarification of the rules of evidence employed within the paradigm that dominates a discipline, while simultaneously analyzing historically how that paradigm achieved hegemony and where it is likely to confront its limits.

As stated above, dialectical analyses of courtship, break-ups, inter-generational value disagreements, and frustrations of college do not preclude formal analyses. But with respect to social reasoning it is important to note that in each case dialectical analyses provide alternatives to views of the problem that are destructive to self or others. In one of the examples, the mother's formalistic analysis leaves her with two emotionally self-destructive alternatives. The dialectical analysis provides an alternative that affirms the self within the context of historical change. In other cases, the constraints of formal analysis are oppressive to other people. The "formalistic" approach to courtship, which attempts to evaluate the traits of potential partners, may be experienced by a potential partner as a barrier to emotional closeness as well as to the partner's influence. The "dialectical" approach, which anticipates the possibility of development resulting from interaction with partners, is, in contrast, likely to be experienced as a warm invitation to interact.

In general, formal analyses that establish categories of analysis from the thinker's own perspective tend to remain relatively impermeable to the differing perspectives of others.[1] Dialectical thinking, in contrast, is actively oriented toward shifting categories of analysis and creating more inclusive categories, in response to the perspectives of others.

I do not want to present dialectical thinking as either an intellectual or psychological panacea. Dialectical analyses are not without costs. The willingness to question the permanence and intransigence of the boundary conditions of a problem and to ask about situations that lie beyond those boundaries characterizes each of the dialectical analyses cited above. In one case the boundaries were the capitalist form of production; in another, existing paradigms; in a third, existing conceptions of one's own personality; in a fourth, the social conditions in which one's moral principles were formed; and in a fifth, the assumption that educational practice follows from educational theory. In questioning these boundaries, we may be questioning precisely those points of reference that provide us with a sense of intellectual stability and coherence about our world.

To think dialectically, is, in a certain sense, to trade off a degree of intellectual security for a freedom from intellectually imposing limitations on oneself or other people. The open-mindedness thus gained is extremely important from the perspective of a concern with sociocognitive development because it facilitates the joining in collective meaning-making efforts with others whose reasoning is shaped by very different world-views or life-contexts. However, if our concern were only with individual psychological well-being, and not with sociocognitive development, we might not be so quick to advocate this tradeoff. If might well depend on the likelihood of the individual being able to organize his or her life in such a way as to avoid encountering events that shatter his or her particular sources of intellectual security.

We face sources of limitations other than intellectual ones, and other sources of pain as well. In the example of the relationship breaking up, loss of the reassuring presence of someone one loves and whom one may have expected to spend one's life with is painful, usually excruciating, no matter how one thinks about it. Dialectical thinking can not free one from that pain. However, the kind of formalistic analysis of the break-up that I presented before intellectually reinforces the pain. It adds to the pain of loss the self-punitive pain of failure or inadequate judgment or the divisive pain of blame and hatred. The dialectical analysis is more likely to allow one to experience the pain as loss and to mourn the loss. At the same time the pain of loss may be counterbalanced by an emotionally positive intellectual awareness of (1) order in the developmental process, (2) new discovery, and (3) the opening of new possibilities.

In the case of the Marxian analysis presented above, if one is embedded in the midst of a capitalist economy, whether as a government economic advisor or as an individual laborer and consumer, it may seem far more worthwhile to spend one's time analyzing the laws of that economy formalistically than analyzing how it got to be that way, how it maintains itself, and where it could be going, dialectically. Granted, not being able to imagine what living under different laws of economic behavior would be like is a limitation; but needing to live among other people, all operating according to the current laws, poses a more serious limitation. Again, if we were arguing solely about individual welfare, the tradeoff between analyses that help one make predictions given boundary conditions that are unlikely to change in the near future and analyses that might help one to change or prepare for change in those conditions would be tough to evaluate. But from the point of view of humanity, as a socioepistemic subject, involved in an ongoing pursuit of truth, the added power made possible by the capacity for dialectical analyses seems important to recognize. While recognizing the importance of seriously addressing the question, Who has time for what kind of dialectical analyses when I do want to claim that dialectical thinking is an important phenomenon of young adult sociocognitive development.

To review, the following general characteristics of dialectical thinking have been cited above.

1. Dialectical thinking is thinking that looks for and recognizes instances of dialectic—developmental transformation occurring via constitutive and interactive relationships.
2. Dialectical thinking is philosophically rooted in a family of world outlooks in which knowledge and existence are viewed as essentially dialectical processes and in which change, wholeness, and internal relations are emphasized.
3. Dialectical analyses draw attention to the limits of the contexts in which formal analyses are applicable.
4. As a result, dialectical analyses have a power to deal with relationships and transformations beyond the boundary conditions of a formal analysis, while still making use of the power of the formal analysis within those boundaries.
5. Dialectical approaches are more permeable than formalistic approaches to the perspectives of other people who may define a problem in fundamentally different ways.

Dialectical Schemata

In order to operationalize the concept of dialectical thinking and make it accessible to psychological research, I developed the dialectical schemata (DS) framework. The DS framework breaks dialectical thinking down into 24 component *schemata*—specific types of moves-in-thought that dialectical thinkers tend to make (see Table 2.1). These 24 patterned moves-in-thought can then be readily identified in an individual's explanations,

TABLE 2.1. THE DIALECTICAL SCHEMA FRAMEWORK

A. Motion-orientated schemata

1. Thesis-antithesis-synthesis movement in thought
2. Affirmation of the primacy of motion
3. Recognition and description of thesis-antithesis-synthesis movement
4. Recognition of correlativity of a thing and its other
5. Recognition of ongoing interaction as a source of movement
6. Affirmation of the practical or active character of knowledge
7. Avoidance or exposure of objectification, hypostatization, and reification
8. Understanding events or situations as moments (of development) of a process

B. Form-oriented schemata

9. Location of an element or phenomenon with the whole(s) of which it is a part
10. Description of a whole (system, form) in structural, functional, or equilibrational terms
11. Assumption of contextual relativism

C. Relationship-oriented schemata

12. Assertion of the existence of relations, the limits of separation and the value of relatedness
13. Criticism of multiplicity, subjectivism, and pluralism
14. Description of a two-way reciprocal relationship
15. Assertion of internal relations

D. Meta-formal schemata

16. Location (or description of the process of emergence) of contradictions or sources of disequilibrium within a system (form) or between a system (form) and external forces or elements that are antithetical to the system's (form's) structure
17. Understanding the resolution of disequilibrium or contradiction in terms of a notion of transformation in developmental direction
18. Relating value to (a) movement in developmental direction and/or (b) stability through developmental movement
19. Evaluative comparison of forms (systems)
20. Attention to problems of coordinating systems (forms) in relation to each other
21. Description of open self-transforming systems
22. Description of qualitative change as a result of quantitative change within a form
23. Criticism of formalism based on the interdependence of form and content
24. Multiplication of perspectives as a concreteness-preserving approach to inclusiveness.

Source: Basseches 1984, 74.

analyses, or arguments. I have described these specific schemata and the research using the DS framework in detail elsewhere (see Basseches 1978, 1980, 1984) and will not review them here. However, to summarize, this research has indicated that a sample of college faculty members, on the average, use a broader range of dialectical schemata in their thinking than do college seniors, who in turn use a broader range than do college freshman.

The dialectical schemata resemble Piagetian operations, in that both are hypothetical constructs presumed to regulate thought. Also, both perform this regulatory function in coordination with other schemata or operations.

However, there is a fundamental difference between the way in which Piagetian operations are coordinated with one another and the way in which dialectical schemata eventually become coordinated within the organization of dialectical thinking as a whole. Operations are organized into closed systems ("structures") of reversible operations in which the effects of any operation can be undone by the use of an inverse operation, and no operation or combination of operations yields a result external to the system as a whole. In contrast, the dialectical schemata are organized into a coherent whole by an underlying model of dialectic. Whereas a structure is a closed system, resistant to fundamental change, a dialectic is an ongoing process of developmental transformation. Thus, when dialectical schemata are applied in coordination, new thoughts are built upon old ones in nonreversible fashion, and unlike the case of reversible operations, the contents of thought are irrevocably changed. This means the dialectical schemata regulate a much more free, less conservative kind of movement in thought than Piagetian operations. Dialectical schemata refer to moves in thought in which even the constraints associated with formal operations are broken free of, while at the same time the order provided by formal operations is in part maintained.

Whereas formal operations and concrete operations describe how thought is structured and made to move within a closed system, dialectical schemata describe how thought frees itself to transcend closed systems and thereby to create and comprehend change of a greater scope in itself and in the world. The examples of dialectical thinking thus far presented all involved challenging the boundary conditions of formal analyses and dealing with what lies beyond those boundaries.

Dialectic as an Organizing Principle

The organizing principle for formal operational thought is the structured whole, or system. In contrast, the organizing principle for dialectical thinking is the dialectic. If we equate the notion of form in the definition of dialectic with that of structured whole or system we see how the concept of dialectic builds upon, but is more complex than, the concept of system. Dialectic refers to the developmental transformation of systems over time, via constitutive and interactive relationships.

Thus, whereas formal thinking is systematic, dialectical thinking is metasystematic. In formal operational thought, an underlying (closed) system organizes a *logic of propositions* into a coherent whole. It enables the thinker to deal systematically with various propositions and their necessary interrelationships. It also makes possible the analysis of phenomena that can be effectively modeled as comprising closed systems. But the closed-system model is not adequate for problems requiring analysis of (1) multiple systems and their relationships to each other, or (2) open systems that undergo radical transformation.

In contrast, in dialectical thinking, an underlying model of dialectic organizes a *logic of systems* into a coherent whole. It enables the thinker to deal with various systems and their relationships to each other over time dialectically. The model of dialectic does provide a basis for analysis of (1) multiple systems and their relationships to each other, as well as (2) open systems that undergo radical transformation.

Dialectical Thinking as a Level of Equilibrium

According to Piaget's strict definition of a structure (1970), a structure *must* be a closed system. Since a dialectic is a system that changes in fundamental and irreversible ways over time, as a result of dynamic relationships both within the system and between the system and its context (which may include other systems), a dialectic is clearly not a structure in the traditional Piagetian sense. Nor is thought organized by the concept of dialectic a Piagetian structure. Nevertheless, there is a formation of equilibrium provided by dialectical cognitive organization. In fact, dialectical thinking allows the recognition of something as remaining constant amidst a far broader range of changes than formal reasoning can equilibrate. Let us explore the nature of that equilibrium.

The whole study of equilibration in genetic epistemology (Piaget 1952, 1978) is based on the recognition of two properties of human cognition. First, there is a human need to imposed stability on the reality that people experience. Cognitive schemata allow one to make sense of—cognize and re-cognize—what without those structures would be nothing more than James's "blooming, buzzing, confusion." Second, there is a human process of applying and extending one's cognitive schemata by putting them into practice in the world (assimilation), which tends to result in changes (accommodation). Structures of equilibrium allow this process of extension and change to occur, while keeping something constant.

Consider the various structures of equilibrium that Piaget describes.

The permanent-object concept (sensorimotor stage) allows one to recognize an object as constant, amidst continual change in its appearance resulting from the new perspectives from which it is viewed. Conservation of volume (concrete operations stage) allows one to recognize the abstract concept of volume as remaining constant through the various transformations that occur in pouring a quantity of liquid from one receptacle to another. Propositional logic (formal operations stage) describes rules for keeping the truth values of simple propositions (p, q) constant, and for transforming them into determinate truth values of complex propositions as the simple propositions are recombined into complex propositions in various way (e.g., $p \wedge q$; $p \vee q$; $\sim p \wedge q$; $q \rightarrow p$; etc.).

In dialectical thinking, what it is that remains recognizable across a range of changes is the historical process as an evolving whole. Any change at all, no matter how radical, can be equilibrated if it can be conceptualized as a moment in a dialectical process of evolution. New events are integrated within a dialectical conception of a process as later steps in the evolution of that process; old constructions are conserved— they remain part of the process of dialectic—although their historical role is reconstructed in the light of subsequent transformations.

For example, consider this dialectical analysis of sex roles. Systematic regularities have existed throughout history in male and female sex roles. In each era, the description of regularities in male and female sex roles has led to abstractions about how women's nature and temperament is on the whole different from men's. Now that certain changes in society have occurred (e.g., overpopulation), phenomena occur more regularly that are discrepant with traditional sex roles. The abstract models, as well as social norms and laws that are based upon and support those models, are viewed as no longer adequate. Contradictions or tensions have emerged in the system of sex role–regulated behavior including demands for political, social, and economic equality of the sexes. These contradictions will only be resolved as new more developed conceptions of maleness and femaleness emerge that are consistent with a greater range of male and female activities and with equality between the sexes (see Gilligan 1978, 1982).

The basis of the equilibrium in this way of thinking are (1) the assumption that change is what is most fundamental; and (2) the ability to conceptualize changes as (a) emergences of contradictions within existing systems and (b) formations of new, more inclusive systems. The nature of maleness and femaleness is not viewed as fundamental—it is seen as likely to change through history. At any point in time it may be useful to conceptualize the regularities in male and female roles, but these conceptualizations are meaningful as part of a historical process in which they will be challenged and transcended.

A closed-system model of sex-role behavior, which claims that such behavior derives from fundamental immutable laws of male and female temperament, must necessarily ignore or attempt to suppress what begin an anomalies and later become new patterns of behavior by males and females, if the equilibrium of the system is to be maintained[2] (i.e., if maleness is to continue to be recognized as maleness and femaleness is to continue to be recognized as femaleness). In contrast, a dialectical model can incorporate such anomalies and new patterns while maintaining equilibrium by recognizing them as developments in the continuing dialectic of the relations of the sexes.

I have argued elsewhere (1980, 1984) that dialectical thinking describes a post-formal level of cognitive organization. This argument is based in part on the fact that dialectic as an organizing principle builds upon (and treats at a level of greater complexity by integrating with the dimension of change over time) the concept of system, which is the organizing principle of formal operations. The argument is also based in part on the greater equilibrating power (ability to maintain recognizable continuity in the midst of a broader range of change) of dialectical cognitive organization vis-à-vis formal operational organization. But it should be clear from the above example that my view that dialectical thinking is a necessary advance in equilibrium is also based on the general ontological assumption that people will be confronted with anomalous events that do not conform to prior closed-system laws.

In the natural sciences, this general ontological assumption amounts to the assumption that scientists will have to deal with scientific revolutions (Kuhn). In the life sciences and social sciences, it amounts to the assumption that the phenomena dealt with are highly susceptible to rapid and radical change, which scientists will need to comprehend. In day-to-day life, it amounts to the assumption that for making practical decisions, closed systems (including moral systems) that are constructed on the basis of limited data and from limited perspectives will be inadequate. Social life is complex and requires multiple perspective-taking. People will be confronted with new data and new perspectives, and it is important that their cognitive structures leave them open to taking these new data and perspectives into account, accommodating to them, and dealing with them constructively. Confrontations, in science and in life, with phenomena that demand recognition of multiple interacting systems and radical transformation of systems, will point out the limits of formal thinking and stimulate the construction of more dialectical forms of reasoning.

Facilitating the Development of Dialectical Thinking

The above assumptions imply the importance of dialectical thinking to the achievement of cognitive equilibrium. This does not, however, imply that all young adults in fact achieve this level of equilibrium. Research indicates that just as all adults do not fully develop formal operations, so they may not all develop dialectical thinking. Whether individuals do develop dialectical thinking depends on both environmental factors and developmental characteristics of the person.

First of all, fully developed dialectical thinking presupposes something like what Piaget calls formal operations. The ability to organize the world into an abstract consistent systematic pattern is a prerequisite to providing an account of how such patterns evolve and change. It is certainly possible to recognize the ontological and epistemological centrality of change, as well as the power of relationships, without organizing the world into systems. In fact, these recognitions may constitute preformal precursors and dialectical thinking. However, to do more than assert the importance of change and relationships—to actually describe the course of dialectical change over time—requires the ability to describe the temporary patterns of organization systems that constitute moments in dialectical processes.

When adults systematize the world (1) using sets of fixed categories, and (2) holding to static ontological and epistemological assumptions often associated with formal thought, their maintenance of cognitive equilibrium depends on their power to seal themselves off from anomalous data and discrepant viewpoints. For example, with respect to the analysis of sex roles above, individuals may attempt (1) to force others to conform to their notions of sex-appropriate behavior, or (2) to isolate themselves from individuals whose behavior does not conform, in order to maintain their systematic understandings of the nature of masculinity and femininity. These strategies are surely not optimal from the point of view of a concern with expanding human sociality, but they may succeed in the short term if the individuals employing them are powerful enough. However, if adults cannot seal themselves off from discrepant events, they are likely to experience frustrations and conflicts resulting from the limits of fixed categories of thought for addressing a changing reality.

When this happens one of two things is likely to occur. Either the adults will reject formal operational thinking and resort to less logical forms of thought, or the adults will begin to reorganize their formal operations within the context of the more adequate organization of dialectical thinking. A combination of personal support, exposure to diverse perspectives, and opportunities for careful, critical reflection will facilitate the latter outcome.

Higher education appears to hold considerable potential as an environment for promoting this kind of cognitive development in late adolescents and adults, and writing assignments can play a crucial role in this process.

If we address the specific question, What conditions must prevail in institutions of higher education if they are to serve as effective contexts for the development of dialectical thinking? Several hypotheses suggest themselves.

First these institutions must not be content merely to present students with "established facts." They must present students with multiple frames of reference—multiple justifiable coherent ways of interpreting facts based on diverging assumptions—that can be contrasted to each other. This experience is likely to lead students to recognize the active, relativistic nature of the process of interpretation, a crucial recognition in the movement from formal to dialectical forms of cognitive organization.

Similarly, students should not be presented with single "correct" methods of discovery. Rather, alternative paradigms for research should be contrasted, and all methods should be open to question based on their appropriateness to various human goals. The recognition of the relativity of the very process of research (i.e., the construction of facts) to alternate modes of interpretation forms a crucial foundation for development of dialectical thinking.

At the same time, educational institutions should not be content to leave students in the transitional swamps of relativism. Students should recognize that there are multiple ways of looking at things. However, it is also important to recognize that these multiple ways of looking at things, along with the people who look at things in these ways, interact with each other over history. Advances in human knowledge occur when people succeed in synthesizing valuable aspects of different perspectives so that they function together as a whole, just as advances in history occur as the people who look at things in different ways learn to live together harmoniously.

Multipe conflicting frames of reference and multiple points of view must be presented to students as facts of life and as crucial moments in dialectical processes. But while these facts of life are presented as facts to be recognized, they must not be presented simply as facts to be accepted. Rather, each instance of conflicting points of view must be presented to students as an epistemological challenge—a challenge not only to the student but to the faculty as well. It should not be expected that the student will meet the challenge by resolving such conflicts in the course of the semester, or perhaps even in his or her lifetime, but it should be recognized that to be a seeker of truth means to try. For it is through the efforts of those who have taken on the challenges of trying that knowledge has advanced.

Finally, educational institutions must provide personal support for development, or, as Perry has put it, educators must share "in the costs of growth" (267). They must recognize the pain of letting go of a world where every question has a right answer and either authorities or logic can be counted on to provide the correct answers, to slowly build a world where the only answers one will have are those one has struggled for—a world where in many cases one will struggle and not find any answers at all and where in the rest of the cases the answers one finds only beget new questions. Educators must at least acknowledge their own pain, which comes of being dedicated to truth.

For if teachers hold up a bravado of confidence and comfort, students will have to cope not only with their own pain but also with the feeling that there is something wrong with them for feeling this pain when their teachers appear to breeze through a relativistic world so nonchalantly, so much in command. Beyond acknowledging their own intellectual pain and sharing it with students, educators can actually share in students' pain, if not by holding hands, at least by holding minds. Educators will find themselves with many more opportunities to revel in the joys of their students' growth—to share the release of emancipation that occurs when the students realize new degrees of freedom—if the educators are also willing to share in growth's costs.

It may be informative to compare higher education, a context in which the shared social commitment to rationality is normally taken for granted but where the need for personal support is too often ignored, with a context in which the reverse is true. Psychotherapy is another context in which the development of dialectical thinking in late adolescents and adults may be fostered. In this context, one finds more prevalent recognition of the importance of providing personal support at times when the individual's sense of coherence in the self and world are under attack. However, a greater understanding of, and more explicit commitment to, dialectical rationality on the part of therapists would make psychotherapy a more effective context for development.

The modal source of threat of self/world coherence is somewhat different in psychotherapy and higher education, although there is also significant overlap. Whereas in higher education the challenges to one's way of making rational sense of things are likely to come from exposure to alternative ways of making rational sense, in psychotherapy aspects of one's experience of self and world which are internally in tension with one's ways of making sense are more often the source of the challenge. Comparable to the educator's task of balancing supporting students' realization of the existence of alternative ways of looking at things with the awareness of possibilities for growth from the interaction of perspectives is the therapist's task and supporting both openness to discrepant aspects of one's experience and the desire to build a coherent sense of self and the world that integrates these discrepant "irrational" experiences. While in the social setting of higher education the shared commitment to rationality is built upon to maintain the balancing act between doubt and integration, in psychotherapy a commitment to suspending the demands of rationality is needed to protect the dialectic from "rationalization" and to maintain clients' openness to their own experience. Nevertheless, a commitment to the client as a rational meaning-maker is equally important to support the client's integrative tendencies and capacities, within which dialectical thinking can develop as a crucial tool.

Within higher education, the relationship between theorizing and practice is perhaps analogous to the relationship the therapist must maintain between the client's rational capacities and the fuller reality of the client's experience-in-the-world. The positive effects of the educational process are likely to be limited insofar as it is divorced from practical concerns. If one only studies the systematizations of science and philosophy as abstract objects rather than attempting to systematize the dynamic contradictory realities of life beyond the laboratory and the classroom (students' own lives and those of others), encounters with the discrepant may be limited. On the other hand, if (as happens in much preprofessional education), practical problems are addressed but the definitions of the problems are taken uncritically, from a single point of view, discrepancies may also be avoided (especially if the point of view is that of powerful elements of society—elements strong enough to impose the order of a static system on the lives of others.)

In sum, my assertion that the achievement of dialectical thinking describes the direction of young adult cognitive development is a claim (1) that this achievement normally occurs after the achievement of formal operations, and (2) that this achievement is worthy of being called a "development" in the genetic epistemological sense of providing a more adequate way of understanding the universe than do formal operations alone. My discussion of dialectic as a principle of organization and dialectical thinking from the equilibrium standpoint have addressed the second (2, above) part of this claim (see Basseches 1978, 1984, for an elaboration of this claim). Results from empirical research (Basseches 1980, 1984) have provided initial support for the first (1, above) part of the claim (viz. that there is a tendency for dialectical thinking to be achieved after formal operations).

NOTES

1. This problem is analogous to an oft-discussed problem of social research. When researchers deal with data by sorting subjects' responses into categories predetermined by the researchers, this excludes the possibility of the subjcts contributing from their own perspectives to the definition of the problem and the shape of the results.
2. Note the arguments of the "Moral Majority" here.

WORKS CITED

Adorno, T.W., and M. Horkheimer. *Dialectic of Enlightenment*. Trans. John Cumming. London: NLB, 1979.

Basseches, M. *Beyond Closed-System Problem Solving: A Study of Metasystematic Aspects of Mature Thought*. Ph.D. diss. Harvard University, 1978. Ann Arbor, MI: UMI, 1979. 79/8210.

———. "Dialectical Schematas: A Framework for the Empirical Study of the Development of Dialectical Thinking." *Human Development* 23 (1980): 400–421.

———. *Dialectical Thinking and Adult Development*. Norwood, NJ: Ablex, 1984.

Feyerabend, P. *Against Method: Outline of an Anarchist Theory of Knowledge*. London: NLB, 1975.

Fowler, J.W. *Stages of Faith*. New York: Harper & Row, 1981.

Gilligan, C. "In a Different Voice: Women's Conception of the Self and Morality." *Harvard Educational Review* 7.4 (1978): 481–517.

———. *In a Different Voice: Psychological Theory and Women's Development*. Cambridge: Harvard University Press, 1982.

Hegel, G.W.F. *The Philosophy of Right*. Trans. T.M. Knox. *The Philosophy of History*. Trans. J. Sibree. Vol. 46 of *Great Books of the Western World*. Ed. R.M. Hutchins and M.J. Adler. Chicago: Encyclopedia Britannica, 1952.

Horz, H., H. Poltz, H. Parthey, U. Rosenbert, and K. Wessel. *Philosophical Problems in Physical Science*. Minneapolis: Marxist Educational Press, 1980.

Jameson, F. *Marxism and Form: 20th Century Dialectical Theories of Literature*. Princeton: Princeton University Press, 1971.

Jay, M. *The Dialectical Imagination*. Boston: Little, Brown, 1973.

Kilminster, R. *Praxis and Method: A Sociological Dialogue with Lukacs, Gramsci, and the Early Frankforth School*. London: Routledge & Kegan Paul, 1979.

Kuhn, T.S. *The Structure of Scientific Revolutions*. 2nd ed. Chicago: University of Chicago Press, 1970.

Mandel, E. *An Introduction to Marxist Economic Theory*. New York: Pathfinder Press, 1973.

Marx, K. *Writings of the Young Marx on Philosophy and Society*. Ed. L.D. Easton and K.H. Guddat. Garden City: Anchor, 1967.

Marx, K. and F. Engels. *The Communist Manifesto*. 1948. Norwalk, CT: Appleton-Century-Crofts, 1955.

Perry, W.G. "Sharing in the Costs of Growth." *Encouraging Development in College Students*. Ed. Clyde A. Parker. Minneapolis, MN; University of Minnesota Press, 1978. 267–273.

Piaget, J. *The Origins of Intelligence in Children*. New York: Norton, 1952.

———. *Structuralism*. New York: Basic Books, 1970.

———. *The Development of Thought*. Oxford: Blackwell, 1978.

Popper, K. *The Logic of Scientific Discovery*. New York: Basic Books, 1959.

Provine, W. *The Origins of Theoretical Population Genetics*. Chicago: University of Chicago Press, 1971.

Reichenbach, H. *Experience and Prediction*. Chicago: University of Chicago Press, 1938.

Smith, A. *An Inquiry into the Nature and Causes of the Wealth of Nations*. 1776. New York: Modern Library, 1937.

CHAPTER 3

A Model of the Mature Thinker

Edith D. Neimark

Any attempt at a definitive description of "the mature thinker" involves, of necessity, the exercise of temerity. Certainly there is no accepted scale of maturity on file at the National Bureau of Standards in Washington against which to calibrate it. Rather, what I have to offer is a personal view, albeit an informed one reflective of current theory and evidence in the areas of cognitive psychology and cognitive development. Other writers would doubtless have a different evaluation of what features are central and the nature of their relationship. I shall try to provide some indication of possible alternative interpretations in the discussion that follows. It should be added that this description is also an exercise in ethnocentrism. Industrialized Western societies with their emphasis upon achievement, individual initiative, and technological advance have different value systems than do other cultures. This caveat is well to bear in mind in evaluating one's students; sometimes apparent shortcomings are better attributed to a different value system rather than a lack of ability (cf. Goodnow and Cashmore).

In the discussion that follows I offer my model of the mature thinker described in terms of desirable qualities of behavior rather than the actual behaviors themselves, along with relevant information to justify the characteristics selected. I shall then suggest some procedures for developing those characteristics in oneself and in one's students. The term *model* is used advisedly, partly because its connotations of schematic summary and idealization (that aims at encompassing all possible instances while providing accurate description of no specific example) are appropriate, and partly because the construction of models and other organizing frame-

47

TABLE 3.1. SOME SAMPLE PROBLEMS FOR YOU TO SOLVE

1. You have four separate lengths of chain, each consisting of three links. Your task is to join them into one continuous necklace as cheaply as possible. It costs 2 cents to open a link and 3 cents to close it. Can you make a necklace for 15 cents?
2. A father and son were involved in an auto crash in which the father was killed and the son seriously injured. The son was rushed to a hospital where the neurosurgeon said in dismay, "I can't operate on him: he's my son." How could that be?
3. At a celebration for two fathers and two sons each honoree has a cake. There are a total of three cakes. How can that be?
4. If a unique number is substituted for each letter in the problems below it will yield a correct arithmetic sum. Break the code.

$$
\begin{array}{r}
\text{F O U R} \\
+ \text{ F I V E} \\
\hline
\text{N I N E}
\end{array}
\qquad
\begin{array}{r}
\text{S E N D} \\
+ \text{ M O R E} \\
\hline
\text{M O N E Y}
\end{array}
$$

Box 1–1, "Five Classic Problems" from *Adventures in Thinking* by Edith D. Neimark, copyright © 1987 by Harcourt Brace Jovanovich, Inc. Reprinted by permission of the publisher.

works is a major activity of the mature thinker. Finally, it is worth noting that although "mature" connotes the result of aging, the process of growing older is insufficient in and of itself to produce the qualities to be described. Many inadequacies in thinking can appropriately be viewed as the persistence of immature behavior and outlooks. To provide a concrete context for discussion a number of old chestnuts from the problem-solving literature are presented in Table 3.1. Do them and also record your thought processes in the course of solution.

CHARACTERISTICS OF THE MATURE THINKER

In couching my description in terms of characteristics of the individual thinker rather than in terms of properties of the thought process itself I am adopting a less popular view of which the reader should be aware. By dealing with individual characteristics as habitual orientations somewhat analogous to personality traits, I am suggesting that mature thought is better viewed as an approach to life rather than as a specific skill that can be developed and applied as the need arises. This view has widespread and pervasive ramifications. I am also acknowledging the reality of individual differences. Although the mature thinker is a different kind of person than the immature thinker, there are differences among mature thinkers. For any given individual some characteristics will be more prominent and more easily developed than others, and they may be manifest in different ways. The four necessary characteristics that I have identified are transformative, systematic, detached, and evaluative. Let's consider each in turn, although it is hard to deal with any one independent of the others.

Transformative

Thought is by its very nature symbolic. In thinking one does not deal directly and exclusively with concrete objects and events of the here and now but, rather, with some representation of them expressed symbolically through images, words, diagrams, implicit actions, and so on (cf. Mandler). Thought transforms experience by actively endowing it with meaning. In so doing it removes events from the concrete context of direct experience and places them in a symbolic framework (e.g., an object is labeled as a member of a class or an event is understood in terms of some theoretical principle). Symbolic frameworks differ with respect to their level of abstraction. Moshman and Franks (Chapter 1) identify the levels distinguished by Piaget and describe how the stage of formal operations differs from the preceding stage of concrete operations in (1) the shift of focus from content to form, (2) the nature of the operations applied, and (3) the closed-system structure relating operations.

Although the Piagetian view of cognitive development is not universally accepted, all cognitive psychologists agree that understanding is an individual construction: that each individual develops his or her own world view through a process of transforming experience via the mechanism of thought and testing that view against reality. Of necessity, therefore, the thinker is actively engaged in a process of transformation at progressively higher levels of abstraction as connections are formed and new experience is related to existing knowledge. This process may be illustrated in your approach to the necklace problem. At first you probably dealt with it in terms of the four presented lengths, opening the end link of each and connecting them. But that solution would cost 20 cents and exceed the allowed amount. That realization should shift your focus away from the actual lengths and toward the constraint upon them: only three links can be opened and reconnected. How may that be achieved? By using one length as the source of connectors for the remaining three. As you go through the other problems you may begin to notice a similarity among them: all contain inducements to automatic habitual response patterns that will lead you down a cul-de-sac and prevent solution. As a result of this insight you may begin to classify problems not in terms of their content, as the necklace problem or the surgeon problem, but in terms of their structure, for instance, problems involving negative set. Many, but by no means all problems, are of this form; a more abstract categorization of them helps to develop solutions for the general class (cf. Mayer). There is an obvious implication of this discovery for teaching practice: although a good example is helpful in introducing material, one should always go beyond specific examples and encourage the generation of alternative examples by the student to help him or her identify central features and formulate more abstract categories with respect to them. It might be noted that abstract formulations are not only more general but also more neutral and, therefore, less subject to constraint and more conducive to the generation of many alternatives for consideration. Since the present discussion has, itself, been pretty abstract, you may want to construct alternative examples of your own (e.g., instances of subject matter concepts).

Systematic

The central feature of a systematic approach is the search for an organizing framework, be it a general classification, relevant principles, apt analogy, appropriate model, set of procedures, or outline. For example, I suggested that in dealing with the problems of Table 3.1 it is helpful to view them as instances of a general class of problems: One solution procedure, working from maximal to lesser constraints, is a good way to deal with many problems, such as the crypt-arithmetic problem. To take another example, Donne's celebrated sermon is constructed on a geographic metaphor, "No man is an island," from which the conclusion "Seek not to know for whom the bell tolls It tolls for thee" is derived. Darwin's use of the analogy of a branching tree (Gruber) in which to couch his theory of evolution is yet another example of the power of an organizing framework. Voss's discussion (Chapter 4) of the difference between the novice and the expert provides yet other examples. Doubtless you can generate additional examples of your own.

Most contemporary approaches to the training of thinking—and there are a great many of them—tend to focus almost exclusively upon the importance of a systematic approach by providing prescribed procedures as tools of efficient thought. Two good examples are presented in Table 3.2, the systematic procedures for problem solving proposed by Polya and by Hayes. They are very useful and the interested reader is urged to pursue them in greater detail (see also Bransford and Stein). Comparable procedures have been described to enhance creativity, in general, by increasing the number of alternatives considered or by adopting a generative framework (Adams; DeBono; Parnes, Noller, and Biondi are all useful examples). To appreciate more fully the role of a systematic approach, you might review your description of your thought processes in solving the problems of Table 3.1. Did you have a system, or was your procedure more accurately described as trial and error?

In characterizing the mature thinker as systematic, I want to emphasize not only that he or she has a practiced repertoire of systematic procedures, but also that he or she has a general orientation toward proceeding systematically whatever the enterprise, through prior planning and search for organization. The novice writer, for example, discovers what he or she has to say in the course of writing it, whereas the expert devotes much time to creating a focus or organizing framework and an outline in which to develop it. It is the orienting quest for coherence, a conscious intent to impose order and meaning that motivates and guides the acquisition and use of one's armamentarium of conceptual machinery (formalized knowledge and procedural rules). A great many writers have made this point (Bruner; deCharms; Dewey; Rogers; Wertheimer, to cite a few of many possible examples). It underlies much discussion of education, inveighing against rote learning, and my introductory observation on the importance of model building.

Hayes's analysis of the procedure of problem solving makes the orienting aspect of a systematic approach more explicit than does Polya's analysis (which it incorporates) through the addition of an initial and a final step. Problem finding, the first step, has been proposed as a characteristic of mature thought (Getzels) that marks an advance beyond the level of formal operations (Arlin). The term contrasts problem solving, a readiness for coping with presented problems, to a deliberate set for provoking challenging questions, in effect, anticipating problems before they arise. Perhaps the best-known examples of problem finding are Fleming's discovery of antibiotics as a consequence of his questioning why mold should kill bacterial cultures and Newton's reflections on a falling apple. In both cases systematic questioning of a commonplace event led to significant advances in knowledge. Hayes's final step, consolidation of gains, reflects a comparable effect of the quest for understanding beyond the attainment of a solution to an immediate problem that is, relating the resultant finding to existing knowledge to broaden, or, if need be, modify it accordingly (or, perhaps, to progress to problem finding in an ever-widening spiral of meaning-making).

Detached

The term *detached* has several connotations, all of them relevant to the description of a mature thinker. One connotation, detachment from immediate content and context, has already been considered and its relevance to problem solving demonstrated. One of the major cognitive styles identified in the psychological literature, field independence as contrasted with the opposite pole of the continuum, field dependence (Witkin; Witkin, Moore, Goodenough, and Cox) focuses upon this aspect of behavior (cf. Neimark, 1981, for its implication for cognitive performance). In general, individuals with a field dependent style have been shown to be more limited thinkers on a variety of tasks. Figure 3.1 contains items of the sort often used to assess cognitive style.

A second connotation, impersonal, is also relevant. The mature thinker is able to detach from his or her emotional reactions and personal values and to appreciate the possible viewpoints of other individuals. The attainment of relativism has been discussed by both Moshman and Franks

TABLE 3.2. TWO PROBLEM-SOLVING ANALYSES

	Polya's	Hayes's
First. You have to *understand* the problem.	UNDERSTANDING THE PROBLEM • *What is the unknown? What are the data? What is the condition?* • Is it possible to satisfy the condition? Is the condition sufficient to determine the unknown? Or is it insufficient? Or redundant? Or contradictory? • Draw a figure. Introduce suitable notation. • Separate the various parts of the condition. Can you write them down?	Finding the problem. What state of affairs is unsatisfactory or unclear? Representing the problem. What is the goal? How can it be reached? What are the constraints on an acceptable solution?
Second. Find the connection between the data and the unknown. You may be obliged to consider auxiliary problems if an immediate connection cannot be found. You should obtain eventually a *plan* of the solution.	DEVISING A PLAN • Have you seen it before? Or have you seen the same problem in a slightly different form? • *Do you know a related problem?* Do you know a theorem that could be useful? • *Look at the unknown!* And try to think of a familiar problem having the same or a similar unknown. • *Here is a problem related to yours and solved before. Could you use it?* Could you use its results? Could you use its method? Should you introduce some auxiliary element in order to make its use possible? • Could you restate the problem? Could you restate it still differently? Go back to definitions. • If you cannot solve the proposed problem, try to solve first some related problem. Could you imagine a more accessible related problem? A more general problem. A more special problem? An analogous problem? Could you solve a part of the problem? Keep only a part of the condition, drop the other part; how far is the unknown then determined, how can it vary? Could you derive something	Planning the solution. List steps and courses of action contingent on alternative outcomes.

	useful from the data? Could you think of other data appropriate to determine the unknown? Could you think of other data appropriate to determine the unknown? Could you change the unknown or the data, or both if necessary, so that the new unknowns and the new data are nearer to each other? Did you use all the data? • Did you use the whole condition? Have you taken into account all essential notions involved in the problem?	
Third. *Carry out* your plan.	CARRYING OUT THE PLAN • Carrying out your plan of the solution, check each step. Can you see clearly that the step is correct? Can you prove that it is correct?	Carry out the plan.
Fourth. *Examine* the solution obtained.	LOOKING BACK • Can you *check the result?* Can you check the argument? • Can you derive the result differently? Can you see it at a glance? • Can you use the result, or the method, for some other problem?	Evaluate the solution. Does it satisfy the demands and constraints of the representation? Consolidating gains. What have you learned?

Polya, G. (1957). *How to Solve It: A New Aspect of Mathematical Method.* Copyright 1945, © 1973 renewed by Princeton University Press, second edition copyright © 1957 by G. Polya. Table on pp. xvi–xvii reprinted by permission of Princeton University Press.

and by Basseches (Chapters 1 and 2, respectively). These authors have demonstrated the movement away from an egocentric framework as a characteristic of mature thought and some of its wide ramifications for improved interpersonal relations. To cite but one of many possible examples, the responsible authorities of every society—its judges, mediators, and leader—must find a common ground among contending positions. Their failure to do so, as in the case of Mr. Botha and other South African officials, is at the heart of serious social upheavals. In more academic enterprises, this aspect of detachment has led to significant scientific advance (e.g., Einstein's theory of relativity, or the field of cultural anthropology) as well as memorable literary works (e.g., the dramatic tension in the Japanese film *Rashomon*).

A third connotation, leading to much current research in cognitive

A. Match the top skater with one exactly alike in the bottom row.

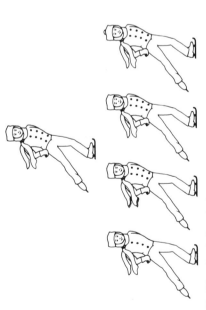

B. Find the simple form below in the complex figure to its right.

C. For each of the bottles pictured below imagine that it is half full of wine and closed tightly. Draw in a line showing the fluid level. The first one has been completed as an example.

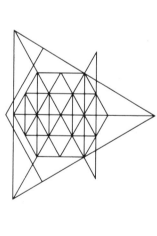

D. Answer yes or no to each of the items below:
  1. I find it difficult to handle questions requiring a comparison of different concepts.
  2. I have trouble making inferences.
  3. I have trouble organizing the information I remember.
  4. I find it difficult to handle questions requiring critical evaluation.
  5. I do well on essay tests.
  6. I look for reasons behind the facts.
  7. New concepts usually make me think of similar concepts.
  8. While studying, I attempt to find answers to questions I have in mind.
  9. I am usually able to design procedures for solving problems.
  10. After reading a unit of material I sit and think about it. (After Schmeck, 1983)

Figure 3.1 Some Sample Cognitive Style Test Items (A–C: "Some Style Test Items," from *Adventures in Thinking*, Box 1–4, by Edith D. Neimark, copyright © 1987 by Harcourt Brace Jovanovich, Inc. Reprinted by permission of the publisher. D: From Ronald R. Schmeck, "Learning Styles of College Students," in *Individual Differences in Cognition*, Vol. I, ed. R.R. Dillon and R.R. Schmeck, Academic Press, 1983. By permission of the publisher and of the author.)

psychology (Brown, Bransford, Ferrara, and Campione; Lefebvre-Pinard; Piaget 1976, 1978; Vygotsky), focuses upon self-awareness or, to use the technical term, metacognition. As implied by use of the prefix *meta*, metacognition refers to cognition about one's own cognitive processes, that is, the ability to detach from one's own thought processes in order to assess them objectively as one would any other items of experience. Just as it is common practice to differentiate two aspects of understanding, into knowledge about substantive domains (declarative knowledge), and systematic procedures for dealing with knowledge (procedural knowledge), a comparable differentation is made with respect to metacognition. That term encompasses both one's knowledge about one's own thought processes (e.g., that long lists of unrelated items are difficult to memorize) as well as the systematic procedures for assessing and directing those processes (executive routines, e.g., for processing text for understanding by summarizing the gist of successive units, relating them to each other, anticipating future points, etc.).

To the extent that any understanding is viewed as the product of the individual's transformation of experience, the reader may be experiencing some justifiable confusion as to the role of conscious regulation. Piaget (1976, 1978) describes three levels of consciousness in self-regulation: autonomous regulation, active regulation, and conscious regulation. He concludes from this analysis that the quality of understanding is a function of its level of conscious regulation; understanding at the level of deliberate conscious regulation is different from and more mature than understanding at the lower levels. To cite a homely example, the novice tennis player's understanding of the game is confined to his or her actions on the court (plus an ability to describe the rules of the game). The top-seeded player, on the other hand, freely describes the game in terms of analysis of the opponent's game and a planned strategy for countering it, all of which are elaborated mentally prior to picking up a racket (although the plan may be changed during the course of the game as a result of conscious monitoring of its effectiveness).

Evaluative

Conscious regulation implies a continual process of judgment and evaluation (What does that mean? Is that true? Does it contradict any earlier statement? are all examples of evaluation of text). Even the simplest everyday actions, such as driving through traffic, tying one's shoes, making breakfast, require judgment and evaluation. Those processes are both inescapable and fallible by their very nature. What characterizes the mature thinker, therefore, is not the frequency or, even, the accuracy of judgments but, rather, their basis. All judgment implies a criterion: some scale, standard, or framework against which it is made. The mature thinker consciously employs the most objective, appropriate, and consistent criteria available. Moreover, explicit formulation of such criteria is an important component of his or her thinking. To express it another way, actions are placed in perspective where, in the broadest sense, that perspective is an explicit, coherent value system. The formulation of such a value system is one of the major continuing tasks of the mature thinker. For the young adult, problems of identity and ethical code are certainly the most pressing (Erikson). Perry and his associates have traced the evolution of an evaluative framework by Harvard undergraduates from the security of absolute right and wrong (a position Perry terms dualism) through the confusions of relativism to dawning awareness of the need for personal commitment. Their scheme is summarized in Figure 3.2. A comparable developmental course in the evolution of a personal moral code has been outlined by Kohlberg and his associates (Colby, Kohlberg, Gibbs, and Lieberman; Kohlberg, Levine, and Hewer). A chilling case history on the failure to attain mature evaluative thought, on the other hand, is provided by Arendt in her analysis of Adolf Eichmann.

Putting it All Together

In attempting to characterize the mature thinker in terms of four salient characteristics, I have drawn upon a variety of literatures differing widely in their domain and breadth of application, vocabulary, underlying assumptions, and empirical base. The resulting idealization is of an individual who actively transforms experience in thought in a deliberate, systematic manner in order to organize and evaluate it within a coherent broader framework. Although my personal model may not violate the reader's own preconceptions, to what extent does it provide a substantive advance over culturally shared common sense? That is a legitimate question to which I cannot now give an adequate answer. What I can do is to identify some important critical questions for this model and some implications for the practical enterprise of transforming students into mature thinkers (see also Neimark 1987)

ISSUES AND IMPLICATIONS

Definition of Terms

The serious reader who employs the four characteristics of the model by deliberately transforming key concepts into his or her own words and examples to identify the defining features and evaluate the uniqueness or utility of the concepts in some systematic fashion will no doubt be very unhappy with the imprecision of the foregoing discussion. What is thinking? Is there only one kind of thinking, independent of what one is thinking about? With respect to what criterion does one identify maturity? Can the four qualities be defined more precisely? These are obvious questions that must be answered. I'll consider the first three and postpone the fourth to the next section.

With respect to the definition of thinking I believe it is accurate to say that all investigators accept the symbolic nature of the process as its central defining property, although, as previously noted, the degree of conscious awareness of the process or the particular symbolic medium may—and do—vary. It is also the case that many typologies of thinking have been proposed: for example, the differentiation of inductive from deductive reasoning has been widely accepted (although philosophers still argue as to the meaningfulness of the distinction). Another proposed differentiation with some empirical support (Guilford) contrasts convergent and divergent thinking: convergent is directed toward a unique solution, whereas divergent looks for many alternatives, ramifications, and novelty. Structurally there are differences among proposed varieties of thought; in terms of performance on appropriate tests, correlations among them may not be very high. Even within a coherent framework, such as Piaget's stages, there is abundant evidence that alternative measures of concrete or of formal operations do not co-vary in an orderly fashion. These data certainly provide ground for caution in speaking globally about thinking as though it were a simple unitary phenomenon. That caution is further emphasized by theorists holding a contextualist position (e.g., Laboratory of Human Cognition) that behavior is intrinsically context-tied and content-specific and that one cannot legitimately generalize across contexts and cultures. Nevertheless, it seems to me meaningful to refer to the relative propensity for engaging in thought regardless of context or occasion as a characteristic in which individuals vary. The reality of this dimension is acknowledged by everyday practice (e.g., letters of recommendation and other occasions for listing individual attributes) if not by current laboratory evidence. We can agree that some people are thoughtful and that others are not and could, if forced to do so, place individuals on a continuum with respect to that dimension.

With respect to the definition of maturity we are on much firmer ground. Rapidly accumulating developmental evidence clearly shows systematic directional change toward greater abstraction, increasing conscious regulation, or the use of more powerful organizing frameworks with advancing age or domain-specific experience (as in the comparison of novice with expert). More difficult questions arise, however, when one attempts to analyze developmental changes into their independent com-

THE SCHEME

Position 1	Authorities know, and if we work hard, read every word, and learn Right Answers, all will be well.
Transition	But what about those Others I hear about? And different opinions? And Uncertainties? Some of our own Authorities disagree with each other or don't seem to know, and some give us problems instead of Answers.
Position 2	True Authorities must be Right, the others are frauds. We remain Right. Others must be different and Wrong. Good Authorities give us problems so we can learn to find the Right Answer by our own independent thought.
Transition	But even Good Authorities admit they don't know all the answers yet!
Position 3	Then some uncertainties and different opinions are real and legitimate *temporarily*, even for Authorities. They're working on them to get to the Truth.
Transition	But there are *so many* things they don't know the Answers to! And they won't for a long time.
Position 4a	Where Authorities don't know the Right answers, everyone has a right to his own opinion; no one is wrong!
Transition (and/or)	But some of my friends ask me to support my opinions with facts and reasons.
Transition	Then what right have They to grade us? About what?
Position 4B	In certain courses Authorities are not asking for the Right Answer; They want us to *think* about things in a certain way, *supporting* opinion with data. That's what they grade us on.

Dualism modified ⟶

Relativism discovered ⟶

Commitments in Relativism developed ⟶

Transition	But this "way" seems to *work* in most courses, and even outside them.
Position 5	Then *all* thinking must be like this, even for Them. Everything is relative but not equally valid. You have to understand how each context works. Theories are not Truth but metaphors to interpret data with. You have to think about your thinking.
Transition	But if everything is relative, am I relative too? How can I know I'm making the Right Choice?
Position 6	I see I'm going to have to make my own decisions in an uncertain world with no one to tell me I'm Right.
Transition	I'm lost if I don't. When I decide on my career (or marriage or values) everything will straighten out.
Position 7	Well, I've made my first Commitment!
Transition	Why didn't that settle everything?
Position 8	I've made several commitments. I've got to balance them—how many, how deep? How certain, how tentative?
Transition	Things are getting contradictory. I can't make logical sense out of life's dilemmas.
Position 9	This is how life will be. I must be wholeheartedly while tentative, fight for my values yet respect others, believe my deepest values right yet be ready to learn. I see that I shall be retracing this whole journey over and over – but, I hope, more wisely.

THE MAP OF DEVELOPMENT

Dualism. Division of meaning into two realms—Good versus Bad, Right versus Wrong. We versus They, All that is not Success is Failure, and the like. Right Answers exist *somewhere* for every problem, and authorities know them. Right Answers are to be memorized by hard work. Knowledge is quantitative. Agency is experienced as "out there" in Authority, test scores, the Right job.

Multiplicity. Diversity of opinion and values is recognized as legitimate in areas where right answers are not yet known. Opinions remain atomistic without pattern or system. No judgments can be made among them so "everyone has a right to his own opinion; none can be called wrong."

Relativism. Diversity of opinion, values, and judgment derived from coherent sources, evidence, logics, systems, and patterns allowing for analysis and comparison.

Some opinions may be found worthless, while there will remain matters about which reasonable people will reasonably disagree. Knowledge is qualitative, dependent on contexts.

Commitment (uppercase C). An affirmation, choice, or decision (career, values, politics, personal relationship) made in the awareness of Relativism (distinct from lower-case c of commitments never questioned). Agency is experienced as within the individual.

Temporizing. Postponement of movement for a year or more.

Escape. Alienation, abandonment of responsibility. Exploitation of Multiplicity and Relativism for avoidance of Commitment.

Retreat. Avoidance of complexity and ambivalence by regression to Dualism colored by hatred of otherness.

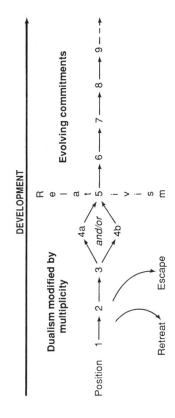

Figure 3.2 Perry's Scheme of Cognitive and Ethical Development in College Students (From William Perry, "Cognitive and Ethical Growth: The Making of Meaning," Figure 1 (pp. 79–80) in *The Modern American College*, ed. A.W. Chickering. Jossey–Bass, 1981.)

ponents as, for instance, in identifying four major properties of mature thought.

Identification of Independent Characteristics

The methodology for identification of components as separable characteristics is relatively advanced. In principle, one administers a battery of tests in which some tests are "pure" tests of the component in question while others are not, and subjects the scores to a factor analysis. The emergence of factors on which the "pure" tests load (i.e., correlate significantly) is viewed as validation of the analysis into components. At the present state of knowledge about thinking, there is no such evidence with which to validate my analysis into precisely four characteristics of mature thought. They are no more than a speculative heuristic framework. Nor is there much likelihood of substantiating that framework in the foreseeable future. I don't even know of any existing scales for measuring propensity for systematizing, or for transforming, and so forth. Nor do I believe that any one characteristic is fully independent of the others. Assuming that independent measures were to be available, presumably there would be low to moderate correlations among them, although the relative position of an individual on any one scale might vary relative to the others: for example, one could be better at detaching than at systematizing or evaluating. How the four characteristics interrelate developmentally is another open question.

Lest this discussion lead the reader to despair, I hasten to note that most of the existing analyses of thinking, typologies of thinkers, or training procedures based upon them have no more solid an empirical foundation. One has no choice but to start with provisional hypotheses and revise in the light of subsequent evidence. Some of the available hypotheses and the directions in which they lead will be outlined in the next section.

Skills versus Styles

That one can deal with thinking as a class of behavior to be analyzed into component skills or focus upon the individual who does the thinking and identify styles has been implicit in the foregoing discussion. It is now time to compare these alternative approaches and their implications for practice more systematically.

What I am calling a skills approach (the word *strategy* is also commonly used to describe the class of behavior under analysis) assumes that thinking is behavior no different, in principle, from other classes of behavior in the mechanisms of its acquisition and modification. It follows from that assumption that thinking skills can be taught in the same manner that any other skills, for example, reading, writing, or arithmetic, are taught: by providing repeated occasions in which the appropriate behavior is evoked and corrected. Typically the component behaviors are identified through a procedure of task analysis, generally for a rather narrowly delimited definition of the skill in question. A good example of this type of approach is Siegler's (1983) analysis of a balance scale task in which various combinations of weights and distance of weight from fulcrum are presented to a subject required to predict what will happen to the balance as a result. In that analysis Siegler assumes (1) that children's strategies are governed by rules that increase in sophistication with age, and (2) that the hypothesized rule progressions are subject to direct test through the use of specific problem sets designed to contrast the response patterns of each rule level. His model of rule levels for this task is shown in Figure 3.3 along with the problems used to identify rule level.

One implication of this type of approach is that, once component strategies and rules have been identified, it should be possible to train people in the use of better strategies or rules. For example, in memorizing lists of items it is helpful to repeat members over and over or to organize them into conceptual categories. There is evidence that one can teach young children who do not spontaneously use these strategies to do so, but it has generally been found that the effects of training do not generalize to similar tasks in which instructions to use the strategy are not continued (e.g., Keeney, Cannizzo, and Flavell; Hagen, Hargrave, and Ross, for rehearsal, and Liberty and Ornstein; Rosner; Williams and Goulet, for organization). Moreover, developmentally advanced children seem to profit more from training than do children at a lower level, with the result that training widens ability differences. Comparable results have been obtained for different kinds of tasks where training was administered (e.g., Danner and Day, for formal operational–level problem solving; Wilkinson, for reading instruction; and Bereiter and Scardamalia, for composition). Thus, laboratory evidence suggests that strategy training in and of itself is of limited effectiveness. Current applications of a skills approach have increasingly tended to focus upon training of metacognitive skills (Brown and Smiley; Baker and Brown). For example, in teaching children to be better readers the authors cited trained them to paraphrase for gist, monitor their own comprehension, and so forth. These broader orientations begin to converge upon a style approach.

The term *cognitive style* is used to refer to the individual's characteristic approach to cognitive tasks. Although a great variety of elements and typologies of style have been proposed (e.g., field dependence/independence, introduced earlier in the discussion of detachment), style theorists share a tendency to view style as a more or less pervasive characteristic of the individual. Two examples of a styles perspective on

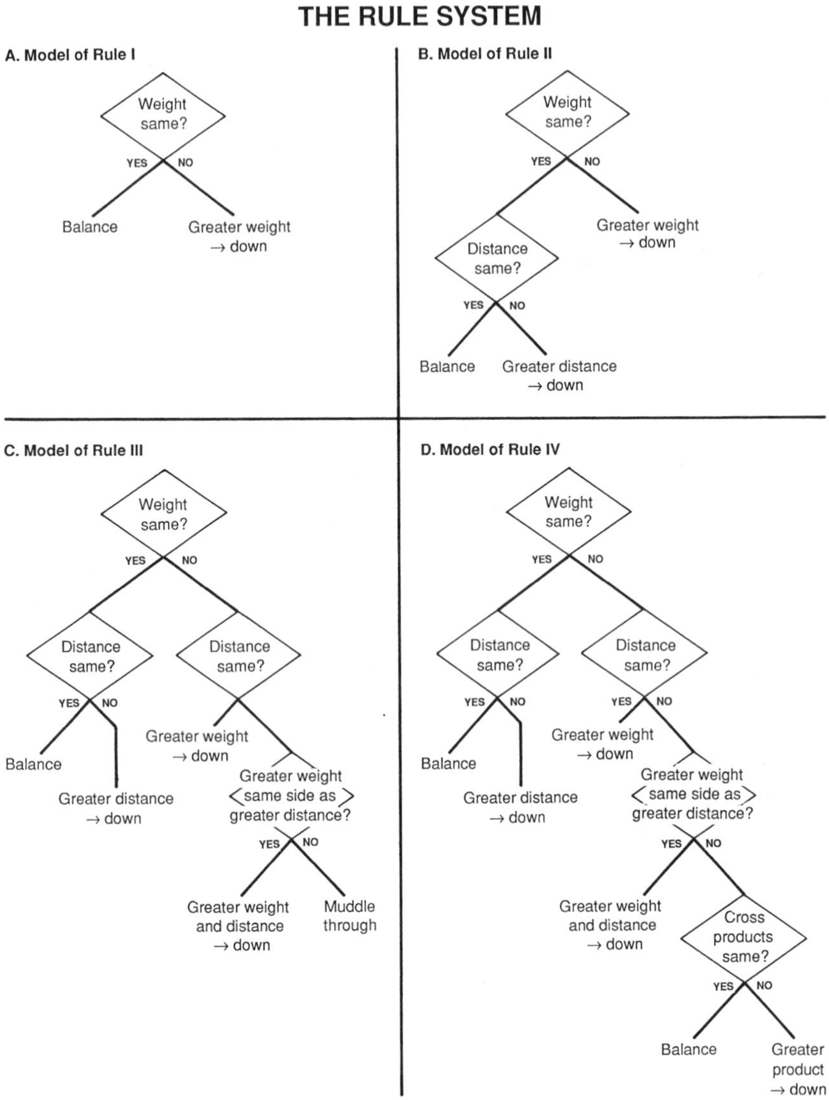

THE RULE SYSTEM

A. Model of Rule I

Weight same?

YES — NO

Balance | Greater weight → down

B. Model of Rule II

Weight same?

YES — NO

Greater weight → down

Distance same?

YES — NO

Balance | Greater distance → down

C. Model of Rule III

Weight same?

YES — NO

Distance same? | Distance same?

YES — NO

Balance

Greater distance → down

Greater weight → down

Greater weight < same side as > greater distance?

YES — NO

Greater weight and distance → down | Muddle through

D. Model of Rule IV

Weight same?

YES — NO

Distance same? | Distance same?

YES — NO

Balance

Greater distance → down

Greater weight → down

Greater weight < same side as > greater distance?

YES — NO

Greater weight and distance → down

Cross products same?

YES — NO

Balance | Greater product → down

Figure 3.3 Siegler's Rule System and the Problem Differentiating Rule (From Robert S. Siegler, "Information Processing Approaches to Development," in *History, Theory, and Methods*. Vol. I of *Handbook of Child Psychology*. Ed. P.H. Mussen. New York: Wiley, 1983. By permission of the publisher.)

THE PROBLEM

PROBLEM TYPE	RULE			
	I	II	III	IV
Balance 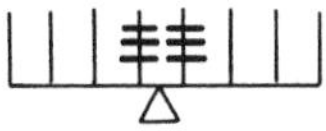	100	100	100	100
Weight 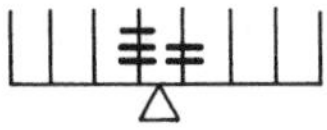	100	100	100	100
Distance 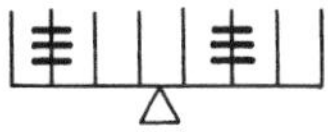	0 (Should say "Balance")	100	100	100
Conflict-Weight 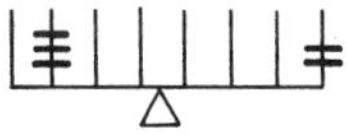	100	100	33 (Chance responding)	100
Conflict-Distance 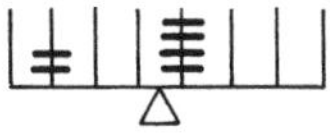	0 (Should say "Right Down")	0 (Should say "Right Down")	33 (Chance responding)	100
Conflict-Balance 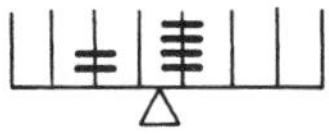	0 (Should say "Right Down")	0 (Should say "Right Down")	33 (Chance responding)	100

Figure 3.3 (*Continued*)

students' approach to study are provided by the work of Schmeck and of Kolb, both of whom employ self report questionnaires for style assessment (cf. also Neimark and Stead). Kolb proposes that there are two primary dimensions to the learning process: (1) a dimension going from concrete experiencing of events at one end to abstract conceptualization at the other; and (2) a dimension from active experimentation at one end to reflective observation at the other. The combination of possible relative standings on both dimensions yields four types of learning style: (1) convergers (abstract conceptualization and active experimentation); (2) divergers (concrete experience and reflective observation); (3) assimilators (abstract conceptualization and reflective observation); and (4) accommodators (concrete experience and active experimentation). The latter two types might also be characterized as theorists and practitioners; the first two differ with respect to breadth of interest. Schmeck's dimensions arise from a factor analysis of his Inventory of Learning Processes. The processes include deep processing, methodical study, fact retention, and elaborative processing, of which the first is the best studied and most potentially relevant. It is defined by a negative response to such items as "I have trouble making inferences" or "I find it difficult to handle questions requiring comparison of different concepts" and positive response to items like "I do well on essay tests" or "I think fast."

As suggested by these two examples, styles approaches are more globally formulated and less empirically based than skills approaches, and they have less optimistic implications for educational practice. To the extent that a style is, like a personality trait, a persistent characteristic of the individual, it should not be subject to drastic modification. To the extent that it is modifiable, the means of its modification should be through social shaping toward emulation of a model rather than by traditional direct instruction. A review of the literature on one proposed cognitive style in children, reflection/impulsivity, by Messer supports that prediction. Another implication of a style approach is that one should "go with the flow," so to speak, by matching the style of instruction to style of the learner (Witkin) and allowing the individual to capitalize upon his or her particular assets. There is some suggestive evidence that groups' differing in career choice (Witkin, Moore, Goodenough, and Cox), or academic major (Kolb), also differ with respect to their group mean style score. That style is a determinant of career orientation is not, however, demonstrated by the reported correlations.

There is, of course, a middle ground between exclusive adherence to a skill or a style approach. Characterization of the mature thinker probably requires a judicious combination of both approaches. That compromise position is proposed by Anderson, and, as noted earlier, the increasing emphasis upon skills of self-regulation suggests that skills approaches are heading in the same direction (Brown).

The Knowledge Base

There is a certain perversity in talking about thinking abstractly as though one could think in a vacuum. Obviously, one has to think about something. Some of those somethings are more conducive to deep mature thought than are others, but regardless of the realm, presumably the more substantive knowledge one has about it, the richer and deeper one's potential thought. On the basis of some recent evidence comparing the memory of novice and expert chess players (Chase and Simon; Chi), some writers have concluded that knowledge base is a major determinant of thought (e.g., expert chess players excel novices in memory for meaningful positions but not random ones). Although such findings do not seem to me to warrant an extreme contextualist position, they should engender a healthy respect for some of the abiding concerns of traditional education. One must provide students with information, but one should also teach how to expand and organize that information independently and outside the classroom setting.

SOME SUGGESTIONS FOR MATURING THINKERS

Given this extensive array of conflicting evidence and directing views, what can one do in the classroom? The nugget I offer is to be as transformative, systematic, detached, and evaluative as possible in analyzing your problem, constructing a model and testing the solution implications deriving from it. The goal should be to develop those same four qualities in your students. The single best vehicle for encouraging transformation is to make students write, not only required assignments on a variety of topics (or on occasion, the same topic from a different angle) but also to encourage them to keep a journal of their own thought processes in the course of doing those assignments (Neimark and Stead). The latter task should also help promote detached awareness. It is also helpful to have class discussion of the observations that result from journal keeping. To the extent that thinking is a style, it is helpful to present anonymous examples of good work as well as poor work for class evaluation and comparison in order to help students develop models to emulate. And that discussion should go beyond the immediate context to encourage development of more general systematic approaches. At the end of the semester, it is always a good idea to have students write a summary of what they learned, how it relates to prior knowledge and beliefs, and what basis it provides for future work. This required summary, in effect, imposes Hayes's final stage of problem solving, consolidation of gains. Finally, always remember that individual differences are a fact of life. Some students will need much more structure and specific direction than others. Try to provide it so that they will have enough experience of success to be motivated to continue on their own toward the goal of being a more mature thinker.

WORKS CITED

Adams, J.L. *Conceptual Blockbusting*. San Francisco: Freeman, 1974.

Anderson, B.F. *The Complete Thinker*. Englewood Cliffs, NJ: Prentice-Hall, 1980.

Arendt, H. *The Life of the Mind: Thinking*. New York: Harcourt Brace Jovanovich, 1978.

Arlin, P.K. "Cognitive Development in Adulthood: A Fifth Stage?" *Developmental Psychology* 11 (1975): 602–606.

Baker, L., and A.L. Brown. "Metacognition and the Reading Process." *Handbook of Reading Research*. Ed. P.D. Pearson. New York: Longman, 1984. 353–394.

Bereiter, C., and M. Scardamalia. "From Conservation to Composition: The Role of Instruction in a Developmental Process." *Advances in Instructional Psychology*. Ed. R. Glaser. Hillsdale, NJ: Erlbaum, 1982. Vol. 2. 1–64.

Bransford, J.D., and B.S. Stein. *The Ideal Problem Solver*. New York: Freeman, 1984.

Brown, A.L. "Metacognition, Executive Control, Self-Regulation, and Other More Mysterious Mechanisms." *Metacognition, Motivation, and Understanding*. Ed. F.E. Weinert and R.H. Kluwe. Hillsdale, NJ: Erlbaum, 1987. 65–116.

Brown, A.L., J.D. Bransford, R.A. Ferrara, and J.C. Campione. "Learning, Remembering, and Understanding." *Cognitive Development*. Vol. 3 of *Handbook of Child Psychology*. Ed. P.H. Mussen. New York: Wiley, 1983. 77–166.

Brown, A.L., and S.S. Smiley. "The Development of Strategies for Studying Texts." *Child Development* 49 (1976): 1076–1088.

Bruner, J.S. *The Relevance of Education*. Bungay, Suffolk: Penguin, 1974.

Chase, W.G., and H.A. Simon. "Perception in Chess." *Cognitive Psychology* 4 (1973): 55–81.

Chi, M.T.H. "Knowledge Structures and Memory Development." *Children's Thinking: What Develops?* Ed. R.S. Siegler. Hillsdale, NJ: Erlbaum, 1978. 73–96.

Colby, A., L. Kohlberg, J. Gibbs, and M. Lieberman. "A Longitudinal Study of Moral Development." *Monographs of the Society for Research in Child Development* 48.1–2 (1983): Serial No. 200.

Danner, F.N., and M.C. Day. "Eliciting Formal Operations." *Child Development* 48 (1977): 1600–1606.

DeBono, E. *New Think: The Use of Lateral Thinking in the Generation of New Ideas*. New York: Basic Books, 1968.

deCharms, R. *Enhancing Motivation: Change in the Classroom.* New York: Irvington, 1976.

Dewey, J. *The School and Society.* Chicago: University of Chicago Press, 1915.

Erikson, E. *Identity: Youth and Crisis.* New York: Norton, 1968.

Getzels, J.W. "Creative Thinking, Problem Solving and Instruction." *The Sixty-Third Yearbook of the National Society for the Study of Education: Theories of Learning and Instruction.* Ed. E. Hilgard. Chicago: University of Chicago Press, 1964.

Goodnow, J.J., and J. Cashmore. "Culture and Performance." *Moderators of Competence.* Ed. E.D. Neimark, R. DeLisi, and J.L. Newman. Hillsdale, NJ: Erlbaum, 1985. 77–98.

Gruber, H.E. *Darwin on Man.* 2nd ed. Chicago: University of Chicago Press, 1981.

Guilford, J.P. *The Nature of Human Intelligence.* New York: McGraw-Hill, 1967.

Hagen, J.W., S. Hargrave, and W. Ross. "Prompting and Rehearsal in Short-term Memory." *Child Development* 44 (1973): 201–204.

Hayes, J.R. *The Complete Problem Solver.* Philadelphia: Franklin Institute Press, 1981.

Keeney, T.J., S.R. Cannizzo, and J.H. Flavell. "Spontaneous and Induced Verbal Rehearsal in a Recall Task." *Child Development* 38 (1967): 953–966.

Kohlberg, L., C. Levine, and A. Hewer. "Moral Stages: A Current Formulation and a Response to Critics." *Contributions to Human Development.* Ed. J.A. Meacham. Basel: Karger, 1983. Vol. 10.

Kolb, D.A. "Learning Styles and Disciplinary Differences." *The Modern American College.* Ed. A.W. Chickering and associates. San Francisco: Jossey-Bass, 1981. 232–255.

Laboratory of Human Cognition. "Culture and Intelligence." *Handbook of Human Intelligence.* Ed. R.J. Sternberg. Cambridge: Cambridge University Press, 1982. 642–719.

Lefebvre-Pinard, M. "Understanding and Auto-control of Cognitive Functions: Implications for the Relationship Between Cognition and Behavior." *International Journal of Behavioral Development* 6 (1983): 15–36.

Liberty, C., and P.A. Ornstein. "Age Differences in Organization and Recall: The Effects of Training in Categorization." *Journal of Experimental Child Psychology* 15 (1973): 169–186.

Mandler, J.M. "Representation." *Cognitive Development.* Vol. 3 of *Handbook of Child Psychology.* Ed. P.H. Mussen. New York: Wiley, 1983. 420–494.

Mayer, R.E. *Thinking, Problem Solving, Cognition.* New York: Freeman, 1983.

Messer, S.B. "Reflection-impulsivity: A Review." *Psychological Bulletin* 83 (1976): 1026–1053.

Neimark, E.D. "Confounding with Cognitive Style Factors: An Artifact Explanation for the Apparent Nonuniversal Incidence of Formal Operations." *New Directions in Piagetian Theory and Practice.* Ed. I.E. Sigel, D.M. Brodzinsky, and R.M. Golinkoff. Hillsdale, NJ: Erlbaum, 1981. 177–180.

———. *Adventures in Thinking.* San Diego: Harcourt Brace Jovanovich, 1987.

Neimark, E.D., and C. Stead. "Everyday Thinking by College Women: Analysis of Journal Entries." *Merrill-Palmer Quarterly* 27 (1981): 417–488.

Parnes, S.J., R.B. Noller, and A.M. Biondi. *Guide to Creative Action: Revised*

Edition of Creative Behavior Guidebook. New York: Scribner's, 1977.

Perry, W.G., Jr. "Cognitive and Ethical Growth: The Making of Meaning." *The Modern American College.* Ed. A.W. Chickering and associates. San Francisco: Jossey-Bass, 1981. 76–116.

Piaget, J. *The Grasp of Consciousness: Action and Concept in the Young Child.* Cambridge; Harvard University Press, 1976.

———. *Success and Understanding.* Cambridge: Harvard University Press, 1978.

Polya, G. *How To Solve It.* 2nd ed. Garden City, NY: Doubleday, 1957.

Rogers, C.R. *A Way of Being.* Boston: Houghton-Mifflin, 1980.

Rosner, S. "The Effects of Rehearsal and Chunking Instructions of Children's Multitrial Free Recall." *Journal of Experimental Child Psychology* 11 (1971): 93–105.

Schmeck, R.R. "Learning Styles of College Students." *Individual Differences in Cognition.* Ed. R.F. Dillon and R.R. Schmeck. New York: Academic Press, 1983. 233–279.

Siegler, R.S. "Information Processing Approaches to Development." *History, Theory, and Methods.* Vol. 1 of *Handbook of Child Psychology.* Ed. P.H. Mussen. New York: Wiley, 1983. 129–212.

———. *Children's Thinking.* Englewood Cliffs, NJ: Prentice-Hall, 1986.

Vygotsky, L.S. *Thought and Language.* Cambridge; M.I.T. Press, 1962.

Wertheimer, M. *Productive Thinking.* New York: Harper & Row, 1945.

Wilkinson, A.C. "Children's Understanding in Reading and Listening." *Journal of Experimental Child Psychology* 72 (1980): 561–574.

Williams, K.G., and L.R. Goulet. "The Effects of Cueing and Constraint Instructions on Children's Free Recall Performance." *Journal of Experimental Child Psychology* 19 (1973): 464–475.

Witkin, H. "Cognitive Styles in Academic Performance and in Teacher-student Relations." *Individuality in Learning: Implications of Cognitive Styles and Creativity for Human Development.* Ed. S. Messick and associates. San Francisco: Jossey-Bass, 1976. 38–72.

Witkin, H.A., C.S. Moore, D.R. Goodenough, and P.W. Cox. "Field-dependent and Field-independent Cognitive Styles and Their Implications." *Review of Educational Research* 47 (1977): 1–64.

CHAPTER 4

On the Composition of Experts and Novices

James F. Voss

The human being performs many complex acts and on occasion even becomes proficient in the execution of one of them. As Herbert Simon points out, some acts, such as hitting a baseball, have complex perceptual-motor components, while others, including those generally regarded as cognitive, emphasize the manipulation of symbols. These mental acts include, at a minimum, reading, writing, speaking, arguing, remembering, calculating, thinking, reasoning, learning, and problem solving.

In recent years, research on the performance of complex acts has been increasing, and one issue that has received considerable attention is how knowledge in the content area or domain influences such performance. The influence of knowledge is typically studied via use of a cross-sectional procedure in which individuals who are either expert or novice with respect to their knowledge of the domain in question are presented with one or more domain-related tasks. Performance of the experts and novices is then compared. (The reader is referred to Voss, Fincher–Kiefer, Greene, and Post for a distinction of the expert-novice comparison procedure).

One area of study in which the expert-novice paradigm has been extensively employed is problem solving, with all of the research involving the use of well-structured problems. Our interest has been in studying the

This chapter was supported by the National Institute of Education via a grant to the Learning Research and Development Center (NIE-G-83-0004) and by the National Science Foundation BNS (8409123). The viewpoints expressed in this chapter do not necessarily constitute the opinion of either organization.

solving of more poorly defined or ill-structured problems, and it is this work that serves as the basis for the present discussion. In addition, our research has led to an interest in reasoning since we found that reasoning was central to the development of a problem solution. Moreover, such reasoning was of an informal, as opposed to formal, nature, a distinction discussed later.

It is a thesis of this essay that, while the research on the solving of well-structured problems and on formal reasoning tasks is important, a better understanding of the complex acts of everyday behavior, including tasks such as writing, will be developed when the processes underlying the solving of ill-defined problems, including the processes of informal reasoning, are better understood. Most mental activity takes place not in reference to solving well-structured tasks and reasoning via formal logic but in relation to the more vaguely structured problems and informal reasoning procedures. Given this thesis, the paper has three objectives: (1) to present a brief summary of research on the solving of ill-structured problems by experts and novices; (2) to describe briefly some research on informal reasoning; (3) to indicate how such research on problem solving and reasoning may enhance our understanding of instruction in other complex tasks such as writing.

WELL-STRUCTURED AND ILL-STRUCTURED PROBLEMS

While psychologists have studied problem solving for many years, recent interest in the topic was largely generated by Newell and Simon's book, *Human Problem Solving*. This problem stated the basic information-processing model of problem solving, the model having had its origins in the theory of Selz, the research of Wertheimer and Duncker, and in the early stages of what has become known as artificial intelligence (Newell, Shaw, and Simon).

Within the general information-processing framework, a problem has three components; the "givens", the initial state of the problem, the goal, and the constraints. Solving a problem thus consists of taking steps that enable the solver to advance from the initial state to the goal state, the possible steps limited by the problem constraints. As an example, consider a missionary-cannibal problem (a type of puzzle) in which there are three missionaries and three cannibals on one side of a river and they need to cross the river. The problem is: How do they all get across the river? In this case the "givens" consist of the number of missionaries and cannibals, the goal of crossing the river, and the constraints of the boat capacity and the restriction that the number of cannibals cannot exceed the number of missionaries on either side. The solver may begin by saying that a missionary and a cannibal cross the river. This move or operation changes the state of the problem with respect to the number of missionaries and cannibals on each side. The next move is the return of the missionary to the initial side. (The cannibal cannot return alone because such a move would violate a constraint.) The solver then continues to make moves until the goal is achieved. Thus, in general, solving the problem consists in taking a number of steps until the goal is attained.

Problem Representation and Problem Solution

For problems that are more complex, the information-processing model distinguishes two phases of problem-solving activity, problem representation and problem solution. Broadly speaking, the representation phase consists of the solver developing an interpretation of the problem, that is, the solver establishes the givens, the goal, and the constraints of the problem. Moreover, the means by which the solver develops the problem representation are a function of whether the problem is well-structured or ill-structured as well as a function of whether the solver is an expert or novice with respect to the subject matter domain in question.

In general, in well-structured problems the givens, the goal, and the constraints are presented in the problem statement or readily derived from it; in ill-structured problems one or more of these components is not presented in the problem statement. (See Reitman; Simon 1973; and Voss and Post for discussions of this distinction.) One relationship that exists with respect to well-structured and ill-structured problems is that the former usually are found in domains that have well-developed procedures of investigation, data bases, and theory. Such areas include mathematics, physics, and chemistry. On the other hand, ill-structured problems are generally found in domains that have less developed investigative procedures, data bases, and theory. These areas include much of economics, sociology, political science, and the humanities. (If the reader wonders what an ill-structured problem may be in the humanities, see Reitman for a discussion of the composition of a fugue as an ill-structured problem.)

THE PROBLEM SOLVING OF EXPERTS

The solving of well-structured problems has received considerable attention in the area of physics (e.g., Larkin; Larkin, McDermott, Simon, and Simon). To illustrate, imagine a physics expert is given a problem from an undergraduate physics text. While the expert will solve the problem more quickly than the novice, the expert will nevertheless spend a relatively large amount of time developing the problem representation. The expert may do this by drawing a diagram of the problem or by studying the relations of the problem parameters in some other way.[1] The expert will then state that it is, for example, an "energy" problem, and, once the problem is so classified, the expert enters the solution phase by providing a series of equations that produces the solution. The expert's interpretation of the problem thus takes place via a pattern-matching operation in which the parameters of the given problem and their interrelationships are matched to the characteristics of a class of problems the expert had stored in memory, and once the problem is classified, the expert is readily able to provide the solution.

With respect to the representation of ill-structured problems, consider a city manager in an urban area where the crime rate has recently increased, and assume that this individual must develop and implement a policy designed to reduce the crime rate. In this case, the givens of the problem are only that there has been an increase in the crime rate. The goal is "reducing the crime rate," and no constraints are provided in the problem statement.

As noted, the development of the representation consists of interpreting the problem. In the case of an ill-structured problem such as that of "reducing the crime rate," representing the problem typically involves establishing the primary factor(s) producing the problem. Determining these factors is not a simple matter, however, and the individual may use a number of strategies to accomplish this objective. One of the most common is to analyze the problem history and from such an analysis determine what the major factors may be. This procedure is reasonably standard in a number of disciplines, that is, the introductory section in social science papers often develops the problem in terms of the problem's history. In addition to establishing the factors producing the problem, the solver also needs to establish the constraints, which in the "crime rate" case could involve the budget or perhaps the attitudes of council members and/or the police force and the public. Finally, the goal often needs to be made more specific, since what constitute a "significant decrease in crime rate" is vague.

But what about the solution phase? After developing the representation, the solver typically proposes a solution, the specific solution usually depending upon the particular representation developed. The solution, of course, is usually aimed at eliminating or alleviating the problem by reducing the influence of the factors producing the problem. Moreover, an important characteristic of the solving of ill-structured problems by experts is that the solution is relatively abstract, that is, the solver will attempt to provide a single solution designed to deal with the factors that constitute components of the problem. For example, the solver may propose a single policy to reduce the crime rate, but the implementation of the policy will include handling factors that may be contributing to the crime rate increase, factors such as inadequate police protection, drug usage, and lack of community awareness.

In the solving of ill-structured problems, the expert, quite importantly, not only provides a solution to the problem but also typically "builds a case" for the solution. The justification usually takes place in two ways. First, the individual will show how the proposed solution will work in eliminating the factors producing the problem. Second, the solver will attempt to anticipate criticisms of the solution as well as possible problems that may arise if the proposed solution is implemented. Thus, the solver of an ill-structured problem usually justifies the proposed solution via verbal argument. (This description of the solving of an ill-structured problem is based upon the analyses of Voss, Tyler, and Yengo and Voss, Greene, Post, and Penner.)

A comparison of the solving of well-structured and ill-structured problems by experts in the respective domains thus suggests the following similarities and differences. (1) Probably the most obvious similarity is that each solution has a representation and a solution phase. (2) Considering the representation phase, there is a difference in the way the representations are developed in the two types of problems. In the physics problem, the solver establishes the representation by classification, whereas the social policy solver needs to generate the representation via isolation of the factors producing the crime rate. The solver likely had to search his or her memory to determine these factors or perhaps had to obtain information from other (external) sources. It may of course be the case that the solver had stored in memory the results of studies on urban crime, but if there were empirically established and accepted procedures on reducing urban crime and if the solver had knowledge of such procedures, then the problem would have been well-structured.

Setting aside the crime rate example, the fact is that problems found in social sciences are not neatly organized and classified. The basic parameters of particular problems are not known and/or there often is a lack of consensual agreement among individuals knowledgeable in a field regarding what parameters are important. Indeed, Reitman indicated that lack of consensual agreement is a common characteristic of the solutions to ill-structured problems. Consider, for example, two political scientists debating over the current or possibly the future U.S. policy toward Nicaragua. Assume one person viewed Nicaragua as a case of exporting communism and represented the problem by "classifying" it as another instance of

"Munich." This person would quite likely advocate a strong U.S. policy and involvement. On the other hand, if a person "classified" Nicaragua as another "Vietnam," then the advocated policy would likely emphasize disengagement. In fact, this type of result has been obtained in relation to issues of Central America (Gilovich). Indeed, such an example not only shows that there often is a lack of consensual agreement among experts but also demonstrates how a person's beliefs or attitudes may influence how the problem is represented. (See Voss, Greene, Post, and Penner for a discussion of this issue.)

Strong and Weak Methods. Consideration of how the problem representation is developed also raises the important distinction of weak and strong problem-solving methods (Newell). Weak methods are strategies useful in a variety of subject matter domains, but these methods are regarded as weak because they lack power rather than generality, that is, they are not applicable for the more specific problems within the respective domains. One of the most commonly used weak methods is decomposition, that is, breaking up a problem into component subproblems and subsequently solving the problem by solving each subproblem. Another weak method is analogy. Typically analogies are helpful in seeing relationships between two problem domains, but analogy tends to break down when it is pushed to the specifics of the domain in which the problem is to be solved. Another weak method that we have observed is problem conversion (Voss, Greene, Post, and Penner). In this case, a given problem is transformed into another problem, the latter being easier to solve than the former. These three and other methods constitute strategies that provide the solver with a way to take initial steps in the solving of a problem, but, as noted, the methods typically do not provide for the solving of the more specific, domain-related problems. In contrast, strong problem-solving methods tend to be domain-specific and usually are not applicable to other domains. Subtraction is an example of a strong method, as is a procedure for solving a "distance = rate × time" algebra word problem. Interestingly, with the possible exception of economics, social sciences seem to have few strong methods. Examining the history of a problem, for example, seems to be more of a weak than a strong method.

(3) Returning to the third comparison of expert problem solving of well-structured and ill-structured problems we find that, with respect to the solution phase, the physicist needs only to state the appropriate equations that produce the solution, and this of course is a strong method. Moreover, when the physicist or mathematician solves the problem by generating the appropriate equations, the solution, in a sense, is the justification. This is an interesting point, for in mathematics and physics, solutions seem to require no justification when the solution involves formal reasoning. In

contrast, the social scientist, as previously noted, typically generates a solution and subsequently justifies it by verbal argument. The argument usually consists of two previously mentioned components, providing support by showing how the solution would resolve the problem and anticipating and addressing possible criticisms or problems that may arise if the solution is implemented. The probable reason that such support is provided is that the social scientist needs to convince and persuade others (and also perhaps himself or herself) that the solution is the best available or perhaps that it is simply workable. Finally, in physics, when the solution is arrived at, it is usually obvious, but the "solution" to an ill-structured problem is typically an arbitrary decision.

A question that may be asked at this point is whether the previously described differences in the problem solving of well-structured and ill-structured problems means that problem solving in physical sciences and in social sciences is basically different. The answer offered here is no. The reason for this answer is shown by referring to Tweney's account of the discovery of electromagnetic induction by Michael Faraday. While Tweney's interests were in the hypothesis-testing procedures employed by Faraday, Tweney's account also indicated that the "protocol" provided by Faraday's notes shows that Faraday, in a manner quite similar to the solution process obtained in social science problem solving, spent considerable time representing the problem and developing an abstract solution. Faraday then generated hypotheses based upon the solution and subsequently tested the hypotheses by experimentation.

The Faraday account leads to a number of interesting points. One is that, in general, there is no fundamental difference in the overall problem-solving process used in social science and in physics when the solver is dealing with an ill-structured problem. The same approaches to the representation and solution phases are observed. A second point is that there is a difference in the way solutions are supported. The expert physicist generates a solution, develops hypotheses based upon the solution, and tests the hypotheses in the laboratory. Moreover, in conducting such tests the physicist most often is testing hypotheses that will provide support for the solution, in the sense that findings consistent with the hypothesis would support the solution. Thus, the physicist designs experiments that effectively do what the social scientist is doing via argument, that is, supporting solutions, and anticipating criticisms or subproblems and providing answers to them. The difference, of course, between Faraday's developing the support for the solution of a structured problem via experimentation and the social scientist's attempt to support a solution without experimentation is that the latter generally does not have the possibility of experimental verification. In lieu of this support, the solution is built by argumentation.

Indeed, sometimes in considering the "logic" and "objectivity" of science, we sometimes forget that having a paper published is an exercise in rhetoric. The physicist, or for that matter the person in any experimentally based discipline, must "build the case" to have the work published. The scientist must show via argument that the hypotheses indeed follow from the theory, that the experiments are reasonable tests of the hypotheses, and failure to provide a convincing argument in this regard more often than not results in an editor's noting the omissions and/or questionable claims and rejecting the paper.

THE PROBLEM SOLVING OF NOVICES

Thus far we have been speaking of experts. What type of solutions are provided by novices in the area of physics and social science? Novices in physics tend to spend relatively less time on problem representation than physics experts, and the novice also tends to process the problem statement not in terms of underlying principles but instead according to the surface structure of the problem, that is, the novice may select some parameter of the problem, generate equations that contain a parameter needed in the solution, try to work backward to the givens, and eventually reach the solution (Larkin, McDermott, Simon, and Simon). The novice thus does not tend to classify the problem, quite likely because the novice does not have problem classes and their characteristics stored in memory and thus is not able to match a pattern in memory with the parameters of the problem. In addition, the novice does not show a differentiation of the representation and solution phases of the problem-solving activity. The social science novice similarly tends to address relatively specific aspects of the problem at hand and also does not provide differentiated representation and solution phases. Thus, in a "crime rate" problem, the novice solver may say that the police force should be increased or make similar statements that may be appropriate but do not provide a more general solution that encompasses all such items. Also, the social science novice typically provides little, if any, support for the solutions offered.

The novice data point to three conclusions. One is that in a particular subject matter domain, novices have relatively isolated bits of information. Furthermore, in contrast to experts, what the novice knows generally lacks the hierarchical organization of subject matter found in experts (Chi, Feltovich, and Glaser). A second factor is that novices tend not to use information that they know though the utilization of the known information would be appropriate (Larkin; Simon 1980; Voss, Greene, Post, and Penner). Such findings suggest that experience plays a major role in the development of experts in that expertise does not simply involve knowing information but also the ability to utilize such information. It usually takes considerable experience to develop expertise, and such development in- volves not only learning new information but learning how to use what you know in various problem contexts. Moreover, such experience may pro- vide at least two results. First, when subsequent problems occur, the in- dividual may relate such problems to those already experienced and thus be able to address them accordingly. Second, the problem-solving expe- rience may also provide opportunities for the learner to utilize particular strategies.

Verbal Reasoning. To this point the solving of well-structured and ill- structured problems by individuals who are expert or novice has been considered. One point made in relation to the solving of ill-structured problems, especially for problems in the social sciences, is that verbal reasoning is a central component of the problem-solving process. The nature of the reasoning is now considered.

In their analysis of the solving of ill-structured problems, Voss, Greene, Post, and Penner delineated two control structures that guided the problem- solving activity, the problem-solving structure, and the reasoning struc- ture. The former was of a higher order and involved the delineation of the solution into the representation and solution phases, the isolation of con- straints, the statement of subproblems, and the providing of support. In a sense, these mechanisms constitute goals, and the reasoning operators used as means to reach these goals. The reasoning operators that were delineated are state argument, state assertion, state fact, present specific case, state reason, state outcome, compare and/or contrast, elaborate and/ or clarify, state conclusion, and state quantifiers. (See Penner and Voss for a description of how the protocols were analyzed in relation to these operators.) The important point is that the solving of the ill-structured problem involves not only the (implicit or explicit) knowledge of weak problem-solving methods and the ability to utilize such knowledge in the context of a particular subject matter domain but also skill in the verbal reasoning procedures one associates with rhetorical skill and with the type of argumentation often taught in writing courses. Having related reasoning skills to those of problem solving, it is appropriate to briefly consider the topic of informal reasoning.

ON THE NATURE OF INFORMAL REASONING

While the topic of reasoning has been of interest to psychologists for many years, research in this area has largely involved the use of formal reasoning tasks (cf. Mayer). Psychologists have been enamored with the syllogism and more recently have conducted research on issues raised by propositional calculus such as the four-card problem (Johnson-Laird and Wason). A third type of task that may be considered as more or less a study of formal reasoning is that employed in some decision-making research. Individuals are given choices and they select among the alternatives, the choices of representing particular formal models such as the Bayesian (cf. Einhorn and Hogarth). Investigators using formal reasoning tasks have typically focused on two related questions. One is whether individuals perform in a "rational" or "logical" manner; the other is that, if they do not, why is there a lack of "rationality" or "logic"? Interestingly, the work reflects the longstanding question of whether mental performance indicates that human thought is by nature logical and rational (cf. Henle).

While the psychological study of reasoning has given rise to important theoretical issues (cf. Johnson-Laird), there has been a lack of research on informal reasoning. (Exceptions include the work of Perkins, Allen, and Hafner, and of Collins 1978, 1985). Moreover, while social psychologists have been interested in argumentation, the work has generally been concerned with how argumentation produces change in one's attitude and/or opinion, rather than upon the processes of reasoning per se (cf. Petty and Cacioppo).

The differences between formal and informal reasoning, at least from our point of view, largely involve Aristotle's distinction of dialectic and rhetoric (cf. Cooper). Dialectic is associated with the syllogism, while rhetoric is associated with the enthymeme. The syllogism, of course, consists of a major premise, minor premise, and conclusion, and the validity of the conclusion is determined by whether it violates any rules of the formal system. The enthymeme consists of a single statement that essentially includes both a premise and a conclusion. The second premise is implicit. In crude form, a syllogism may state, "Good political candidates are assertive. John Doe is assertive. Therefore John Doe would make a good political candidate." An enthymeme may state, "John Doe would make a good political candidate because he is assertive." The implicit premise is that good political candidates are assertive. The important point for present purposes is that the validity of the assertion is to be judged on the basis of how it can be supported. Indeed, Aristotle listed over 20 "topics," or ways to support an enthymeme. In the present example, evidence may be stated that shows John Doe is assertive or shows that particularly good candidates have been assertive. Of course, evidence may also be cited that opposes the assertion.

Other somewhat similar analyses of reasoning include those of Peirce, whose concept of abduction is similar in function to the implicit premise of the enthymeme, and more recently the work of Toulmin. Basically, Toulmin describes an assertion as consisting of a data-claim statement, with the warrant being what enables one to make the claim from the datum (the implicit premise). Moreover, while the warrant is almost always implicit, backing for the warrant, and correspondingly for the data-claim, is explicit. In the present context it should be noted that the statements are often probabilistic and individuals of course frequently differ with respect to the perceived probability. Thus, as pointed out by Perkins, Allen, and Hafner, a person may state, "If A, then B," and later the same person or another individual may state, "No, if A, then C." Under such conditions the warrants generally would be different, as would be the backing.

As previously noted, informal reasoning has received little empirical study. However, Blais, Means, Greene, Ahwesh and I have been conducting a study on informal reasoning in economics by novices (individuals having taken one or two courses in economics) and naive individuals (no courses in economics). The study has the additional feature that some of the naive individuals were college educated, while others were not. We focused on three economics issues: (1) changes in the price of automobiles; (2) the federal deficit; and (3) changes in interest rates. We asked the participants to indicate what factors influenced each of the above phenomena and in what way the influence is exerted. Subsequently we provided scenarios related to each of the three topics, asking individuals to answer scenario-related questions. For example, we asked how an arms control treaty could influence the federal deficit or how import controls on steel could influence automobile prices.

The results I want to describe briefly are those on how rules are used by the novices or naive individuals. Individuals who have studied economics tend to interpret the questions in an economic context and apply a rule of economics, such as supply and demand, to provide an answer. Individuals without a college education often provide a rule but it may be from personal experience rather than based upon economics. Use of such rules, moreover, often distort the nature of the question. Probably the most interesting set of results involves individuals who have a college education but who have not taken economics courses. (No claim is made about what factors are or are not correlated with a college education.) These individuals apparently know that they do not know the economics rules required to answer the question, and they often establish an involved reasoning process that enables them to try to reach a suitable answer. For example, they will set up a hypothetical situation and try to work out an answer. Or they will convert the problem to a more general or more specific case and work via inference to a conclusion. The point is that these individuals seem to use reasoning as a substitute for domain knowledge in an effort to generate answers, the reasoning involving a rather sophisticated use of weak reasoning methods. (See Voss, Blais, Means, Greene, and Ahwesh for a discussion of this issue.)

These preliminary results suggest that individuals who have had experience in using weak problem-solving methods are able to use such methods even in domains where they have limited domain knowledge. In a broader sense, they use reasoning to try to compensate for lack of knowledge. Yet, because of the lack of a data base, they usually fall short of reaching an answer comparable to that of a person more versed in economics. But the reasoning process does provide better answers than those generated by individuals who have had no college education. Such results at least suggest that studying the performance of the naive and novice individuals may provide a better understanding of how reasoning may be used in various task situations when one's domain-related knowledge is limited.

This brief discussion of informal reasoning, apart from pointing to the need for further study, suggests that we need to develop a better understanding of how domain knowledge and strategies such as weak problem-solving methods are used in relation to the goals of the reasoner or solver. The problem-solving goals essentially drive the reasoning process, and reasoning thus is used as a tool. But it is the process of reasoning integrated with one's domain knowledge that provides for the problem representation and problem solution in the solving of an ill-structured problem and the need to understand this interaction of reasoning and knowledge constitutes an important theoretical challenge.

SOME CONCLUSIONS

The study of the solving of ill-structured problems as well as the study of informal reasoning has not been extensive. Yet the research that has been conducted provides for some conclusions (conclusions which are speculations or guesses).

1. Weak problem-solving methods and the strategies or mechanisms of informal reasoning are probably acquired by most people. However, although such learning takes place, the ability to use such strategies is greater when the individual has stronger intellectual ability and/or more formal education. This finding at least suggests that reasoning strategies are acquired, perhaps somewhat indirectly, during schooling. Evidence regarding how such learning takes place is lacking, that is, the question of the extent to which strategies are or may be taught in a general, context-free manner and the extent to which the strategies are taught via subject matter learning is an unresolved issue. Instructors of a course often have their own ideas and anecdotes regarding how they teach reasoning, but experimental evidence that "builds a case" for the effectiveness of such teaching seems to be in short supply.

Perhaps the best guess at this point is that instruction in reasoning strategies in a content-free course is probably not effective because experience in the effective use of the strategies often requires subject matter content. Indeed, it would seem inappropriate to instruct students in weak methods of problem solving, for example, and ask them to take a problem and "fit" it to a method. Under such conditions, one could envision a student not solving a problem while deciding which weak method to use. Interestingly, when solving problems, individuals, including experts, almost invariably do not verbalize anything about the strategies they are using to solve the problems.

2. Although strategy instruction in a content-free format is likely not effective, instruction in a particular context may be quite effective for learning to use that strategy *in that particular content domain.* Such instruction may provide for the learning of that strategy as well as for the experience in assessing the knowledge that is involved. The question then becomes how readily individuals transfer the strategy across domains.

In an application of these conclusions, a study on text generation shows the impact of knowledge differences on the writing of and subsequent recall of a passage. Voss, Vesonder, and Spilich had individuals with high or low baseball knowledge generate a one-half inning description of a baseball game. (The high knowledge and low knowledge groups were equated on reading comprehension text scores.) Two weeks later each individual recalled the text that he or she had generated. The high knowledge individuals were better in recalling the self-generated text than were the low knowledge individuals (even though the high knowledge texts were longer.) In addition, another group of high knowledge individuals read and recalled the contents of texts generated by either high or low knowledge individuals while low knowledge individuals read and recalled the same texts. As expected, the recall by high knowledge individuals was superior to the recall by low knowledge individuals for texts generated by high knowledge individuals. However, for texts generated by low knowledge individuals, there was no difference in the recall by high knowledge or low knowledge individuals. Inspection of the texts revealed that the texts written by high knowledge individuals provided a coherent account of the half-inning of the game with the actions of the game readily depicting how the game moved from one state to the next. Moreover, comments made by the high knowledge individuals while generating the texts suggested that their major problem was selection; they could include many facets of a baseball account and needed to select what should be included. On the other hand, the text of the low knowledge individuals was quite choppy, listing successive game states, but usually not providing for state transitions or being consistent and accurate in the account.

These findings thus indicate that there is no substitute for domain knowledge when performing a complex task in that domain. The generation of text, viewed as a problem-solving activity (Flower and Hayes 1977,

1980), readily shows that knowledgeable people are better able to represent the problem and solve it and that the text coherence and structure is a function of germane strategies being integrated with the domain knowledge.

NOTE

1. The word *parameter* is problematic for some readers. Voss uses it in its original meaning as a variable or set of variables affecting the distribution of a set of scores. Later usage came to include guideline or boundary or aspect. (Editors' note.)

WORKS CITED

Chi, M.T.H., P. Feltovich, and G. Glaser. "Categorization and Representation of Physics Problems by Experts and Novices." *Cognitive Science* 5 (1981): 121–152.

Collins, A. "Fragments of a Theory of Human Plausible Reasoning." *Theoretical Issues in Natural Language Processing-2*. Ed. D.L. Waltz. Urbana-Champaign: University of Illinois Press, 1978.

———. "Teaching Reasoning Skills." *Research and Open Questions*. Vol. 2 of *Thinking and Learning Skills*. Ed. S.F. Chipman, J.W. Segal, and R. Glaser. Hillsdale, NJ: Erlbaum, 1985. 579–586.

Cooper. L. Introduction. *The Rhetoric of Aristotle*. Englewood Cliffs, NJ: Prentice-Hall, 1932, xvii–xxxv.

Duncker, K. "On Problem Solving." *Psychological Monographs 58* (1945): whole no. 270.

Einhorn, H.J., and R.M. Hogarth. "Behavioral Decision Theory: Processes of Judgment and Choice." *Annual Review of Psychology* 32 (1981): 53–88.

Flower, L.S., and J.R. Hayes. "Problem Solving and the Writing Process." *College English* 39 (1977): 449–461.

———. "The Dynamics of Composing: Making Plans and Juggling Constraints." *Cognitive Processes in Writing*. Ed. L. Gregg and E. Steinberg. Hillsdale, NJ: Erlbaum, 1980. 31–50.

Gilovich, T. "Seeing the Past in the Present: The Effect of Associations to Familiar Events on Judgments and Decisions." *Journal of Personality and Social Psychology* 40 (1981): 797–808.

Henle, M. "On the Relation Between Logic and Thinking." *Psychological Review* 69 (1962): 366–378.

Johnson-Laird, P.N. *Mental Models*. Cambridge: Harvard University Press, 1983.

Johnson-Laird, P.N., and P.C. Wason. "Insight Into a Logical Relation." *Quarterly Journal of Experimental Psychology* 22 (1970): 49–61.

Larkin, J.H. "The Role of Problem Representation in Physics." *Mental Models*. Ed. D. Gentner and A.L. Stevens. Hillsdale, NJ: Erlbaum, 1893. 75–98.

Larkin, J.H., J. McDermott, D.P. Simon, and H. Simon. "Expert and Novice

Performance in Solving Physics Problems." *Science* 208 (1980): 1335–1342.

Mayer, R.E. *Thinking, Problem Solving, Cognition.* New York: Freeman, 1983.

Newell, A "One Final Word." *Problem Solving and Education: Issues in Teaching and Research.* Ed. D.T. Tuma and F. Reif. Hillsdale, NJ: Erlbaum, 1980. 175–189.

Newell, A., J.C. Shaw, and H.A. Simon. "Elements of a Theory of Human Problem Solving." *Psychological Review* 65 (1958): 151–166.

Newell, A., and H. Simon. *Human Problem Solving.* Englewood Cliffs, NJ: Prentice-Hall, 1972.

Peirce, C.S. "The Logic of Drawing History from Ancient Documents." *Collected Papers of Charles Sanders Peirce.* Ed. A. Burks. 8 vols. Cambridge: Harvard University Press, 1958. 7:89–164.

Penner, B.C., and J.F. Voss. "Problem Solving Skills in the Social Sciences: Methodological Considerations." *Learning Research and Development Center Publication Series.* Pittsburgh: University of Pittsburgh, 1983. Vol. 15.

Perkins, D.N., R. Allen, and J. Hafner. "Difficulties in Everyday Reasoning." *Thinking: The Expanding Frontier.* Ed. W. Maxwell. Philadelphia: Franklin Institute Press, 1983. 177–189.

Petty, R.E., and J.F. Cacioppo. *Attitude and Persuasion: Classic and Contemporary Approaches.* Dubuque, IA: William C. Brown, 1981.

Reitman, W. *Cognition and Thought.* New York: Wiley, 1965.

Selz, O. *Zur Psychologie des Productiven Denkens.* Bonn: Cohen, 1922.

Simon, H.A. "The Structure of Ill-Structured Problems." *Artifical Intelligence* 4 (1973): 181–201.

———. *Models of Discovery.* Boston: Reidel, 1977.

———. "Problem Solving and Education." *Problem Solving and Education: Issues in Teaching and Research.* Ed. D.T. Tuma and F. Reif. Hillsdale, NJ: Erlbaum, 1980. 81–96.

Toulmin, S.E. *The Uses of Argument.* Cambridge: Cambridge University Press, 1958.

Tweney, R.D. "Confirmatory and Disconfirmatory Heuristics in Michael Faraday's Scientific Research." Paper presented at the meeting of the Psychonomic Society, Philadelphia, 1981.

———. "How Did Faraday Discover Induction?" *Faraday Rediscovered.* Ed. D. Gooding and F. James. London: Macmillan, 1985. 189–209.

Voss, J.F., J. Blais, M.L. Means, T.R. Greene, and E. Ahwesh. "Informal Reasoning and Subject Matter Knowlege in the Solving of Economics Problems by Naive and Novice Individuals." *Cognition and Instruction* 3.4 (1986): 269–302.

Voss, J.F., R.H. Fincher–Kiefer, T.R. Greene, and T.A. Post. "Individual Differences in Performance: The Contrastive Approach to Knowledge." *Advances in the Psychology of Human Intelligence.* Ed. R.J. Sternberg. New York: Academic Press, 1986. 297–334.

Voss, J.F., T.R. Greene, T.A. Post, and B.C. Penner. "Problem Solving Skill in the Social Sciences." *The Psychology of Learning and Motivation: Advances in Research Theory.* New York: Academic Press, 1983: Vol 17. 165–213.

Voss, J.F., and T.A. Post. "On the Solving of Ill-structured Problems." *The*

Nature of Expertise. Ed. M.T.H. Chi, R. Glaser, and M. Farr. Hillsdale, NJ: Erlbaum, 1988.

Voss, J.F., S.W. Tyler, and L.A. Yengo. "Individual Differences in the Solving of Social Science Problems." *Individual Differences in Cognition*. Ed. R.F. Dillon and R.R. Schmeck. New York: Academic Press, 1983. 205–232.

Voss, J.F., G.T. Vesonder, and G.J. Spilich. "Text Generation and Recall by High Knowledge and Low Knowledge Individuals." *Journal of Verbal Learning and Verbal Behavior* 19 (1980): 651–667.

Wertheimer, M. *Productive Thinking*. New York: Harper & Row, 1959.

PART 2

Reasoning

FROM THE PERSPECTIVE OF LOGICIANS

One of the most salutary books published recently is *The Experts Speak*, which collects predications of experts that turned out to be gloriously incorrect. One prediction it missed is one well known to philosophers— Immanuel Kant's statement that of all the disciplines, logic alone was complete; Aristotle, he said, had done it all.[1] Kant has been subjected to many a "tsk! tsk!" for this monumental misjudgment. He had not anticipated what was to become in the late 19th and early 20th centuries mathematical or symbolic logic, which relegated Aristotelian logic to a restricted portion of a wider and more powerful theory.

It took some time for the symbolization of logic to penetrate the textbooks. Russell and Whitehead's influential *Principia Mathematica* was (and is) an extraordinarily intimidating work, not easily transferrable to the classroom. But when logicians found ways to make symbolic logic accessible, it carried all before it. Until the 1950s symbolic logic dominated the field.

We are now witnessing a reaction against that dominance. The motivation is primarily pedagogical: many teachers of logic came to doubt that introducing students to reasoning exclusively from symbolic logic was achieving the traditional aims of the logic course, and so sought an alternative.

In the first essay of this section Blair and Johnson, themselves key figures as founders and editors of *Informal Logic*, describe the various ways that logicians have rebelled against the formal strictures of abstract logic. As one might expect of a reactive movement, there is greater agreement on what not to do than on what to do. As one might also expect, as the movement spreads, the conflicting intellectual underpinnings of the various approaches become both better clarified and more assertive. Thus, it is an easy move away from standard presentations of symbolic logic to insist on the greater use of "real life examples," for pedagogical reasons; it is a more radical step to argue (as Blair and Johnson do) that the theory of symbolic logic is inadequate to deal with the subtleties of everyday reasoning. It is especially noteworthy, though, that, as Blair and Johnson demonstrate, it is through textbooks that the domain is best portrayed. While one might expect the movement eventually to harden into competing intellectual schools, right now the uneasy peace among informal logicians is maintained by a common concern with pedagogy.

The second essay by Johnson and Blair presents their own stance, which centers the teaching of logic on fallacies. This approach has the most celebrated of antecedents, reaching back to Aristotle, and has never been entirely lost in logic. Even in the middle years of the 20th century, when symbolic logic textbooks dominated, other textbooks of classical logic were available that included the topic of fallacies, although sometimes with something of an apologetic air, as if to acknowledge the old-fashioned character of the subject. Yet throughout the history of logic the place of fallacies has been enveloped with continual controversy. Time and again the whole subject has been displaced from logic and "killed off," usually on the ground that it lacks a satisfactory theoretical foundation—a symptom being the multitude of taxonomies offered over the centuries. Recently informal logicians, and especially Blair and Johnson, restoring fallacies to a pivotal role, have injected new energy into the topic. They offer a reinterpretation of how fallacies might be used and defend their use against standard criticisms.

Although the reaction against symbolic logic is called "informal logic," Blair and Johnson make a useful distinction inside the movement between "applied logic" and "informal logic." Applied logic tends to use techniques of formal logic, but searches out practical uses for them. Thus, within applied logic the concept of validity is central; whereas informal logic tends to cut back, or even discount, the role of validity as a crucial concept. O'Connor's chapter might be termed an exercise in applied logic. He takes from Aristotle a model of logical thinker as methodical thinker and from more recent literature a notion of thinking as a dynamic process of successive representations. He argues that concepts and techniques of formal logic could be presented not as subject matter but as tools. These tools can be used to aid even the process of discovery and to represent options for solving problems.

If O'Connor is right in seeing the aim to be the generation of possibilities, there arises the difficult question of what happens when the student is left confronting conflicting choices. Jerry Cederblom's chapter points to the all too familiar case of the student who, to all appearances, is incapable of seriously entertaining two points of view at the same time. How are we to understand this phenomenon? Cederblom's exploration of the case suggests two approaches, one epistemological, the other psychological. The issue is a critical one especially for those who take change in students' attitude (from unexamined certitude to reflective skepticism) as the goal of the logic course. In Cederblom's analysis, the difficulty that students experience in entertaining a conflicting possibility may be due to an incapacity to adopt a detached attitude toward the beliefs one identifies as one's own. To give them up is to threaten the self, because the self is taken to be identical with those beliefs. In that case, Cederblom suggests, the solution might be to reconceptualize the self and to think of self not as the content of beliefs but as the process by which beliefs are formed. On the other hand, the problem may be a developmental incapacity. In that case it lies in the psychologist's domain.

FROM THE PERSPECTIVE OF PSYCHOLOGISTS

In response to Cederblom, psychologists are ready, indeed eager, to interpret the student's difficulty in terms of developmental stages. The description of the student confronting two conflicting beliefs fits both the viewpoint offered by Perry and that of Kitchener and King (see Moshman and Franks, pp. 17–21, and Neimark, pp. 56–58). Cederblom's interpretation of students' intellectual immobility as an identification of self with the content of one's beliefs finds a parallel in Kitchener and King's description of early developmental stages, which will yield to more mature intellectual processes. Or, as Perry would say, the student shifts from dualism to relativism to commitment. The developmentalists, however, are describing the changing relation of individual beliefs to a larger set of assumptions about the world in general and not just the changing relationship of beliefs to the self. If we turn to Piagetian theory for another developmental view, we can provide an explanatory mechanism for the transition from stage to stage. Cederblom's belief-forming process suggests Piaget's notion of disequilibrium: a learner is in disequilibrium when her present scheme is inadequate to explain the information she is obtaining about the world. In Piaget's view, the state is sufficiently discomforting to motivate the learner to readjust her schema for understanding the world. Students and teachers can find in this temporary disequilibrium a motivational source for productive movement.

Those beliefs which, in Cederblom's terms, are particularly resistant to change are those formed early in life, highly familiar, and emotionally significant. Students may therefore vary in flexibility as a function of the personal significance of their beliefs. This egocentric lack of flexibility characterizes the less mature thinking that Neimark describes as lack of detachment.

Some psychologists are less interested in the maturation of problem-solvers than in the problems themselves. Thus, a great deal of research has been devoted to syllogisms and other problems of formal logic. Solving this kind of logic problem requires a narrow focus. For example, subjects might be asked whether "Sandy is well paid" follows from "Only physicians are well paid, and Sandy is a physician." The subject must leave aside any views about salaries of physicians in the real world. Ignoring actual information is difficult for many people. So when people answer incorrectly about Sandy's salary, psychologists cannot easily determine whether their mistake is in their logic or in their inappropriate reference to previously held information (i.e., all physicians are well paid).

There is not a corresponding body of research in informal logic, on argument analysis in natural language text. Blair and Johnson raise some challenging questions for the psychologist, which might be approached through research on level of difficulty: Do students find it equally difficult to apply each of the three criteria of relevance, sufficiency, and acceptability? Are some fallacies more difficult to recognize than others? And if there are variations of difficulty, what accounts for them?

Human reasoning cannot be confined to what logicians would recognize as arguments. Psychologists are also interested in the problems involved in reading any text, not just argumentative text. The processing of a text could be considered a superordinate category for which analyzing an argument and detecting a fallacy are subordinate tasks. Psychological research text-processing includes tasks such as: writing a summary, giving verbatim recall, answering comprehension or factual questions on the material, applying the information to a new problem. The texts are usually stories or essays, although, as in most discourse, readers could identify arguments if they looked for them. This deemphasis on argument identifies one of the many significant differences between the interests of the logician and the text-processing researcher. Even so, some conclusions from text-processing research bear on the concerns of the logician. Some of the results are no surprise—for example, a learner performs better when criteria of evaluation are presented in advance. Researchers have also reinforced the assumption that familiarity of the content affects how the text is processed.

Both logicians and educational psychologists would like to believe that skills can be taught to students that will be useful to them in a variety of tasks. But extensive research has shown that the difference in performance with familiar material is so great that it looks like a qualitatively different activity, as Voss describes in terms of novice and expert. Abundant Piagetian research also shows that the familiarity of the task affects the manifestation of formal operations. These varied lines of psychological research should point the logicians' attention to the importance of familiarity of subject matter on the students' capacity to deal with arguments.

Perhaps more germane to logicians' concern with argument analysis is the research that shows that people remember outlines and summaries better than specific details, in other words, that subjects process hierarchically or top-down. By providing a hierarchy of the paragraphs (not sentences) of a larger text, research has shown the power of hierarchy on comprehension. If the location of the premises is "higher" in the organization of the text, drawing inferences from the text is likely to be more correct (Reder). Argument analysis that concentrates on the structure of the text thus is apt to improve comprehension.

Other research has investigated teaching methods for improving reading. Common to programs that are effective is that they teach students to have a conscious awareness of the strategies they are using. For example, Dansereau uses networking to teach students to identify and diagram relationships among concepts in the text. The visual representations of networking or Venn diagrams are a common tool of expert logicians and physicists. It is interesting, though, that even when students are taught to use these tools and find them successful, they do not always continue to make use of them spontaneously. Thus the kind of diagrammatic representation O'Connor discusses may not describe the activities of the typical student until he or she becomes a mature thinker and is able to be transformative, in Neimark's terms.

FROM THE PERSPECTIVE
OF COMPOSITION SCHOLARS

The essays by the logicians serve as a reassuring reminder to composition teachers that reading and writing are inseparably interrelated. We can incorporate insights from various schools of informal logic when we teach students to reason well, as they respond to the writing of others (whether published authors or peers). Even more important, however, composition teachers can find guidance in the essays in this section for helping students re-envision their own early drafts. Such re-envisioning not only makes revision both critical and creative but makes it an activity different in kind from mere tinkering.

When reading and rewriting critical or analytic discourse, students can be alert to the arguments presented and can then ask the questions suggested by Johnson and Blair: Are the arguments relevant, jointly sufficient, and acceptable? Such questions can guide small group discussions and peer review sessions along the lines suggested by Bruffee and Haney-Peritz. Even when working alone at their desks, students can invoke internalized voices that ask these critical and generative questions.

Composition instructors will be sure to note that changes in their own field in the last 15 years are analogous to changes in informal logic. Both disciplines have evolved emphases on the generative rather than on the corrective. Johnson and Blair's discussion of fallacies is a case in point. Whereas fallacies might once have been studied as the names for mistakes, Johnson and Blair approach the identification of fallacies as a means to an end. Just so, composition textbooks in the past might have borrowed the mistake-oriented treatment of fallacies. Now we have available to us an approach to fallacies that can help students read their own work-in-progress, searching for opportunities for generative revision.

In their essay, Blair and Johnson reconsider conventional wisdom about logic's most important contribution to composition studies: the supposed distinction between deductive reasoning and inductive reasoning. The idea that deduction is reasoning from the general to the particular and that induction is reasoning from the particular to the general entered composition texts decades ago when logicians did indeed hold these conceptions of deduction and induction. Logicians, both formal and informal, draw the distinction far differently today. Deduction involves the logical necessity that a conclusion be true if the premises are true, while induction requires only the probability that the conclusion be true. Since composition texts in this decade persist in making the distinction of deduction-as-equivalent-to-generalization and induction-as-equivalent-to-particularity, Blair and Johnson point out that the terms have simply come to mean something different in composition from what these terms now convey to contemporary logicians.

These outdated definitions for deduction and induction do, however, function within composition studies as ways to identify organizational patterns within a text. The tenacity of these concepts indicates their ongoing utility in describing the structure of a text. In that sense, composition scholars have understood the spirit (if not the up-to-date substance) of appropriate applications from logic to composition: the perception of structure, relational features, organization as distinct from and sometimes divorced from substance.

Likewise, O'Connor's clarification of logic as focusing on structures, not substance, helps composition teachers to use logical concepts as a way for students read and revise the organizational principles of their drafts. O'Connor's explanation of logic's limitations also liberates the composition teacher to transcend logical strictures to take into account audience, context, purpose, and plausibility. Logic, as O'Connor says, may not always be rational or ethical. Nonetheless, students can gain objectivity in reading their own drafted statements by learning to draw Euler and Venn diagrams. They can also prepare for systematic analysis by logically mapping the possibilities and variables.

Jerry Cederblom expands the discussion of informal logic from ways to perceive structural principles to an attitude of mind, what he calls "the willingness to reason." Cederblom pinpoints the underlying difficulty that many inexperienced writers find with the requirement to reread, to reimagine, and to revise their work. As Cederblom says, they wish "*already* to be right." The now outmoded practice in composition studies of requiring revision only for poor or unacceptable papers served to indoctrinate in students the erroneous belief that revision is punishment for not getting it right the first time.

Cederblom places this misleading assumption about writing in the larger context of the self and its relationship to previously unincorporated ideas. In effect, composition instructors who teach writing as process ask students to identify the self, "not as a set of beliefs" but as "a belief-forming process." Only through the latter self-image will students adopt the "willingness to reason" that makes revision possible. The willingness to revise is then closely related to what Cederblom calls "the disposition to become educated." Cederblom also wisely points out the price that one can pay in the loss of passionate commitment in exchange for an image of the self as a belief-forming process. Experienced writers learn to shift perspective, from the detachment that generates revision to the commitment that sustains the energy necessary to write and revise.

In the last two decades, the fields of logic and composition have developed in parallel, without sufficient opportunity for cross-fertilization. We hope that *Thinking, Reasoning, and Writing* may in a small way revive the ancient complementarity between logic and rhetoric.

NOTES

1. "[S]ince Aristotle, [logic] has been unable to advance a step, and thus to all appearance has reached its completion" (Preface to the Second Edition, xxiv).

WORKS CITED

Cerf, Christopher and Victor Navasky. *The Experts Speak: The Definitive Compendium of Authoritative Misinformation.* New York: Pantheon, 1984.

Dansereau, Donald F. "Learning Strategy Research." *Relating Instruction to Research*. Vol. 1 of *Thinking and Learning Skills*. Ed. Judith W. Segal, Susan F. Chipman, and Robert Glaser. Hillsdale, NJ: Erlbaum, 1985. 209–240.

Kant, Immanuel. *Critique of Pure Reason*. Trans. J. M. D. Meiklejohn. London: G. Bell, 1924.

Reder, Lynne M. "Techniques Available to Author, Teacher, and Reader to Improve Retention of Main Ideas of a Chapter." *Research and Open Questions*. Vol. 2 of *Thinking and Learning Skills*. Ed. Susan F. Chipman, Judith W. Segal, and Robert Glaser. Hillsdale, NJ: Erlbaum, 1985. 37–64.

Russell, Bertrand, and Alfred N. Whitehead. *Principia Mathematica*. 3 vols. Cambridge: Cambridge University Press, 1910–1913.

CHAPTER 5

Informal Logic:
A Thematic Account

J. Anthony Blair and Ralph H. Johnson

ON THE HISTORY OF INFORMAL LOGIC

Offered a history of French Impressionism or of the Gothic novel, one would expect fairly early on a definition or at least an explanation of its subject. Mindful of this entirely legitimate expectation, we find ourselves embarrassed to be unable to offer a standard, widely accepted definition of "informal logic."[1] "Informal Logic" does not designate a subject or a discipline, not in the way "formal logic" and "cognitive psychology" do. Nor does it denote a school of thought (e.g., rationalism), or a theory (e.g., utilitarianism), or a style (e.g., Art Nouveau), or a methodology (e.g., behaviorism). We could extend this negative list but hope it suffices to warn against the danger of a premature classification and hence a misclassification and consequent systematic misunderstanding of the phenomenon we wish to describe.

A "phenomenon" is, in a way, what informal logic is. As such, its history is what defines it. That is why we think a useful way to explain informal logic is by describing the developments from which it emerged and then showing how they exhibit a rough coherence.

In the first instance this phenomenon grows out of the history of the teaching of logic in the philosophy departments of English North American colleges and universities. (Its outer and visible sign has been the introductory textbook, so our account will cite as its evidence the changes found in the new textbooks that began to appear around 1970.) "Informal logic" is the name given to the subject of courses introduced in the early 1970s as alternatives to the standard introductory logic course. The intent of the new logic course was to provide a superior way of training undergraduates to analyze and evaluate reasoning. Its goal was to prepare students to be able to interpret and assess critically the persuasive reasoning they would encounter in their daily lives in school and on graduation as voters, consumers, employees, parents, and in general as informed citizens. This development is intelligible only against the background of the formal logic in the philosophy curriculum in the 1960s.

In our view, formal logic is the study of entailment, or deductive inference. However, this description is not sufficiently specific to distinguish between two dimensions of this study. When Aristotle invented formal logic, he discovered that it is possible to abstract from the entailment relations that hold between sets of statements in natural language (Greek, in his case) to patterns of entailment (see the *Prior Analytics*).[2] Thus, not only do "All Greeks are human" and "All humans are mortal" entail "All Greeks are mortal," but, substituting A, B, and C for the subject and predicate classes or categories, every instantiation of "'All A is B' and 'All B is C' entails 'All A is C'" is true. One aspect of formal logic, then, is the study of the patterns or forms of entailment that apply in English or any other natural language. This is much like studying algebra with a view to its applications to the calculation of financial transactions. Generally, the goal is the improvement of that reasoning which uses deductive implications, or of the assessment of such reasoning.[3]

Formal logic, however, has another dimension. Formulae such as "'All A is B' and 'All B is C' entail 'All A is C'" are detachable from any particular application and deducible from sets of primitive terms by rules of inference governing the transformations permitted using the operators "all," "some," "not," and the "is" or copula of class membership. Such formulae, in short, belong to purely formal "logistic systems." One project that occupies formal logicians as theorists is constructing different logistic systems and studying their formal properties, often without any particular or immediate view to their possible applications or "interpretations." This is analogous to the study of algebra without immediate interest in using it to do the calculations for the construction of a bridge. Formal logicians have discovered, for example, that Aristotle's system of categorical or class logic can be more elegantly expressed in a system called first-order predicate calculus, and they have developed many other logistic systems as well. That such systems can developed and studied quite independently of their interpretations is shown by the fact that some of them that were originally developed as abstractions from and applicable to inferences in English do not fit all the applications for which they were intended, yet the systems are not therefore rejected.

The study that has as its primary goal the development of formal, logistic systems, with the interpretations of such systems as a derivative interest, is the second dimension of formal logic (see Copi and Gould).

The development of informal logic that began in the late 1960s occurred against a background in which the study of logistic systems was well entrenched as the theoretical interest of formal logicians, as well as the subject matter of advanced undergraduate, and graduate, logic courses. The most that could generally be accomplished even in such courses was an introduction to one or two of these systems and their salient properties, and a prerequisite had to be an introductory course that taught the beginning elements and concepts. As a result, the introductory logic course—the only logic course that most college undergraduates would take—acquired a double mandate. It was expected by students and instructors alike to introduce in some systematic way the standards of logical reasoning, understanding "logical" in its ordinary, nontechnical sense to refer to the standards employed in good arguments, good explanations, and (sometimes) good decision procedures and good problem-solving strategies. As well, however, the introductory logic course was typically expected, at least by the instructor, to prepare students for the advanced theory courses, by introducing the concepts of deductive entailment, logical form and symbolization, rules of inference and proof. In many introductory logic courses, this latter function became the predominant one, and in some it became the exclusive function (cf. texts by Carney and Scheer; Hacking; Lambert and Ulrich; Leblanc and Wisdom; and Posposel).

What we call the informal logic movement was in the first instance a reaction against this state of affairs. Students, and some instructors, began to become disenchanted with the emphasis on formal systems. The practical applications of logic to reasoning that the students wanted to learn and the sympathetic instructors to teach were missing in several respects. The political climate in North American universities in the 1960s permitted these dissatisfactions to be voiced, and frequently heeded.

The disaffection was due to a combination of theoretical and educational considerations, though not all who welcomed or took part in the informal logic developments agreed on all points. We believe that at least the following four factors figured in the emergence of informal logic.

First, formal logic studies the deductive inferences between statements, but this is just one of a variety of features or aspects of everyday reasoning needing critical attention. For instance, an inference in an argument can be deductively acceptable (i.e., valid) but the premises false or dubious, or the argument question-begging, or the position refuted by the valid argument may be a distortion of the position actually held by the arguer's opponent (cf. texts by Kahane 1984; Johnson and Blair 1983; and Govier 1988).

Second, at least some of those who took part in the informal logic reaction against formal logic believed that the distinction between deductive and nondeductive inferences that is essential to formal logic applications is neither necessary nor illuminating so far as the teaching of reasoning goes and so could safely and profitably be ignored or downplayed (cf. texts by Thomas; Scriven).

Third, some of those who were part of the informal logic movement argued that even for those inferences that are correctly interpreted as deductive, the deployment of the formal apparatus to assess them is cumbersome, requires a number of difficult and problematic judgments to implement, and is not a superior substitute for natural language (e.g., ordinary English) logic intuitions, especially if these are sharpened by practice on reasoning in natural language (i.e., in English, as opposed to the artificial language of a symbolic system—cf. Thomas's and Scriven's textbooks).

Finally, doubts were emerging about the efficacy for logical practice of teaching logical theory alone. Students and teachers began to question whether a student who understood and could manipulate the propositional calculus was thereby being trained effectively to analyze critically the arguments of everyday social and political rhetoric. Howard Kahane put this point graphically:

> In class a few years back, while I was going over the (to me) fascinating intricacies of the predicate logic quantifier rules, a student asked in disgust how anything he's learned all semester long had any bearing whatever on President Johnson's decision to escalate again in Vietnam. I mumbled something about bad logic on Johnson's part, and then stated that *Introduction to Logic* was not that kind of course. His reply was to ask what courses did take up such matters, and I had to admit that so far as I knew none did. (1971, vii)

Informal logic is difficult to define partly because, as we have said, not all those who reacted against the teaching of formal logic as the means of introducing students to the standards of good reasoning did so for exactly the same reasons, but furthermore because not all moved forward in the same direction. The innovations that modified the old logic course were more varied than the reasons for rejecting it. The positive denotation of "informal logic" is best seen in terms of the designs of the new logic courses and the textbooks developed for them.

To prevent misunderstanding, we must emphasize before proceeding that we do not mean to convey the impression that logic is no longer taught in the traditional way, or that courses in formal logic are no longer to be found. Not at all. What has happened is that the new informal logic courses are being taught alongside those continuing in the earlier paradigm, or else the older courses have been modified to include some of the informal logic innovations while at the same time retaining some—or even considerable—training in formal logic. In general, it is our impression that introductory logic courses tend to have at least an informal logic component now, or else students are offered the choice between an informal logic and a formal logic course at the introductory level. Most philosophy departments big enough to do so also offer upper-level students an advanced formal logic course. So formal logic has not been replaced in the philosophy curriculum; it has been supplemented by informal logic, and in some cases supplanted as the introductory course or the course expected to be the only logic course most students take.

INFORMAL LOGIC TEXTBOOKS

The direction for the new logic course was set in 1971 by Kahane's text, *Logic and Contemporary Rhetoric* (now in its fourth edition). Kahane focuses on the critique of the arguments of everyday political and social rhetoric, using an extensive, modernized set of informal fallacies as his main critical tool. He applies these fallacies to short arguments but also introduces a method for interpreting and assessing longer or "extended" arguments. As well, he addresses advertising, the news media, and text-books as sources of our information and our world views requiring critical attention.

Stephen Thomas followed in 1973 with *Practical Reasoning in Natural Language* (now in its third edition). Thomas's emphasis is on extracting arguments from their natural language settings and displaying them so as to reveal perspicuously their logical structures. He emphasizes the modeling of good reasoning and analyzes shortcomings mostly as failures to meet these standards, although he does include a chapter of informal fallacies. Like Kahane, he offers a method for analyzing extended arguments.

The third of the ground-breaking informal logic texts was Michael Scriven's *Reasoning*, published in 1976. Scriven concentrates on argument analysis and evaluation, too, but differs from Kahane and from Thomas. His text is organized around a seven-step "method" of argument analysis for both short and extended arguments, beginning with the clarification of meaning, moving on through the identification and portrayal of structure and the criticism of separate premises and inferences, to overall assess-ment. Scriven's analytical and critical tools are the critical terms of ordinary English (often sharpened and clarified). He eschews a "fallacies approach" as unhelpful. Like Thomas, he uses a tree-diagramming technique for evaluating argument structure.

These three textbooks launched, and solidified, the informal logic movement, but they by no means circumscribed it. Logic teachers were working up their own syllabuses independently of one another all over the United States and Canada. When we prepared a bibliography in 1978 we counted at least a dozen other textbooks that had appeared since 1970 (see Blair and Johnson 1980), and in reviewing the subsequent five-year period we counted 41 new texts or new editions appearing between 1978 and 1983 (see Johnson and Blair 1985). Nevertheless, we would argue that an examination of Kahane's, Thomas's, and Scriven's texts is necessary for an understanding of informal logic. A study of all these texts discloses a number of recurring topics.

Real-life Examples of Arguments. It has become *de rigueur* to use as examples, to illustrate and explain, and in exercises, arguments that people have actually used, in their own words, and that are taken from newspapers, magazines, books, and transcripts. These tend to be not exclusively academic and consequently less complete and tidy than the polished arguments of academic prose. Unlike the invented examples of the earlier textbooks, they bring out the difficulties of applying logical principles and also force the textbook author to be more empirical when devising advice for argument interpretation and criticism.

The use of such examples has led to the development of various techniques for deciding when arguments are present and for extricating and displaying or stating such arguments for the purpose of evaluating them. Using tree diagrams to display argument structure, for example, reveals not only a variety of premise-conclusion patterns but also a variety of argument roles (e.g., arguments answering doubts about the claim at issue, arguments answering objections to the claim at issue, arguments answering doubts or objections about the premises or the inferences of the arguments of the first two kinds).

Using real arguments as examples has also required the creation of policies for supplying unexpressed premises and conclusions, and these in turn have promoted theoretical inquiry. For instance, it becomes clear that a decision has to be made about whether to reconstruct an argument so as to make its inferences deductive entailments or not. This has led to investigation of different types of inference and of argument. Also, a distinction must be made between reconstructing the best possible argument (thus necessarily employing some "ideal" of argument), or the argument that the writer intended, or some compromise (e.g., the most plausible argument, given the author's probable beliefs) (see Scriven 1976;

Hitchcock 1983; or Govier 1988 for good discussions of this issue). This has led in turn to discussions of the "ethics" of argument analysis, centering around the principle of charity ("Be charitable in reconstructing an argument"). There are disagreements about what charity specifically entails, or whether it should be used at all (see Scriven 1976; Johnson 1981; Govier 1981, 1983; and Adler).

Treatment of Fallacies. The individual fallacies deployed and the classifications of fallacies used vary widely among informal logic textbooks. Many texts offer apparently random selections of fallacies culled from the fallacy tradition, and organized capriciously (see Fearnside and Holther; Michalos; and Engel 1980, 1986). However, some texts have general theories of fallacy. For instance Kahane, and Johnson and Blair, characterize fallacies as failures to employ the standards of good and cogent reasoning. Thus, for Kahane, "we reason fallaciously whenever we (1) reason from unjustified premises, (2) fail to use relevant information, or (3) reason invalidly" (1984, 47), while for Johnson and Blair, "an argument which fails to satisfy one (or more) of [the]...requirements [of relevant, sufficient, and acceptable support for the conclusion] is fallacious" (1983, 34). Woods and Walton's text, *Argument: The Logic of the Fallacies*, is organized around a theory of argument, in terms of which different kinds of fallacy are violations of the canons appropriate to different kinds of argument. The more usual definition of "fallacy," however, is "an argument which appears to be valid (or cogent) but is not," which has the support of the widely-respected monograph on the subject, C.L. Hamblin's *Fallacies* (see 12).

As a generalization, the more detailed and careful treatments of fallacies hold that certain patterns of reasoning employed under certain specified conditions are fallacious. Thus, for example, criticizing a person, whether it is called an *ad hominem* attack or not, is not per se fallacious. To be *fallacious*, an *ad hominem* attack must occur in the context of an attempt to refute or discredit a position held by the person under attack, and the substance of the attack must be irrelevant to the assessment of the position in question (see Johnson and Blair 1983, 79ff.; Govier 1986, 116). We discuss the treatment of fallacies more fully, and offer an extended example of the sort of fallacy analysis we endorse, in our chapter on the fallacy approach in this book (Chapter 6).

Emphasis on Argument Construction. The informal logic texts that have appeared in the last five years have tended to pay more than lip service to the importance of constructing arguments, alongside the importance of analyzing and criticizing them. This is a very recent development. Earlier texts mentioned this topic but did not offer detailed guidelines for argument construction the way composition texts like Fahnestock and

Secor's do. Barry, Cederblom and Paulsen, Govier (1988), Nosich, and Johnson and Blair (1983), however, present either continuous advice about argument construction or a chapter or section devoted to this advice. Some of this material aims to help students organize their thinking and construct cogent arguments; some of it advises them about strategies of argumentation in dispute-type or adversary contexts. In other words, some seems akin to the advice about writing persuasive essays found in some composition texts, whereas some seems closer to the advice about how to make a case, available in speech or debate texts. As far as we can tell, however, the recommendations offered in the informal logic texts have been generated without the benefit of familiarity with the literature in composition, rhetoric, speech communication, or debate.

The emphasis on actual arguments, the treatments of fallacies, and the new attention to the construction of arguments are some of the highlights of informal logic as it is displayed in the textbooks. The point we would emphasize is that anyone who makes reference to "logic" or to "logic instruction" cannot assume that concepts and approaches learned as an undergraduate or graduate student 10 or more years ago still apply today. For instance, treatments of inductive logic or of scientific reasoning would profit from reference to Merrilee Salmon's *Introduction to Logic and Critical Thinking* (1984), to Ronald Giere's *Understanding Scientific Reasoning* (1984), or to Larry Wright's *Better Reasoning* (1982). (Moreover up-to-date edition must be consulted; for example, we understand Giere is planning a radical change in his theoretical approach for his third edition.) Govier's treatments of arguments from analogy and the slippery slope fallacy represent a major advance. The latest treatment of begging-the-question in the literature is incorporated in Woods and Walton's text. The treatment of the role of language in reasoning and argument, and the analysis of vagueness and meaning in Wright's text are outstanding. Nowhere is the handling of tacit premises and of statement strength more meticulous and thorough than in Hitchocock's text. We no doubt do injustice to other authors by failing to include them in this list, but the point has, we trust, been made: the informal logic textbooks contain part of the literature that must be consulted by anyone claiming familiarity with recent developments in informal logic. *A fortiori* no one is justified in speaking of "logic" in general without a solid acquaintance with the texts contributing to this most recent reform movement.

Disagreements within Informal Logic

We earlier intimated that there is theoretical diversity in the work we identify as informal logic. By describing some of the points of disagreement, we hope to extend our readers' understanding of the movement.

The Role of Formal Logic. Although there are informal logic textbooks that contain no units on formal logic (cf. Kahane; Thomas; Scriven; Johnson and Blair 1983; Hitchcock 1983), no one contends that formal logic is, in its proper domain, mistaken or useless. The controversy arises over the location and extent of its proper domain. Some, such as the above-mentioned authors, think that an educationally responsible logic course can be taught without teaching any formal logic. Many others, however, regard formal logic as sufficiently important for purposes of argument interpretation and assessment or for the contribution to a student's general education for which an introductory logic course is re-sponsible, to give it a chapter or more in their textbook (e.g., Cederblom and Paulsen; Fogelin; Govier 1988; Nolt; Schwartz). The first point of view is perhaps most dramatically expressed by Scriven:

> ...the emergence of informal logic marks the end of the reign of formal logic. Not by any means the end of the *subject*, just its relegation to its proper place in the academic zoo, somewhere over there just north of mathematics and west of computer science, and far away from the children's part of the zoo. (1980, 147)
> ...one has to view with great skepticism the very idea that formal logic is likely to help improve reasoning skill. What it improves is skill in doing formal logic. The syllogism was probably nearer to reality (though not to comprehensiveness) than the propositional calculus, but not near enough to make it useful in handling the average editorial or columnist today. (1976, xv)

The second is put more prosaically by Govier:

> I have tried to combine some elementary formal logic with an informal approach to natural argument. This is because I believe that there are *some* natural arguments that do exemplify logically valid forms, and for these, the understanding of basic formal patterns is very useful. I also believe that the basic concept of deductive entailment is extremely important for the correct interpretation of arguments—whether or not those arguments are themselves deductive. (1988, ix)

The controversy is partly empirical: at issue is just how extensively deductive inferences occur in everyday reasoning and argumentation. It is also partly pedagogical: people disagree about whether students can be taught to recognize and assess deductive inferences without having been taught some of the theory of formal logic, including some of the forms or patterns of deductive entailment. Finally, the disagreement is educational: the value of learning the theory of formal logic, which is conceded by all to be advanced and elegant, is disputed.

Informal Logic versus Applied Logic. Some who see themselves as doing and teaching informal logic are interested primarily in applying the results of formal logic to everyday argument. (We regard Finbarr O'Connor's essay in this volume as a good example of such an approach. A text that nicely illustrates it is John Nolt's *Informal Logic*.) These logic teachers consider logic as the science of deductive inferences and of arguments using such inferences. The laws of logic are most perspicuously expressed in formal language; informal logic is the application of these laws to "natural language" (e.g., everyday English) reasoning. Hence "informal logic" is "applied logic."

Others—among whom we include ourselves—regard logic as the study of cogent argumentation, with the standards of cogency an open question. For them, "formal logic" denotes the study, usually in artificial or formal languages, of deductive systems. "Informal logic," in their view, then denotes all that is left over, which includes the discovery, elucidation, and application of a variety of standards of cogent argument in addition to the deductive validity of inferences. These theorists hold, then, that informal logic is an autonomous branch of logic, not the application of logic proper to practical matters. Logical theory, on this second understanding of informal logic, will not necessarily be formalized; and certainly informal logic is not the application of formal logic.

These two conceptions of informal logic can be found in the textbooks and the literature. Our sense is, however, that teachers and theorists in the field are insufficiently aware of the distinction we have just drawn.

The Deductive-Inductive Distinction. Some hold that arguments may be classified as either inductive or deductive. Others hold that it is not arguments but inferences that are so classifiable and distinguishable. Some hold that whatever the referent of these predicates may be—arguments or inferences—there is a distinction and it is exhaustive. (This is the conventional wisdom.) Others hold that the distinction is not exhaustive— that there are other classes of inferences (or arguments) (e.g., "conductive": a conclusion about some individual case is drawn nonconclusively from premises about the same case and without appeal to other cases). Yet others deny that the distinction is always clearly applicable, so there is a class of arguments that cannot be assigned to one or the other category. (See the exchange in the *Informal Logic Newsletter* between Weddle 1979; Fohr 1980 (a) (b); Hitchcock 1980, 1981; Govier 1978, 1980 (a) (b); Freeman 1983, 1984; and F. Johnson.)

Many English composition texts define "deduction" or "deductive reasoning" as reasoning from a general thesis or truth to particulars, and "induction" or "inductive reasoning" as reasoning from specific facts or particulars to a general conclusion (see McDonald; Messenger and Taylor; Parker). This is not how logicians, formal or informal, draw the distinction today. Here is the way the distinction is drawn by one highly respected logician:

There are certain fundamental characteristics which distinguish between correct deductive and correct inductive arguments. We will mention two primary ones. Deductive: I. If all the premises are true, the conclusion *must be true*. II. All of the information or factual content in the conclusion was already contained, at least implicitly, in the premises. Inductive: I. If all the premises are true, the conclusion is probably true but not necessarily true. II. The conclusion contains information not present, even implicitly, in the premises. (W. Salmon 14)

By this definition, deductive reasoning can be between particular statements (e.g., "Sal is in the library or at the pub, and she is not in the library, so she must be at the pub") or from particulars to general statements (e.g., "Book 1 in this room has Ev's bookplate; Book 2 in this room has Ev's bookplate; ...; book n in this room has Ev's bookplate; there are exactly n books in this room; so all the books in this room have Ev's bookplate"). Similarly, inductive reasoning can move from particulars to particulars (e.g., "This fire is hot, so probably the next fire will be hot") or from general statements to general statements (e.g., "Crows are black, black absorbs heat, so crows' color helps to keep them warm"). Are logicians right and composition texts wrong?

We suspect that the "particulars-to-general = induction" and the "general-to-particulars = deduction" formulas entered the composition literature at a time when these conceptions of induction and deduction *were* the conventional wisdom among logicians and became in turn the conventional wisdom in composition. What has subsequently happened, though—judging by the composition texts we have examined—is that "induction" and "deduction" have acquired their own independent meanings in the composition field. They now refer to two ways of organizing an argumentative discourse: moving from a general proposition at the outset to particular instances of it subsequently (deductive organization), and moving from particular examples to a generalization based on them (inductive organization). In other words, these terms, in spite of a common origin, now simply mean different things to logicians and to composition teachers.

We conclude, then, that there need be no correct and mistaken sides in this difference. So long as composition authors do *not* suggest that the two formulas for "deduction" and "induction" correctly define logical types of argument, there is no mistake.

Fallacies. Opinions about the existence, nature, and value of teaching informal fallacies vary widely. Since we discuss these views in some detail in our later chapter on the fallacy approach (Chapter 6), we will here do no more than refer readers forward for the details, while noting that this is a significant area of disagreement among informal logic theorists and practitioners.

Premise Criteria. There are different views about what standards the premises of a good argument should meet. Most texts state that the premises of a good argument must be true (e.g., Browne and Keeley; Cederblom and Paulsen; Crossley and Wilson; Fogelin; Hoaglund; Nolt; Nosich; Thomas). Others would countenance a variety of norms, depending on the context, including plausibility as well as probability and truth (e.g., Barker; Woods and Walton; Govier, 1988). Yet others have argued that acceptability, defined in terms of the capacity of meet plausible objections, should be the criterion (e.g., Johnson and Blair 1983).

Inference Criteria. Most hold that deductive entailments and probabilistic inferences are acceptable as inferences. Yet others would tolerate a range of kinds of inferences: plausible inference, conductive inference, and dialectically acceptable inferences (i.e., an inference that can be defended against plausible objections) (cf. Woods and Walton; Johnson and Blair 1983; Govier 1988).

Domain Dependence and Independence. While most theorists would agree that the background knowledge needed for evaluating premises will be to a large degree dependent on the areas of knowledge or the subject matter involved, almost all hold that the inferences from the premises to the conclusion can be assessed without reference to subject matter. There are those, however, who argue that the standards which inferences must satisfy depend on warrants or inference "licenses" that are domain-specific, so that what may count as a legitimate pattern of inference in one subject area would not be acceptable in others (see Toulmin, Rieke, and Janik; or McPeck 1981, 1985).

Abilities and Attitudes. Many texts are written as if the mastery that informal logic tries to teach and that is intended to have practical value consists of a set of abilities or skills. The goal of the enterprise is to impart these abilities, and it is they that prove useful to the student upon leaving the course (e.g., Annis 1962, 1981; Engel 1986). Others argue that in addition to abilities (or skills, or aptitudes), a certain attitude or outlook or disposition is essential (cf. Binkley; Paul; Ennis). This outlook has been called reflective skepticism, the love of reason, and a dialogical perspective. Proponents of this position argue that egocentric and sociocentric outlooks promote self-deception and rationalization. The skills learned, they contend, can be used to reinforce prejudice unless taught in concert with an attitude of openness and self-criticism.

This list gives the lie to any simple-minded assumption that informal logic is a unified theory (see McPeck 1985). At the same time, it indicates a partial agenda for future research in the area. We hope as well that it conveys a sense for the kinds of issue that concern those who identify themselves as working in informal logic.

CRITICAL THINKING AND INFORMAL LOGIC

We have so far said nothing about critical thinking and what its relationship to informal logic might be. This is simply because, vague though the designation *informal logic* is, we have tended to identify our own work and interest as belonging to informal logic and are not accustomed to thinking of it as falling under the rubric *critical thinking*. The latter has a much longer history and wider application than the former, and an even vaguer denotation. Scolding his colleagues in education circles for the imprecision of their use of the label *critical thinking*, Barry Beyer remarked recently, "Defining critical thinking as virtually all forms of thinking fails to distinguish its unique features and function, and is about as useful as no definition at all" (270). But in that article Beyer cites just such a range of uses of the term as to tempt skepticism about its utility.

Like Beyer, we believe critical thinking can be defined in a way that makes it a useful concept, but definitions of critical thinking, like those of informal logic, must perforce be persuasive—that is, be recommendations about how the term should henceforth be used, supported (ideally) by reasons for embracing such conceptual legislation. Beyer himself recommends that critical thinking be understood as "the process of determining the authenticity, accuracy and worth of information or knowledge claims" and a critical thinker as one who possesses a number of discrete, identifiable skills plus the inclination to use them to assess information and knowledge claims (276). Robert Ennis, perhaps the leading researcher in critical thinking testing, recommends a similar definition: "The process of reasonably deciding what to believe and do" (see Ennis 1962).

If these specifications of "critical thinking" are accepted, then critical thinking turns out to have connections with informal logic but it is not the same thing. Our prescriptive definition of informal logic is that it should be understood as the study of the nonformal methods and standards for analyzing, evaluating, and constructing arguments and argumentation in natural language. As such, informal logic is a field of study, not a process. An informal logician is a theorist and teacher, whereas a critical thinker may be any person, and ideally is Everyone. Insofar as the assessment of information, beliefs, and actions requires the use or analysis and assessment of arguments, the methods and advice of the informal logician will be useful to the critical thinker. A good critical thinker will be a good informal logician. Moreover, one goal of courses in formal logic is to improve and foster critical thinking, especially insofar as critical thinking requires being able to work intelligently with arguments. Furthermore, we believe that many courses currently identified as informal logic courses are in fact intended as critical thinking courses, and many courses labeled critical thinking teach mostly informal logic.

There is not a one-to-one correspondence here, however, because not all beliefs or claims are to be assessed using argumentation. The artist or musician, the poet or novelist, may think critically about his or her craft and about work in process, but we doubt that the critical judgments made need to, or always can, deploy argumentation. Presumably the careful problem-solver or decision-maker thinks critically, but we are far from certain about the role of argumentation in such reasoning. Certainly all these people reason—draw inferences—critically, but not all reasoning takes place through the medium of argument. If informal logic is correctly tied down to argumentation, then critical thinking, we contend, covers a broader area.

The informal logic movement is a reform movement in philosophy, and more narrowly, in logic. The critical thinking movement is a reform movement in education generally. It is a movement that we, as educators, welcome. We think it deserves encouragement, support, and theoretical nurture. As we understand things, informal logic has a central contribution to make to the critical thinking movement. The two, however, are distinct.

Concluding Remarks

We have had three aims in mind when writing this chapter. First, we have encountered from colleagues in a variety of fields including composition and cognitive psychology a conception of logic that is inaccurate. It is often out of date with respect of the more recent developments in formal and in inductive logic, but more seriously from our point of view it displays complete ignorance of the branching out of informal logic from the historical paradigm. We hope to have begun to remove that ignorance and to have made our readers aware that there is a literature on informal logic to be investigated. Second, we hope that an understanding of what informal logic is will make it possible for our colleagues in cognitive psychology and composition to see how their work may relate to ours and alert us to regions of their literature with which we and other informal logicians should familiarize ourselves. Finally, we want to stimulate theorists in composition and cognitive psychology to identify topics and problems in informal logic cognate to their own fields to which they might devote research attention. For instance, we find ourselves in a vacuum as far as empirical knowledge related to the teaching and learning of informal logic goes. Similarly, we sense that prescriptive and descriptive theories of composition would enhance our understanding of argumentation, both its analysis and construction. In general we sense an increasing awareness of cognate fields; we want to contribute to that process.

NOTES

1. In our introduction to *Informal Logic*, the preceedings of the first International Symposium, we offered a working definition: a subject matter characterized by an interest in the theory and pedagogy connected with reasoning and argumentation in directions outside the scope of formal logic (Blair and Johnson 1980, x). The capsule definition we gave in the inaugural issue of the journal *Informal Logic* was: "the logic used in the analysis and evaluation of arguments and other forms of reasoning used in the practice of rational life" (Blair and Johnson 1984, 1). We hazard yet another working definition in Chapter 6 on fallacies in this volume.
2. Logicians use the term *natural language* to refer to a language that has evolved as a means of verbal communication of a cultural group—in other words, the language that a people speaks (e.g., English, French, Swahili). These are contrasted with artificial or technical languages invented for special purposes, such as computer languages (e.g., Basic, Fortran).
3. See the texts listed in the references by Carney and Scheer, Hacking, Jeffrey, Lambert and Ulrich, Leblanc and Wisdom, and Posposel. We should note, however, that there is a strong dissenting voice from some formal logic teachers. See the essays published in Covey.

WORKS CITED

Adler, Jonathan E. "Why Be Charitable?" *Informal Logic Newsletter* 4.2 (May 1982): 15–16.

Annis, David B. *Techniques of Critical Reasoning*. Columbus, OH: Charles E. Merrill, 1974.

Aristotle. *Prior Analytics. The Complete Works of Aristotle*. Ed. Jonathan Barnes. Princeton: Princeton University Press, 1948.

Barker, Evelyn M. *Everyday Reasoning*. Englewood Cliffs, NJ: Prentice-Hall, 1981.

Barry, Vincent. *Invitation to Critical Thinking*. New York: Holt, Rinehart and Winston, 1984.

Beyer, Barry K. "Critical Thinking? What Is It?" *Social Education* 49.4 (April 1985): 270–276.

———, guest editor. "Critical Thinking Revisited" *Social Education* 49.4 (April 1985): 268–310.

Binkley, Robert W. "Can the Ability To Reason Well Be Taught?" *Informal Logic: The First International Symposium.* Ed. J. Anthony Blair and Ralph H. Johnson. Inverness, CA: Edgepress, 1980. 79–92.

Blair, J. Anthony, and Ralph H. Johnson, eds. *Informal Logic: The First International Symposium.* Inverness, CA: Edgepress, 1980.

―――. "From the Editors." *Informal Logic* 6.1 (January 1984): 1–2.

Browne, M. Neil, and Stuart M. Keeley. *Asking the Right Questions: A Guide to Critical Thinking.* 2nd ed. Englewood Cliffs, NJ: Prentice-Hall 1986.

Carney, James D., and Richard K. Scheer. *Fundamentals of Logic.* 3rd ed. New York: Macmillan, 1980.

Cederblom, Jerry, and David W. Paulsen. *Critical Reasoning: Understanding and Criticizing Arguments and Theories.* Belmont, CA: Wadsworth, 1986.

Copi, Irving M., and James A. Gould, eds. *Contemporary Philosophical Logic.* New York: St. Martin's Press, 1978.

Covey, Preston, ed. *Formal Logic and the Liberal Arts.* Special issue of *Teaching Philosophy* 4.3–4 (July–October 1981): 207–427.

Crossley, David J., and Peter A. Wilson. *How To Argue: An Introduction to Logical Thinking.* New York: Random House, 1979.

Engel, S. Morris. *Analyzing Informal Fallacies.* Englewood Cliffs, NJ: Prentice-Hall, 1980.

―――. *With Good Reason: An Introduction to Informal Fallacies.* 3rd ed. New York: St. Martin's Press, 1986.

Ennis, Robert H. "A Concept of Critical Thinking." *Harvard Educational Review* 32.1 (1962): 83–111.

―――. "Rational Thinking and Educational Practice." *Philosophy and Education: Eightieth Yearbook of the National Society for the Study of Education, Part I.* Ed. Jonas F. Soltis. Chicago: NSSE, 1981. 143–183.

Fahnestock, Jeanne, and Marie Secor. *A Rhetoric of Argument.* New York: Random House, 1982.

Fearnside, W. Ward, and William B. Holther. *Fallacy: The Counterfeit of Argument.* Englewood Cliffs, NJ: Prentice-Hall, 1959.

Fogelin, Robert J. *Understanding Arguments: An Introduction to Informal Logic.* 2nd ed. New York: Harcourt Brace Jovanovich, 1982.

Fohr, Samuel. (a) "The Deductive-Inductive Distinction." *Informal Logic Newsletter* 2.2 (April 1980): 5–9.

―――. (b) "Deductive-Inductive: Reply to Criticisms." *Informal Logic Newsletter* 3.1 (October 1980): 5–10.

Freeman, James B. "Logical Form, Probability Interpretations, and the Inductive/Deductive Distinction." *Informal Logic Newsletter* 4.2 (June 1983): 2–10.

―――. "Reply to Englebretsen." *Informal Logic Newsletter* 6.3 (December 1984): 34–40.

Giere, Ronald N. *Understanding Scientific Reasoning.* 2nd ed. New York: Holt, Rinehart and Winston, 1984.

Govier, Trudy. "Alternative to Inductive-Deductive Paradigm." *Informal Logic Newsletter* 1.2 (December 1978): 4.

―――. (a) "More on Deductive and Inductive Arguments." *Informal Logic Newsletter* 2.3 (June 1980):7–8.

———. (b) "Assessing Arguments: What Range of Standards?" *Informal Logic Newsletter* 3.1 (October 1980): 2–4.

———. "Uncharitable Thoughts About Charity." *Informal Logic Newsletter* 4.1 (December 1981): 10–11.

———. "On Adler on Charity." *Informal Logic Newsletter* 4.3 (December 1983): 10–11.

———. *A Practical Study of Argument*. 2nd ed. Belmont, CA: Wadsworth, 1988.

Hacking, Ian. *A Concise Introduction to Logic*. New York: Random House, 1972.

Hamblin, C.L. *Fallacies*. London: Methuen, 1970.

Hitchcock, David. "Deductive and Inductive: Types of Validity, Not Types of Argument." *Informal Logic Newsletter* 2.3 (June 1980): 9–10.

———. "Deduction, Induction and Conduction." *Informal Logic Newsletter* 3.2 (March 1981): 7–15.

———. *Critical Thinking: A Guide to Evaluating Information*. Toronto: Methuen, 1983.

Hoaglund, John. *Critical Thinking: An Introduction to Informal Logic*. Newport News, VA: Vale Press, 1984.

Jeffrey, Richard. *Formal Logic: Its Scope and Limits*. 2nd ed. New York: McGraw-Hill, 1981.

Johnson, Fred. "Deductively-Inductively." *Informal Logic Newsletter* 3.1 (October 1980): 4–5.

Johnson, Ralph H. "Charity Begins at Home." *Informal Logic Newsletter* 3.3 (June 1981): 4–9.

Johnson, Ralph H., and J. Anthony Blair. "The Recent Development of Informal Logic." *Informal Logic: The First International Symposium*. Ed. J. Anthony Blair and Ralph H. Johnson. Inverness, CA: Edgepress, 1980. 3–28.

———. *Logical Self-Defense*. 2nd ed. Toronto: McGraw-Hill Ryerson, 1983.

———. "Informal Logic: The Past Five Years, 1978–1983." *American Philosophical Quarterly* 22.3 (July 1985): 181–196.

Kahane, Howard. *Logic and Contemporary Rhetoric: The Use of Reason in Everyday Life*. Belmont, CA: Wadsworth, 1971.

———. *Logic and Contemporary Rhetoric: The Use of Reason in Everyday Life*. 4th ed. Belmont, CA: Wadsworth, 1984.

Lambert, Karel, and William Ulrich. *The Nature of Argument*. New York: Macmillan, 1980.

Leblanc, Hughes, and William A. Wisdom. *Deductive Logic*. 2nd ed. Boston: Allyn and Bacon, 1976.

McDonald, Daniel. *The Language of Argument*. 4th ed. New York: Harper & Row, 1983.

McPeck, John E. *Critical Thinking and Education*. Oxford: Martin Robertson, 1981.

———. "Critical Thinking and the 'Trivial Pursuit' Theory of Knowledge." *Teaching Philosophy* 8.4 (October 1985): 295–308.

Messenger, William E., and Peter A. Taylor. *Elements of Writing*. Scarborough, Ontario: Prentice-Hall Canada, 1984.

Michalos, Alex C. *Improving Your Reasoning*. Englewood Cliffs, NJ: Prentice-

Hall, 1970.

Nolt, John Eric. *Informal Logic: Possible Worlds and Imagination.* New York: McGraw-Hill, 1984.

Nosich, Gerald M. *Reasons and Arguments.* Belmont, CA: Wadsworth, 1982.

Parker, John F. *The Process of Writing.* Don Mills, Ontario: Addison-Wesley, 1983.

Paul, Richard. "Teaching Critical Thinking in the 'Strong' Sense: A Focus on Self-Deception, World Views, and a Dialectical Mode of Analysis." *Informal Logic Newsletter* 4.2 (May 1982): 2–7.

Posposel, Howard. *An Introduction to Propositional Logic.* Englewood Cliffs, NJ: Prentice-Hall, 1974.

Salmon, Merrilee H. *An Introduction to Logic and Critical Thinking.* San Diego: Harcourt Brace Jovanovich, 1984.

Salmon, Wesley C. *Logic.* 2nd ed. Englewood Cliffs, NJ: Prentice-Hall, 1973.

Schwartz, Thomas. *The Art of Logical Reasoning.* New York: Random House, 1980.

Scriven, Michael. *Reasoning.* New York: McGraw-Hill, 1976.

———. "The Philosophical and Pragmatic Significance of Informal Logic." *Informal Logic: The First International Symposium.* Ed. J. Anthony Blair and Ralph H. Johnson. Inverness, CA: Edgepress, 1980. 147–160.

Thomas, Stephen N. *Practical Reasoning in Natural Language.* 3rd ed. Englewood Cliffs, NJ: Prentice-Hall, 1986.

Toulmin, Steven, Richard Rieke, and Allen Janik. *An Introduction to Reasoning.* New York: Macmillan, 1979.

Weddle, Perry. *Argument: A Guide to Critical Thinking.* New York: McGraw-Hill, 1978.

———. "Inductive, Deductive." *Informal Logic Newsletter* 2.1 (November 1979): 1–5.

———. "Good Grief! More on Deduction/Induction." *Informal Logic Newsletter* 3.1 (October 1980): 10–13.

Woods, John, and Douglas Walton. *Argument: The Logic of the Fallacies.* Toronto: McGraw-Hill Ryerson, 1982.

Wright, Larry. *Better Reasoning: Techniques for Handling Argument, Evidence, and Abstraction.* New York: Holt, Rinehart and Winston, 1982.

CHAPTER 6

The Fallacy Approach to Criticizing Arguments

Ralph H. Johnson and J. Anthony Blair

The last 15 years have been exciting ones in logic. The emergence of critical thinking and informal logic have called into question the mathematical model that has dominated logic for the past century. It is our belief that these developments deserve to be brought to the attention of those interested in an integrated approach to thinking, reading, and writing. Others in this volume will attempt to show the utility of traditional logic (i.e., Aristotelian syllogistic) and modern (symbolic) logic to the enterprise. Our focus will be different: within the general confines of informal logic (which we have to some degree already explained in Chapter 5 but shall say just a bit more about below in our section on the fallacy approach to criticism.

We shall begin our contribution by briefly discussing the crucial terms—logic, informal logic, applied logic, critical thinking. We will then present our version of the fallacy approach. We shall conclude by indicating why, in our years of teaching, we have found that the fallacy approach works best with our students and why we recommend it to others.

CRITICAL THINKING AND INFORMAL LOGIC

Logic can be thought of as that discipline which treats normative questions about reasoning: under what circumstances is reasoning good reasoning? If one is interested in appraising reasoning as it occurs in a natural language setting, and if in particular one is interested in appraising an argument (conceived of here as that form of discourse in which reasons/evidence are offered on behalf of a conclusion), then there are three separate tasks that one must be prepared to undertake. First, the discourse must be identified as argumentative and as worthy of evaluation. Second, the argument must be extracted from the wider text and perhaps reconstructed. Third, the argument must be subjected to critique. The differences between formal and informal logic stem principally from different ideas about what standards an argument should be held to and hence what are legitimate modes of criticism.

By "informal logic" we mean that inquiry within the field of logic which seeks to develop nonformal standards, criteria, and procedures to aid in the evaluation of arguments. Historically formal logic has been primarily interested in inference, implication, and syntactical transformations, and it has been for the most part deductive in character.

The term *applied logic* may be said to take its meaning from this context. Thus, "applied logic" might be taken as referring either to formal logic or to informal logic, as that logic is applied in some context. Another way to put it is this: both formal and informal logic have a theoretical and a practical or applied dimension.

"Critical thinking" is a term that has great predominance these days and a wide variety of applications, but precious little agreement exists among its users about its content. We understand by it a specific kind of intellectual orientation and set of skills and attitudes that enable its possessor to reason well about something.

In closing this section, the authors would be remiss if they did not stress that none of terms discussed above (with the possible exception of "formal logic") has a determinate meaning that is universally or almost universally agreed on. Consequently it is not surprising that there are strong differences of opinion about whether formal logic or informal logic or some combination of both is needed for the development of critical thinking or reasoning skills.

THE FALLACY APPROACH TO CRITICISM

In this section we shall present the reader with the fallacy approach to the criticism of arguments. To understand what is meant by the fallacy approach and where it fits into the subject of argumentation, we refer to the previous section and the three tasks outlined there. The fallacy approach is a response to the third of these tasks. It is the view that a profitable way of criticizing an argument is by the detection of fallacy. The root idea of fallacy is that of a logical error in the argument. Hence, the presence of fallacy invalidates the argument, although it does not mean that the conclusion of the argument is false. We begin with a brief history of fallacies and then discuss several topics pertinent to this essay.

A Very Short History of Fallacies

The study of fallacy dates back at least as far as Aristotle, who devised the original treatment of fallacy in two places in the *Organon*: in the *De Sophisticis Elenchis* and in the *Rhetoric*. Aristotle's treatment was the standard for centuries, though the medieval logicians made important contributions that are just now being appreciated.[1] The *ad* fallacies—*ad hominem, ad verecundiam, ad populum*—are customarily dated from the time of Locke (Hamblin, 158 ff.). There is a long and established tradition of the use of fallacy labels in philosophical argumentation (e.g., *petitio principii*—or begging the question—equivocation, composition),[2] and logic courses have usually paid lip service to this ancient approach to the study of argumentation. However, beginning with the 20th century we see the emergence of a powerful new approach to logic: the logistic approach stemming from the work of Frege and later of Russell and Whitehead. It is safe to say that the formal, logistic approach to argument analysis has dominated the 20th century. However, the last 15 years have witnessed increased attention on the part of many logicians to the fallacy approach as a vehicle for teaching logic.

Outlines of a Viable Approach

Let us begin this section with the question: What are the assumptions on which a fallacy approach is based? Or: What conditions would have to be satisfied in order for a fallacy approach to be viable? It seems to us that for the fallacy approach to have plausibility five assumptions are needed:

1. That people do make logical mistakes in reasoning and arguing;
2. That at least one important category of these mistakes can be described as nonformal;
3. That nonformal mistakes can be identified according to type;
4. That such mistakes in reasoning occur with sufficient frequency to warrant the utility of a list of such mistakes;
5. That a fallacy is a type of logical flaw in an argument that displays a certain frequency of occurrence.

If these assumptions are true, and we believe they are, then a fallacy approach to the critique of everyday reasoning makes sense. We are about to outline one such approach. But we believe that those who agree with

our assumptions will find themselves in basic agreement with what we have
to say about fallacies.

The Current State of the Fallacy Approach

1. There is no generally agreed upon definition or conception of
   fallacy. One common definition is that a fallacy is a deceptive argument.[3] Another related conception is that of fallacy as an argument
   that appears to be valid but is not (Hamblin, 12). Later in this essay
   we shall present a third.
2. There is no universally agreed upon list or inventory of the fallacies. One author's list will contain some but not all of the entries
   in another's (cf. Johnson and Blair 1980, 15–17). And even when
   two authors list the same fallacy, their accounts of the fallacy may
   differ. For example, most writers will treat the *ad hominem* fallacy,
   but seldom do their treatments of it exhibit the uniformity one
   might expect (8).
3. There is lack of agreement, too, among theoreticians about just
   what is required to solidify the fallacy approach. Some believe that
   formal accounts of the so-called informal fallacies are both possible
   and desirable (Woods and Walton); others at least agree that a
   theory of argument underlying a conception of fallacy is necessary
   (Govier); many use fallacies without making any theoretical
   declarations.[4]

It must be admitted that although there are manifest signs of improvement
in the treatments of fallacy in textbooks, still the fallacy approach presents
a rather inelegant picture to the outsider, and indeed to some insiders.

Alternative Approaches to Criticism

What, one may ask, is the alternative to the fallacy approach to criticism?
What other ways are there to criticize an argument? To answer these
questions we must again refer the reader back to our first section on critical
thinking and informal logic. The fallacy approach is an effort within the
third phase or moment of argument analysis. It can be contrasted with the
formal approach on the one hand; and within informal logic, there are
those (like Scriven 76) who eschew the fallacy approach. Its alternative
does not have a well-established name, but it might be called the critical
reasoning approach. As presented in Scriven, this approach means being
prepared to ask two questions: First, are the premises true? Second, are
the inferences "valid"? This brings it quite close to the formalist view,

for which there are but two ways to criticize an argument. Either one criticizes the truth of one or more of the premises, or else one criticizes the inferences (the pattern or form of the argument). The main differences between Scriven's approach and that of the formalist are these. First, Scriven spends a great deal more time on the question of how to evaluate the premises. Second, he does not resort to formal procedures for his answers to the second. In fact, many logic and critical thinking texts contain a mixture of these approaches. Some, for reasons we shall indicate, are unhappy with the fallacy approach.

Illustration of the Fallacy Approach

The conception of fallacy that we wish to defend and that underscores the approach we are about to outline is related to but different from both of the definitions cited earlier. We define a fallacy as an argument that violates one or more of the criteria a good argument must display. The root notion is that of a breakdown in the argumentative process, a defect in the reasoning process.

This conception does not impute malice to the reasoner in the way that it would if fallacy were defined as an attempt to deceive. Doubtless there are such malicious reasoners about. But it seems unwise to build moral turpitude into the definition. Nor does this conception require that the fallacious argument appear to be valid.[5] However, there is merit in teaching students to be wary of the numerous fallacies that do counterfeit legitimate argument strategies. At the core of our conception is the idea that there are nonformal criteria for evaluating arguments and that a violation of any of them is a fallacy. It must then be pointed out that the presence of a fallacy does not mean that the conclusion of the argument is false but rather that the conclusion has not been established by that particular argument.

The question with which we must now deal is: What are the criteria a good argument must display? What should we look for in a good argument? In the first place, the premises must be *relevant* to the conclusion. If I can support the claim that one of your premises is irrelevant to the conclusion, then I have shown that yours is not a good argument. Do people with some degree of frequency produce arguments in which a premise is irrelevant to the conclusion? We think so. And there is a name for that sort of malfeasance: *non sequitur*. We say: "That doesn't follow."

Suppose that the premises are relevant to the conclusion. Is that enough to make the argument a good one? Hardly. The premises must also furnish *sufficient* evidence to support the conclusion. It might, for example, be relevant to the determination of guilt that the alleged murderer can be placed at the scene of the crime, but that would hardly be sufficient evidence to convict. Do people in their efforts in everyday reasoning, with some degree of frequency, produce arguments in which the premises taken together, though relevant, are insufficient to yield the conclusion? We think so. People get a notion in their heads, cast about for a few bits of isolated evidence to support it, and then settle into a comfortable position. They promote intuitions and half-truths based on partial evidence to the status of full-blown truths without bothering to consider or to weigh carefully the full body of evidence that bears on the issue. This kind of malfeasance in the argumentative process occurs often enough to warrant having a name. We call it *jumping to a conclusion*, or *hasty conclusion*.

It seems to us that the best way to illustrate the approach we have in mind would be to give the reader a specimen of how we think fallacies should be presented. Below we have reproduced a section from our textbook, *Logical Self-Defense* (Johnson and Blair 1983, 44–46).[1] In this part of the text we are treating three basic fallacies. We begin by stating (in the box) the conditions under which the fallacy may be said to occur.

Hasty Conclusion

1. M presents Q, R, S,...as sufficient support for a conclusion T.
2. Q, R, S,...taken together are not sufficient support for T, because:
   (a) they do not supply sufficiently systematically gathered evidence; and/or
   (b) they do not supply a sufficient sample of the various relevant kinds of evidence; and/or
   (c) they ignore the presence or possibility of contrary evidence.

As in the case of charging *irrelevant reason*, you have two tasks to perform in making a case for hasty conclusion. First, you must properly identify the premises, and from among them note the ones offering evidence to support the conclusion. That's Condition 1. Then you must not only assert but argue for the assertion that the evidence is not sufficient. You may do this in several ways: (1) You may show that what the evidence presented does show is less than what the arguer concluded. Or (2) you may have to indicate what sort of additional evidence is needed to generate the conclusion: (i) whether more evidence of the same sort, or (ii) evidence of a different type. Or (3) you may argue that the arguer has ignored or overlooked evidence that bears on the conclusion. Whatever the case may be, it is never sufficient for you to merely assert that more evidence is needed; you must defend or justify your assertion.

---

[1] From *Logical Self-Defense* by Ralph H. Johnson and J. Anthony Blair. Copyright © McGraw–Hill Ryerson Limited, 1983. Reprinted by permission.

RALPH H. JOHNSON AND J. ANTHONY BLAIR   **117**

Let's work through [an] example showing how the conditions are to be used. Andrew Greeley is [a] U.S. syndicated columnist. This is an excerpt from a column entitled "The Evil of Communism Is Manifest in Poland" (December 1981):

> *As far as political systems go, communism is the worst thing the world has ever known. . . . Were Cubans better off, all things considered, under Fulgencio Batista than they are under Fidel Castro? Were Nicaraguans better off under Anastasio Somoza than they are going to be under the Leninist regime that is shaping up there? Would Salvadorans be better off under a communist rule than they are? One might ask Polish unionists what their advice would be to the Catholic clergy supporting communist or communist-front movements in Latin America or Asia.*

Greeley has drawn his conclusion from a list of examples that he clearly takes as evidence for it. He does so without qualification, so we may take it that he believes these examples suffice to prove that communism is the worst political system the world has ever known. Thus, we contend, Condition 1 of *hasty conclusion* is satisfied here.

Grant, for the sake of argument, that Greeley's premises are true—controversial though they may be. The question is, if they were true, would they provide sufficient support for the conclusion? We think not, for a couple of reasons. There is no mention here of the People's Republic of China, where some immense strides in improving human welfare have been made (though clearly not without human costs and restrictions), or Chile, where progress toward greater freedom and democracy was being made until, as the evidence seems to indicate, the United States interfered. So there is, first, evidence overlooked by Greeley that some countries have done better under a Communist (or at least Marxist) system than other forms of political system. There is also to be considered whether there are certain forms of political system that are not just as bad as, or worse than, communism. Right-wing military dictatorships now in existence, as well as Nazi and fascist systems, come to mind as examples. So, second, evidence of different sorts needs to be produced in order to justify the claim. For these reasons we conclude that Greeley's evidence is not sufficient. Condition 2 is satisfied: Greeley commits *hasty conclusion*.

People commit *hasty conclusion* because we get a notion in our heads, cast about for a few bits of evidence, and settle into our position. We promote intuitions and half-truths to the status of full and incontrovertible truths without bothering to weigh and consider evidence: "Don't confuse me with the facts." We reason from our own personal experience (anecdotal evidence) to draw conclusions that run far in advance of it. We ignore evidence. Sometimes we *suppress* evidence. Or we simply fail to bring all the evidence to bear on the situation.

As critics, though, we need to be reasonable in our demands for sufficient evidence. There is no handy gauge that tells us how much evidence is enough. The onus is on the critic to cite, in each individual case under scrutiny, specific ways the evidence put forward is insufficient. In effect, the evidence advanced in an argument can be fairly challenged as insufficient only when you, the critic, can cite some item of relevant evidence that would make a difference to the verdict and that has not been taken into account in the argument.

Often, too, the argument can be retrieved and made immune from the *hasty conclusion* criticism by a simple qualification added to the conclusion; for example, by changing an "always" to "usually"; or an "in every case" to "in most cases"; or an "entirely" to "partially." And the qualified conclusion may be all the arguer needs to make the point. In such cases the critic needs to be aware of the minimal force of the *hasty conclusion* charged, and the critic can suggest the qualification that would immunize the argument from this criticism.

This advice can be turned around and put to good use when you are the person constructing the argument. You have no business thinking your opinion or claim is sufficiently supported until you have gathered enough evidence to answer all the reasonable challenges you can imagine. You should be careful to qualify your conclusion so that its generality does not go beyond the limits justified by the evidence you have been able to assemble. These two moves—anticipating and trying to meet challenges, and qualifying the conclusion—will nip many a case of *hasty conclusion* in the bud.

Suppose now that we have judged the premises are both relevant and sufficient. (We grant that these are difficult judgments to make and will often have to be made tentatively and provisionally, may not be responsibly asserted without defense, and are subject to revision upon the delivery of new arguments or in the light of new evidence.) Are we then obligated to accept the conclusion? Not necessarily. We must still decide whether we are going to accept the premises as stated. We need to be prepared to press such questions as: Is this a reasonable claim? Is it acceptable in this context? Is it in need of defense itself? Is it true? If the answer to any of these is no, then we have reason to reject the argument as it stands. This situation occurs frequently enough that it is worth baptizing: we give it the name *problematic premise*.

It is our contention that any argument that satisfies these criteria (relevance, acceptability, and sufficiency) is a good argument. Thus, in our view, the fallacy approach reduces to the capacity to ask and to answer these three questions about the premises: Are they relevant? Are they jointly sufficient? Are they acceptable? The student who can do that is equipped to appraise most arguments in everyday discourse without recourse to formal devices. The individual fallacies, such as *straw man* and *ad hominem* are simply more particular patterns instantiating violations of one of these criteria. The fallacy names may thus be viewed as mnemonic devices, words that help the student recall a particular line of criticism he or she may wish to develop. Learning the names of fallacies is thus a means to an end, never the end in itself.

Criticisms of the Fallacy Approach

We must now take account of some of the complaints lodged against the fallacy approach so that the instructor who is thinking about using this approach has an idea of the sort of criticism and/or problems likely to be encountered.

Criticisms tend in our view to be reducible to one of these four:

1. The fallacy approach is theoretically unsatisfying because it is incomplete;
2. The fallacy approach is unwieldy because lists of fallacies disagree or are unmanageable;
3. The fallacy approach is conceptually mistaken because people do not actually commit fallacies; the alleged fallacies are misunderstandings of the critic;
4. The fallacy approach is particularly subject to abuse by students.

We will explain each of these criticisms in turn, responding to each as we proceed.

1. Criticism: The fallacy approach is vitiated by the fact that there is no systematic approach to the study of fallacy. Such a remark is frequently made in the context of defending formal logic as a better instrument or tool of criticism for argument analysis (Massey). A related complaint is that there is not and cannot be a complete list of fallacies (understood as the ways in which the mind can go wrong) because, it will be said, parroting De Morgan,[6] that the ways of error are infinite.

Response: There is some justice to these complaints, though it is doubtful that they can bear the weight often assigned them. For example, one might ask, why must an account of fallacies be complete before it can be useful? Are the possible types of error indeed infinite? Is there no chance of gaining a comprehensive classification of informal fallacies? It is not evident to us that the answer to all these is no. And if it is not, then there is no impediment to bringing fallacy theory into a reputable state of organization and coherence. The teacher must take into account such criticisms and then weigh them against the potential gains (see below) in deciding whether to use fallacy theory or some other instrument of criticism.

2. Criticism: There are no identity criteria for the fallacies. Thus it is not possible to say with precision whether or not a fallacy has occurred in a given instance.[7]

Response: We are not at all convinced that this is true, although admittedly, if the list of fallacies is too large and fine-grained it becomes difficult to distinguish one specimen from another in natural language reasoning. This is an argument for keeping the list small and manageable and for preserving on it those which have achieved clearest usage over the course of time. That list would include at least: *equivocation, begging the question, ad hominem, straw man, non sequitur, jumping to a conclusion.* Any student able to use these labels judiciously as a beacon to guide his own thinking and to evaluate the thinking of others is well prepared, we would argue, to adjudicate a great many arguments in ordinary language.

3. Criticism: Ordinary reasoners do not commit fallacies and fallacies are really creations of the critic (Finocchiaro).

Response: This is a hard claim to defend—or refute! Its proponents can no doubt find cases favorable to their position. We are convinced, on the other hand, that lots of cases of arguments can be found whose most plausible—and most charitable!—interpretation is that their authors reasoned fallaciously. As evidence we offer the approximately 150 passages we discuss in our text together with over 60 examples presented there as exercises.

4. Criticism: It will be argued that students will abuse the fallacy approach by learning only to toss around accusations, without coming to see that this approach seldom gets beyond name-calling (Paul).

Response: Whether such abuse occurs or not depends on how the course is taught. If the instructor makes the labeling process itself the focus of attention, then such abuse is almost inevitable. However, we are convinced that this need not occur, that the instructor can model the use of the labels so that the students learn to appreciate them as devices for probing an argument for potential weaknesses. The instructor must teach students that a charge of fallacy is not a definitive criticism unless and until supplemented by a robust line of reasoning that will then render the use of the label otiose.

APPLICATIONS OF THE FALLACY APPROACH

We believe that the fallacy approach to argument evaluation has definite advantages when attempting to integrate the teaching of reasoning and writing skills. Insofar as writing consists of the assessment of the reasoning or logic behind a position, the fallacy approach provides a straightforwardly applicable method. In other words, it fits critical and analytic writing directly. To the extent that students are being taught writing for the purpose of advancing and defending a thesis, the fallacy approach can be brought to bear at the very least during revision, but will also shape the reasoning that goes into the initial draft. And since these two perspectives are unlikely to be taught in isolation from each other, we think the fallacy approach clearly is generally applicable to critical and persuasive writing.

Let us rehearse some of its virtues. The fallacy names (the labels so often scorned in critical accounts of fallacies) in fact can be made to function as mnemonic devices that call to mind the lines of criticism. Moreover, the fallacy approach has the advantage of not requiring a student to master any techniques or to master a new (a specialized) language. Fallacy theory is not technical. The alternative, that is, formal logic and the theory of validity, is much more difficult to teach and to retain because it involves encoding into symbols. (At least this is the case with most standard approaches.) So when it comes to teaching students how to appraise reasoning, we believe the fallacy approach has clear advantages. Moreover, at least in the way in which we conceptualize the fallacy approach, the general criteria of logically good arguments—relevance, sufficiency, and acceptability—are readily enough mastered and internalized, so that as the student plans a text and writes it out, he or she bring them to bear in a way similar to the application of paragraphing guidelines and grammatical rules.

Our search for a simple and effective argument evaluation approach has been influenced by this consideration: we believe that whatever we teach our students must be capable of being incorporated into their intellectual repertoires so that it not only can, but generally tends to, become part and parcel of their intellectual skills and tendencies—the intellectual survival kit that they take away with them from college study. In our view, the advantage the fallacy approach enjoys is that it is readily incorporated, and—at least so far as our experience indicates—it is in fact absorbed and used outside the classroom and after graduation.

We conclude this chapter with a request to our colleagues in composition and in cognitive psychology. The latter we invite to study the mechanisms of argument assessment as it is conceived by a theoretically grounded fallacy approach such as ours or of others (e.g., Woods and Walton's), to measure the effectiveness of this approach, and to determine through systematic studies whether our anecdotally supported intuitions about its retention and incorporation are indeed correct. The former—teachers and theorists in the field of composition—we invite to experiment with systematic fallacy approaches, to devise ways to incorporate such an approach into the teaching of writing, and to study the effectiveness of doing so. Obviously enough we are enthusiastic about teaching critical thinking about reasoning and about argumentation in particular by making careful use of a theoretically tidy version of this literally age-old tradition. At the same time we believe we could benefit from the findings and experience of practitioners and theorists in these other two fields.

NOTES

1. Our historical account is based on the research done by Hamblin in his landmark study, *Fallacies*. We have recently reread parts of that work and are coming to have some reservations about its thematic sections. But his historical account is as good as anything thus far tabled.
2. The charge of begging the question is often enough met with in philosophical texts, as is equivocation. See, for example, Hume's *Dialogues Concerning Natural Religion*, in which Hume twice uses the phrase "begging the question." Hume also scores reasoning for being guilty of the fallacy of composition; his arguments against design amount to the charge of faulty analogy, and he himself accuses many of the fallacy of anthropomorphism, and in fact uses the term *fallacy* twice (449, 474, 482).
3. This way of conceiving fallacy is suggested, for example, by Fearnside and Holther in the title of their text, *Fallacy: The Counterfeit of Argument*. Of course there is good etymological reason for this way of understanding the term *fallacy*.
4. For example, see Thomas (361 ff.) and Wright (158–160), where Wright discusses the problem of straw man without however raising theoretical issues about fallacy.
5. There is a question as to how we are to take the term *valid* here. Does the ordinary reasoner have a conception of validity? What is it? We don't know the answer to these questions.
6. *Formal Logic*, 276. The same idea is broached by others: Joseph (569) and Cohen and Nagel (382).
7. A vigorous presentation of this view can be found in Lambert and Ulrich (24–29).

WORKS CITED

Cohen, Morris R., and Ernest Nagel. *Introduction to Logic and Scientific Method.* London: Routledge and Kegan Paul, 1926.

De Morgan, August. *Formal Logic.* London: Open Court, 1926.

Fearnside, W. Ward, and William B. Holther. *Fallacy: The Counterfeit of Argument.* Englewood Cliffs, NJ: Prentice-Hall, 1959.

Finocchiaro, Maurice. "Fallacies and the Evaluation of Reasoning." *American Philosophical Quarterly* 18 (January 1981): 13–22.

Frege, Gottlob. *Begriffschrift.* Halle: L. Nebert, 1879.

Govier, Trudy. "Who Says There Are No Fallacies." *Informal Logic Newsletter* 5.1 (December 1982): 2–10.

Hamblin, C.L. *Fallacies.* London: Methuen, 1970.

Hume, David. *Dialogues Concerning Natural Religion. The Empiricists.* Garden City, NY: Doubleday Dolphin, n.d. 431–517.

Johnson, Ralph H., and J. Anthony Blair. "The Recent Development of Informal Logic." *Informal Logic: The First International Symposium.* Ed. J. Anthony

Blair and Ralph H. Johnson. Inverness, CA: Edgepress, 1980. 3–28.

———. *Logical Self-Defense*. 2nd ed. Toronto: McGraw-Hill Ryerson, 1983.

Joseph, H.W. *Introduction to Logic*. 2nd ed. Oxford: Clarendon, 1926.

Lambert, Karel, and William Ulrich. *The Nature of Argument*. New York: Macmillan, 1980.

Massey, Gerald. "The Fallacy Behind Fallacies." *Midwest Studies in Philosophy* 6 (1981): 489–500.

Paul, Richard. "Teaching Critical Thinking in the 'Strong' Sense: A Focus on Self-Deception, World Views, and a Dialectical Mode of Analysis." *Informal Logic Newsletter* 4.2 (May 1982): 2–7.

Russell, Bertrand, and Alfred N. Whitehead. *Principia Mathematica*. 3 vols. Cambridge: Cambridge University Press, 1910–1913.

Scriven, Michael. *Reasoning*. New York: McGraw-Hill, 1976.

Thomas, Stephen N. *Practical Reasoning in Natural Language*. 2nd ed. Englewood Cliffs, NJ: Prentice-Hall, 1981.

Woods, John, and Douglas Walton. *Argument: The Logic of the Fallacies*. Toronto: McGraw-Hill Ryerson, 1982.

Wright, Larry. *Better Reasoning: Techniques for Handling Argument, Evidence, and Abstraction*. New York: Holt, Rinehart and Winston, 1982.

CHAPTER 7

The Logical, the Valid, and the Methodical

Finbarr W. O'Connor

THE LOGICAL

What is it to think logically? Is it to be defined in terms of the product (or output) of the thought or by the way in which the output is produced? Is logical thinking that kind of thinking which produces logical outputs, or is it a distinctive approach to a subject? Alternatively, is it to be defined in terms of characteristics of the thinker, and, if so, what characteristics?

One might expect these questions to be addressed in the discipline of logic. Certainly the popular justification of the presence of a course in logic in the college curriculum is its presumed (positive) effect on students' thinking: as a result of taking a course in logic, students might be expected to become more logical in how they think. Logicians themselves, however, make no such claims; they are reluctant to take as their purpose that of improving "thinking skills" and, for that matter, seldom use the word *logical* at all. Logicians will say, "That's a matter of logic," or "This conforms to the principles of logic"; they will never say, "That's logical," or "This argument is logical," or "This person is logical." There are "laws of logic" but not "logical laws." There is clearly a gap between what logicians understand themselves to be doing and the popular understanding. There are reasons for logicians' reticence. For one, the word *logical* as it occurs in ordinary language is equivocal: sometimes it means "well reasoned" (as in "that's logical, but..."), and sometimes it means "true" (when "that's logical" expresses agreement). Logicians therefore prefer to employ terms that are more precisely defined, for example, "valid," and "sound," and (perhaps) "true."

The avoidance of "logical" also has a rich historical dimension. Much of the development of 20th-century logic is the result of rejecting the "psychologism" of the 19th century, when logic was considered a form of deep psychology and laws of logic were spoken of as laws of thought, laws governing how human beings *must* think. In the tradition of the "method" philosophers of an earlier period—Descartes, Bacon, Locke, and even Newton—advocates of psychologism, such as James Mill, find the question, How *should* we think? both intelligible and a matter in the jurisdiction of logic. Modern logic either assigns the question to psychology or, if it is held that psychology can deal only in description, regards it as unanswerable. What logic *can* deal with, goes the conventional view, is whether the *product* of thought conforms to principles of logic. Whether the *process* leading to that product is "logical" or not has little meaning and, from the point of view of logic, really irrelevant anyway. The properties studied by logic—implication, consistency, for example—are properties of the product, not of the process. Thus, Reichenbach early in the 20th century offered the distinction between the "context of discovery" and the "context of justification" and insisted that logic deals only with the latter, in other words, that logic deals with the evaluation of the product (6). Over the intervening years, Reichenbach's distinction has hardened into dogma.

Readers familiar with debates in composition theory will find the problem familiar: if the properties of good writing are properties of the written product, is the process the writer experiences accessible—whether by direct inspection or by inference from the product—or is it inaccessible and relegated to the realm of the mysterious? And, of course, there is the corresponding question for teaching: Is the process teachable in terms of some properties of its own, or only by imitation of model products?

John Stuart Mill, the most celebrated logician of the 19th century, stands as a transitional figure from his father's psychologism. On the one hand, his famous Methods of Induction are intended partly as rules for thought—as guides for organizing our exploration of phenomena. For him it clearly makes sense to say that a person following, for example, the Method of Agreement, is thinking logically. On the other hand, in his Inaugural Address as Lord Rector of the University of St. Andrews (1867), he combines an appropriately modest 20th-century view of the limits of logic—as a discipline that protects us from error—with the more robust 19th-century view that logic analyzes the "reasoning process" and provides us with rules by which we ought to reason.

> Of Logic, I venture to say, even if limited to that of mere ratiocination, the theory of names, propositions, and the syllogism, that there is no part

of intellectual education which is of greater value, or whose place can so ill be supplied by anything else. Its uses, it is true, are chiefly negative; its function is not so much to teach us to go right, as to keep us from going wrong. But in the operations of the intellect it is so much easier to go wrong than right; it is so utterly impossible for even the most vigorous mind to keep itself in the path but by maintaining a vigilant watch against all deviations, and noting all the byways by which it is possible to go astray—that the chief difference between one reasoner and another consists in their less or greater liability to be misled. Logic points out all the possible ways in which, starting from true premises, we may draw false conclusions. By its analysis of the reasoning process, and the forms it supplies for stating and setting forth our reasonings, it enables us to guard the points at which a fallacy is in danger of slipping in, or to lay our fingers upon the place where it has slipped in....Logic is the great disperser of hazy and confused thinking: it clears up the fogs which hide from us our own ignorance, and make us believe that we understand a subject when we do not....

You will find abundance of people to tell you that logic is no help to thought, and that people cannot be taught to think by rules. Undoubtedly rules by themselves, without practice, go but a little way to teaching anything. But if the practice of thinking is not improved by rules, I venture to say it is the only difficult thing done by human beings that is not so. A man learns to saw wood principally by practice, but there are rules for doing it, grounded on the nature of the operation, and if he is not taught the rules, he will not saw well until he has discovered them for himself. Wherever there is a right way and a wrong, there must be a difference between them, and it must be possible to find out what the difference is; and when found out and expressed in words, it is a rule for the operation. If anyone is inclined to disparage rules, I say to him, try to learn anything which there are rules for, without knowing the rules, and see how you succeed. To those who think lightly of the school logic, I say, take the trouble to learn it. You will easily do so in a few weeks, and you will see whether it is of no use to you in making your mind clear, and keeping you from stumbling in the dark over the most outrageous fallacies. (383–385)

Note that Mill in the latter part of the 19th century is already displaying some defensiveness on whether logic is a "help to thought," whether indeed it belongs in the curriculum (although he has no doubt that it does). His defense of the teaching of logic wavers between the minimalist, product-oriented claim, that it encompasses a study of human error, and the stronger, process-oriented claim, that through logic we learn rules for reasoning. Modern formal logic backed away from both claims.

The informal logic movement (Blair and Johnson, Chapter 5 this volume) can be viewed as an effort to reinstate the practical in logic. But, for the most part, the direction has been rather more in line with Mill's first defense of logic—it protects us from error—than with his second defense. Thus, one way to make logic practical is to reduce its formality or abstractness, to exemplify logical principles in "real world" arguments such as students are likely to meet outside the logic classroom, to apply logic to serious and compelling contemporary political or social issues. This is a welcome development explored elsewhere in this volume. I wish to explore the other avenue toward making logic practical—as a model of how to think. Is it possible that by taking a logic course one can be taught how to think logically?

It is far from obvious that this can be done. To the popular understanding, of course, it is absurd to suggest that a logic course should not teach logical thinking. But the situation is paradoxical: it seems reasonable to say that if "logical thinking" means anything at all, it must have some relation to what logicians take logic to be; but many of them deny that logic deals with thinking at all. Now, I want to argue that logic can be about thinking. To prepare for the argument I need to suggest why logic might be thought not to be about thinking—especially to those who take logic to be formal logic. The problem centers around the concept of "argument" and the concept of "validity."

THE VALID

It is standard for logic books to begin by distinguishing *argument* from other forms of discourse, argument being defined as a set of statements such that one is said to follow from the other(s). Arguments are then distinguished as valid and invalid (see Figure 7.1). *Validity* is a characteristic of arguments, not of individual statements, that is, it is a characteristic of the relationship among statements: an argument is valid if it is *impossible* for its premises to be true and its conclusion false; if its premises are true its conclusion *must* be true. Valid arguments are in turn classified into the *sound* and the *unsound*: an argument is sound if its premises are true. To judge an argument valid is therefore not to commit yourself to the truth of the conclusion; but to judge an argument sound does so commit you.

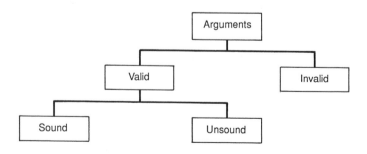

Figure 7.1 Classification of Argument

Therefore, to *establish* the truth of a conclusion by way of argument, the argument must be sound.

Aristotle's discovery was that there are certain *structures* that constrain the possible relations of truth and falsehood among the sentences composing an argument. For example, in the structure,

All A is B
No B is C
Therefore, No A is C

Aristotle noticed that *no* substitution of *any* term for A, B, and C will give a case where "All A is B" is true, "No B is C" is true, and "No A is C" is false. It is simply not possible to find such an example. The structure is therefore *valid*; and any argument in that structure is also valid, for any substitution of A, B, and C. The characterization *valid* is therefore absolute and universal.

By contrast, the structure,

All A is B
All A is C
Therefore, All B is C

is invalid. It is possible to find terms to substitute for A, B, and C that will make the resulting premises true and the conclusion false, for example (substituting "bat" for A, "mammal" for B, and "winged" for C):

All bats are mammals.
All bats are winged.
Therefore, all mammals are winged.

All you need to do to show that a particular structure is invalid is to provide one such case. Of course, there are many arguments whose structure is invalid whose premises and conclusion are true, for example,

All bats are mammals.
All bats are warmblooded.
Therefore, all mammals are warmblooded.

Thus, invalidity does not mean that the conclusion is false; it means only that the premises being true do not guarantee that the conclusion is also true.

Two features of this standard presentation of the concept of validity are to be noted. First, it is the *structure* (formulated above in terms of A,

B, and C—but there are many other kinds of structure) that is the primary bearer of validity, not the arguments expressed in English, or "natural language," statements. The argument in English is valid, if it is, *in virtue* of being an instance of a valid structure. It is in this sense that validity is a formal property: it is a characteristic of forms or structures.

Second, note the artificiality of the examples (bats, mammals, warm-blooded) and how closely they are tied to the form. In such cases there is little room for dispute as to whether these arguments have this structure. But we seldom encounter in real life such arguments conveniently arranged in neat structures.[1] Great effort is involved in determining for most arguments we meet what their structures are. And as the arguments themselves increase in complexity the greater the scope for disagreement on their structure. Determining whether a given structure is valid or not belongs to the science of logic, and logical techniques are very successful in providing an algorithmic answer to this. But how to decide what structure to use for a given argument in English is a matter of the art of logic, and techniques here are not algorithmic.[2]

How to handle validity is a major problem for any logic course. The movement toward informal logic is motivated to a considerable extent by the feeling among teachers of logic that while students were quite capable of applying the techniques of formal logic to argument structures, or to artificially neat examples of argument, they were deficient in the art of logic. But if one cannot use these techniques for ordinary "real life" examples of arguments, it is far from clear that one has come to understand what validity is. Furthermore, it is not clear that outside the logic class-room there is any understanding of validity, even among those one would acknowledge as "good" reasoners. People can see that from "Big cars are more expensive than small cars," "Cadillacs are more expensive than Hondas" follows, without being able to articulate or understand the structure behind the reasoning. In fact, they are likely to be more sure of the reasoning couched in terms of Cadillacs and Hondas than they are of whether "All C's are more E than H's" follows from "All B's are more E than S's," and "All C's are more E than H's." Teaching validity is an uphill struggle because it appears an "unnatural" way of thinking.

If validity presents a problem for the logic classroom, *a fortiori* it presents a problem for the composition classroom. If logic teachers complain that even after a full semester of logic many students still seem not to understand what validity is—perhaps the most discouraging experience for a logic teacher is at the end of the semester to hear a student say, "But how can it be valid? The conclusion is obviously false"—composition teachers, with plenty of other matters to attend to, can hardly be expected to teach validity also, if they wish to employ logic as a tool in teaching writing.

One of the trends of the informal logic movement has been to discount the importance of validity as a concept. Composition teachers, especially, should find this a welcome development. Of the other logicians represented in this volume, Johnson and Blair pass it over entirely in their textbook, without a mention in the index, while Cederblom in his devotes but a few pages to it. Steven Toulmin is another logician whose textbook presents logic without validity.[3]

Even so, validity does have its attractions, at least to the logician. It, and the concepts surrounding it, have an aesthetic appeal, in the way that elegant mathematical systems are pleasing. It represents one of the great intellectual achievements. Second, and perhaps more important, the concept provides the logician with a kind of anchor, a source of certainty for logical judgments. Since validity can be assessed quite independently of content of the argument, the logic teacher can pronounce judgments of validity of arguments in any domain whatever, and in any subject matter whatever, without any specific subject matter knowledge. Thus, arguments involving highly emotional issues—for example, U.S. support of the contras in Nicaragua—can be assessed quite independently of the teacher's or the students' political commitments. Without validity, the emphasis of logical assessment tends to shift toward whether the premises are acceptable or not, which in turn involves some degree of subject matter knowledge and maybe political or social commitments. The practical effect of centering a logic course on validity is to strengthen the teacher's authority (as logician) but also to diminish its scope.

This is not to say that a logic centered on validity does not raise questions about premises. But these questions are raised *later*, after validity has been evaluated. Voss (Chapter 4) discusses the enthymeme, "John Doe would make a good political candidate because he is assertive." A validity-centered logic would analyze this argument by first "reconstructing" it with the implicit premises made explicit, in this case, as "Good political candidates are assertive, and John Doe is assertive, therefore, John Doe would make a good political candidate." Then one would ask if the argument were valid. In this case, it is, if the first premise is interpreted as "*all* good political candidates are assertive." Only then, when one has satisfied oneself that the argument is valid, would one get to the question of whether it is reasonable to believe that all good candidates are assertive. Another logic might ask this question first.

I hope that I have sufficiently shown the array of problems that surround validity, and the extent to which it presents an obstacle to attempts to make logic practical. I am also suggesting (although this is surely an oversimplification) that these problems can be seen as a motivating force for the development of informal logic. One way to make logic more practical is to de-emphasize its formal and abstract character, to deal with "real life" examples, to attend to issues of natural language (such as ambiguity, emotiveness) and to the acceptability of premises. The effect of this direction is, I think, to shift logic toward rhetoric. It introduces into logic concerns that have traditionally been the province of rhetoric—issues of audience, context, purpose, form of presentation, burden of proof, plausibility, and so on. Or, to put it in another way, this direction in informal logic turns logic to face toward one of the fields represented in this book—composition.

There is another possible response to the problems of validity. This involves turning logic to face the other field in this volume—cognitive psychology. Like logicians, psychologists are concerned with reasoning. But if one examines the instances of reasoning psychologists study and contrasts them with the typical exercises of a logic classroom, what one is struck by is not so much the artificial character of the logic problems—in this respect the problems psychologists study are often similar[4]—but the fact that in some sense the logic problems students typically do are already answered for them. What we ask our students is, "Here is an argument. Is it valid (or sound, or good)?" We seldom ask, "Here are some premises. What follows?" We ask, "Does this reasoning justify this decision?" but seldom, "What is the right, or best, decision in this situation (on this evidence)?"

At issue here is a difference over what accounts for the disparity between what students expect of a logic classroom and what is actually delivered. Blair and Johnson (Chapter 5) quote Howard Kahane on his discomfort as a logic teacher on the challenge of a student who demanded what logic had to say about the Vietnam war. This suggests that student dissatisfaction is due to logic's incapacity to deal with "real" problems—it should have something to "say" about important issues. I am drawing attention to a different (though not inconsistent) diagnosis: that logic did not offer guidance on *how* to think. It is this lack I have in mind by saying logic is *product*-oriented. Having the ability to assess validity of an argument is a little like being in a position to assess whether an entry in a crossword puzzle fits the space and clues. Almost anyone can do that. What makes a good crossword puzzle solver, however, is the ability to *find* the appropriate word.

I am now ready to return to the question, What is logical thinking? or, as I now want to interpret it, What contribution to good reasoning does (or can) logic make? Here one must be wary of expanding the concept of logical thinking so that it becomes simply "good" thinking, or thinking in the best way. It does not seem to me obviously true that the "logical approach" to a problem is always the best. Robert Ennis offers a conception of "rational thinking" that seems to encompass all that is good in thinking: a rational thinker, he says, will take into account the whole situation, be well informed, demand as much precision as the subject permits, deal with the parts of a complex situation in an orderly fashion, consider seriously other points of view, withhold judgment when the evidence and/or reasons are insufficient, take (and change) a position when the evidence and reasons are sufficient, and accept the necessity of exercising informed judgment. In addition, the rational thinker will exercise good judgment (145). Who could deny that these are desiderata? But they do not necessarily specify characteristics of logical thinking. They are surely characteristics of a more inclusive idea—the mature thinker (see Neimark, Chapter 3).

I want not to identify logical thinking with all-round correct thinking. The logical thinker can be wrong, and often is. On the other hand, I do not want to identify logical thinking with the ability to deal with some narrow range of logic problems, or just validity assessment. What I want to propose is that what characterizes a logical thinker above all is that he or she thinks *methodically*.

THE METHODICAL

Let me begin, as writings on logic should, with Aristotle. In this instance, I take a passage not from one of his logic works, but from the *Nicomachean Ethics* (Book II, Chapter 4). At this point he has argued that virtues are habits and that virtues are formed by actions. The virtue temperance, for example, is developed by the individual's performing temperate actions, and justice by just actions. Aristotle now considers an objection:

> However, the question may be raised what we mean by saying that men become just by performing just actions and self-controlled by practicing self-control. For if they perform just actions and exercise self-control, they are already just and self-controlled, in the same way as they are literate and musical if they write correctly and practice music.

He responds to the objection:

> But is this objection really valid, even as regards the arts? No, for it is possible for a man to write a piece correctly by chance or at the prompting of another: but he will be literate only if he produces a piece of writing *in a literate way*, and that means doing it in accordance with the skill of literary composition which he has in himself.[5]

Now, Aristotle does not say the writing is literate only if it is produced by a literate person, as correspondingly, I would not wish to say that an argument (a logical product) is logical only if it is produced as a result of logical thinking. The connection between product and process is not that direct.

There is nevertheless a connection. In Aristotelian language, I wish to argue (1) that logical thinking is a virtue, or habit, (2) that it is developed by the exercise of logical techniques—just as you become literate by exercising literacy, (3) that the virtue, logical thinking, is not identical with those techniques. I take habit in Aristotle's sense as a disposition or readiness to act in a certain way, a disposition that is self-reinforcing. I am not claiming that there is a unitary habit or disposition that exhausts the meaning of logical thinking. Rather I take Aristotle's point to be that the exercise of techniques in any domain develops characteristics at some *other* and higher level: the exercise of technique A develops the ability to do X. Thus, the exercise of logical techniques develops the ability to do something else, at another level, and it is the latter that constitutes the nature of logical thinking.

To explore this approach, I will briefly describe three standard techniques of logic and ask what more generally the exercise of these techniques make possible for the person exercising them.

Argument Identification

Most modern logic textbooks begin with a definition of argument, offer some examples of arguments, and ask the student to identify the structure in terms of premise and conclusion. One is usually given a list of terms that indicate which statements are premises and which conclusions, for example, "therefore," "so," "hence," "because," "proves that," "as can be seen from." All that is expected of students at this stage is that they be able to *identify* in these simple terms the argument structure as it is presented by its author. The most popular way of representing the argument is by the device of a tree diagram, in which statements are linked by arrows, the direction of the arrow expressing the direction of the inference being made (see Beardsley; Scriven; and Thomas). The construction of the diagram usually involves a very literal reading of the argument, in the sense that where the author of the argument places a "so" you are to take what follows it as a conclusion without asking whether it should be a conclusion or not. The object is not to assess the argument but only to identify what it is. Instructions on how to construct the diagram usually ask that you circle each of the argument indicators, place each statement in the passage inside numbered brackets, make sure there is an arrow in the diagram corresponding to each indicator term, and draw the diagram using the numbers of the statements (see Figure 7.2).

The argument represented in Figure 7.2 is obviously a relatively simple one, and the language of the tree diagram is spare. Yet very significant information about the passage is conveyed: it shows that there are three lines of argument for one main conclusion. Hence an opponent of

An Argument:

The proposed Delaware Expressway is an abomination; it should not be built. At a minimum, it will cost 2 billion dollars, money that could be used for more pressing needs. So, even if it did no harm, it would still be a huge waste of scarce governmental resources. But there are stronger reasons against building it: the city economy will be seriously damaged, for it will remove valuable income-producing land from the tax rolls. Furthermore, it will affect even the health of the taxpayers of Philadelphia, because it will increase automobile traffic and consequently worsen the already bad pollution problems of center city.

Step 1: "Marking up" the Argument

[The proposed Delaware Expressway is an abomination; it should not be built.] [At a minimum, it will cost $2 billion,] [money that could be used for more pressing needs.] So, [even if it did no harm, it would still be a huge waste of scarce government resources.] But there are stronger reasons against building it: [the city economy will be seriously damaged,] for [it will remove valuable income-producing land from the tax rolls.] Furthermore, [it will affect even the health of the taxpayers of Philadelphia,] because [it will increase automobile traffic] and consequently [worsen the already bad pollution problems of center city.]

Step 2: Drawing the Diagram

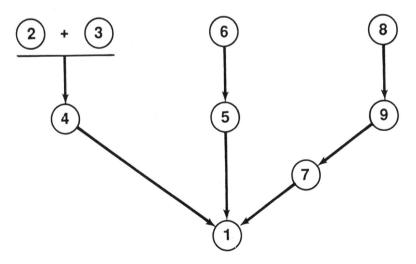

Figure 7.2 Tree Diagram Analysis

the conclusion must deal with all three. It displays the possible moves an opponent must make: in the left hand side, the + between (2) and (3) indicates that both must be true to support the inference to (4), so that to refute the "line of argument" through (4) to (1) it is sufficient to attack one of (2) or (3). In the righthand line, it shows that it would be sufficient to refute one of (8), (9), and (7).

These considerations show what one can do with a tree diagram, what its specific purpose is. What beyond that might the practice of representing arguments in this way encourage? It certainly encourages attention to those phrases that communicate argumentative structure, since you quickly discover that absence of such signals makes it very difficult to diagram the argument. Secondly, it encourages attention to the general feature of structure in arguments. More importantly, I would suggest, since it requires close reading, in that whatever construction you make of the argument is constrained by the language of the author, it encourages a sympathy with the author's intention, the attempt to read the passage as the author intends.[6] In order to use this technique successfully, you must be able to recognize what the argument is without evaluating it.

Logical Relationships

A second standard exercise in logic is to identify the relationship between pairs of statements. There are six possible relationships: independence, equivalence, contradiction, contrariety, subcontrariety, and implication (see Figure 7.3 for definitions by flowchart).[7] This kind of exercise is often used to draw attention to the meaning of "quasi-logical" words, such as "only," "all," "at least," and "unless." Thus, "Only men have been American presidents" is equivalent to "All American presidents have been men." "I won't go unless Barbara is invited" is equivalent to "I will go only if Barbara is invited." "Six students passed the course" implies "At least three students passed the course," while the latter is related by contradiction to "Fewer than three students passed the course."

In this exercise the most common error is to confuse the contrary with the contradictory, that is, to take as contradictory what is really contrary.[8] Thus, there is a tendency to take "Everybody voted for Reagan" to be a contradictory of "No one voted for Reagan." Students see that the first statement and the second statement are incompatible, in the sense that they cannot both be true, and conclude that they are contradictory. But that they cannot both be true is only a necessary condition of the statements being contradictory; it is not sufficient. One needs also to inquire whether they can both be false—contradictories cannot both be false, although contraries can—and of course in this case both statements can be false (and in fact are false). The explanation of the confusion seems to be that whereas people are ready to ask the question, "If x is *true*, what

START HERE

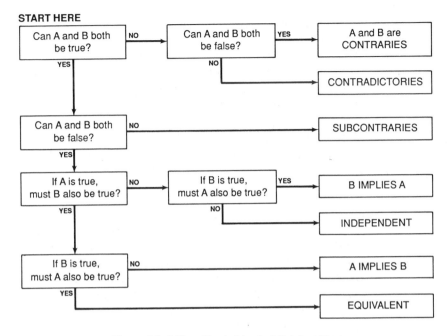

Figure 7.3 A Flow Chart of Logical Relationships

follows for y?" they are less ready to ask, "If x is *false*, what follows for y?" There is something about assuming falsehood—a matter for psychologists to investigate—that makes it difficult to propose. Yet from the point of view of logic, truth and falsehood are simply symmetrical values, neither being preferred to the other.

The larger meaning of this exercise, then, is that it can lead to the habit of asking not just, "What if x were true?" but also, "What if x were false?" The implications of forcing this question are clearest for cases of decision. As I write this, a commission in Philadelphia is investigating the decision process that went into the city's attempt to serve a warrant on members of the radical group MOVE that resulted in the dropping of a bomb on a row house, the deaths of 11 people, and devastation of several blocks. It is clear that the city developed one plan and, when a component of that plan failed, did not have available an alternative. In terms of decision theory, the planners had simply failed to ask themselves, "What if it does not work?" To a planner, it is surely a "logical" question.

Euler and Venn Diagrams

We observed earlier that an argument structure is shown to be invalid ("invalidated") by finding a case of that structure where the premise(s) are true and the conclusion false. This is the most basic of formal logic techniques, underlying almost everything else, and it is decisive when it works. Suppose, though, you are unable to devise an invalidating case for a particular structure, may you conclude that the argument is valid? The failure to find such a case may be due to the fact that the argument structure is in fact valid; but it may also be due simply to a lack of imagination on your part. If you cannot eliminate the latter, you cannot ever use the lack of an invalidating case to conclude the argument structure is valid. Clearly, some method is needed by which defects of imagination can be preempted. One such method was devised by Leonhard Euler in the 18th century, and developed by John Venn in the 19th. They discovered a diagrammatic way of representing statements.

Euler and Venn were concerned with arguments composed of sentences that related one class to another, such as those in the form, "All A is B" and "No A is B." They suggested that if we represent each class by a circle, then the statement can be represented by a spatial relation among circles. In this respect their methods are the same; but in other ways there are significant differences, although this is often misunderstood. For Euler, it is how the circles are located on the page that represents the relationships of the statements. Thus for Euler the relationship "No A is B" is transcribed as two circles that do not touch one another (Figure 7.4a). In the Euler language, two intersecting circles (Figure 7.4b) *assert* that the two classes intersect. It says: Some A is B, and some A is not B, and some B is A and some B is not A. By contrast, when Venn draws A and B as two intersecting circles, there is as yet no assertion of the relationship of A and B; it says only that the universe is divided into four segments: the part that has both properties A and B (or that contains items that have both properties), a part that is A and not B, a part that is B but not A, and a part that is neither A nor B. Thus, the Venn language is a more noncommittal language than Euler's. For Venn, the drawing of the circles does no more than set up possibilities; it works as a classification. To go beyond the classification and make an assertion of how the classes are related requires the additional step of doing something to the diagram. Usually two ways of marking the diagram are available: one (conventionally a dot or an x) says that there is something in the part of the universe so designated; the other (conventionally a shading of some portion of the diagram) indicates that there is nothing in that segment. Thus, in order to assert in a Venn diagram that no A is B, one shades the intersection of A and B (Figure 7.4c). A Venn diagram of an argument shows its validity if once the premises are entered in the diagram the conclusion is also asserted; otherwise it is invalid.

Venn diagrams are less intuitively clear than Euler diagrams: representing "No A is B" by drawing two nonoverlapping circles is clearer than drawing two overlapping circles with the intersection shaded out. But

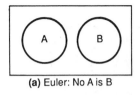
(a) Euler: No A is B

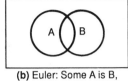
(b) Euler: Some A is B,
some A is not B

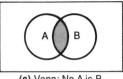
(c) Venn: No A is B

Figure 7.4 Euler and Venn Diagrams

Venn's system is nevertheless superior to Euler's in that it provides a greater neutrality; it distinguishes the initial classification (how many relevant properties does the universe have) from assertions about these properties. It also is technically superior in an interesting way: diagramming "All A is B" in Euler diagrams strictly requires two diagrams, for it can be true where the class A is inside the class B, but it can also be true where the class A and the class B are identical (Figure 7.5a). The Venn diagram representation of the same relationship (Figure 7.5b) can be done in one diagram, because when in the Venn diagram a portion is left empty, no assertion is being made of it. Therefore, the Venn diagram of "All A is B" leaves open each of the two possible interpretations; surprisingly, it may be said that the Venn diagram is superior for its capacity to remain silent.[9]

Logic students have trouble with two kinds of argument: first, valid arguments all of whose statements are false, for they wonder what difference validity can make when the statements are false anyway; and second, invalid arguments whose statements are all true, for they wonder why its invalidity makes a difference. For example, the argument, composed of false statements:[10]

All mammals are bats.
All bats are elephants.
Therefore, all mammals are elephants.

is valid, while

All dogs are mammals.
Some mammals are warmblooded.
Therefore, all dogs are warmblooded.

is invalid.

In both cases the trouble comes from dealing with notions of possibility and necessity. The first argument (shown as a Venn diagram in Figure 7.6a) is valid because *if* the premises were true, the conclusion *must*

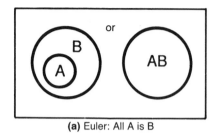

(a) Euler: All A is B

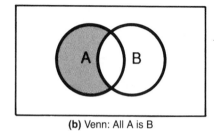

(b) Venn: All A is B

Figure 7.5 Euler and Venn Diagrams Contrasted

be true also (although it is not). The second argument (Figure 7.6b) is invalid because the conclusion *could* be false (although it is not) while the premises are true. The power of the diagram is to show (for valid arguments) that once you have entered the premises—whether true or false—you can see that the conclusion is also there, and to show (for invalid arguments) that entering the premises does not force those marks on the diagram that must be there for the conclusion to be true.

Now, these diagrammatic techniques are usually taught as techniques of validity assessment; and they are used also to decide questions of logical relationship. They can also be seen more generally, however, as a special case of mapping a domain: asking how many variables are relevant, how many possible interrelationships among the variables there are, and searching for a language by which these interrelationships can be expressed. What is actual (actually true) is secondary; what is possible is primary. This is just the kind of reasoning that goes into the solving of nonsyllogistic logic problems of the kind one finds in the literature on problem solving: the so-called Smith-Jones-Robinson problems (you are told there is a fireman, a brakeman, and an engineer of a train; the fireman is from Chicago, the person from Chicago is married, etc.) and so-called detective stories (where you are given names of the suspects and some "tricky" information sufficient to eliminate all but one). But there are many other "real world" situations in which this kind of thinking is exercised, for example, making a decision about buying a car by listing all the possibilities and their variables; or writing an interactive computer program where you need to anticipate all possible responses and misunderstandings.

If you take the view that logical thinking is exclusively the property of logicians, and the subject matter of logicians is argument, then at a minimum logical thinking must be *about* arguments and their characteristics. It does not follow from this that only logicians think logically; but it does follow, for example, that an anthropologist who thinks logically about his or her field must be thinking about the arguments offered within the

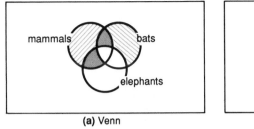
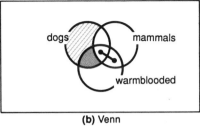

(a) Venn   (b) Venn

Figure 7.6 Using Venn Diagrams to Assess Arguments

field. This seems to me unduly restrictive. Indeed, the kind of thinking that goes into the anthropologist's mapping of the kinship relationships in the society of study seems just the kind of thinking that is the valuable feature of doing a Venn diagram as discussed above. It is true that Venn diagrams find their place in the logic classroom primarily as a device to test arguments; but it does so by providing an abstract model of the (possibly fictional) world described by the statements in the argument. Similarly, it seems to me, the mapping done by the anthropologist is designed to display what relationships are possible and what not possible in the given society. Why, then, cannot that mapping be considered to be an instance of logical thinking?

At issue is, of what are the techniques of logic instances? What are they examples of? The most common view seems to be that they are instances of rigor and precision, and avoidance of error (see Mill above). Instead I wish to suggest, from the techniques looked at above, that to approach a topic logically involves the search for some systematic way of representing the whole domain so that all possibilities are displayed in a useful way. Venn diagrams do just this. The exercise on logical relationships shows it also: to determine what the relationship is one needs to ask *all* the questions in a systematic way. Even the tree diagram technique for displaying the structure of an argument gives a sense of the whole before one engages with specific portions of it.

To approach a subject logically involves approaching it using some method, but not, I think, any method. The method must make some pretension of completeness before its use certifies the approach as logical.[11] Thus the man, in the legendary story, who decides to marry the first woman he meets indeed might be described as exemplifying a decision method; it is scarcely a logical method, in that it lacks any attempt to map out the possibilities in the domain. This conception accounts for why the logical is associated with the reflective, with "stopping to think," and with the abstractive.

There are some consequences to regarding the logical in this manner.

The logical is no longer inherently valuable, since it is not always rational or ethical to deal with subject matter by some systematic method; sometimes we should just act. The "sliding column method" is a systematic way to write a story (see Anderson 160), but it is hardly a good choice of method.[12]

There are also consequences some will find troublesome. It to some extent disengages the logical from the logician and from argument. It also allows methods of creativity, a topic often placed at the opposite end of the continuum from the logical, to be instances of logical thinking, when they make some effort to be exhaustive.[13] A simple checklist would probably not do, nor would free association, although the latter can be adopted as a method. But methods such as Osborn's checklist[14] or morphological analysis probably would do. In the field of composition, certain invention techniques exemplify logical thinking in this sense, the best case being, I think, tagmemic analysis (Young 119–136). Less controversially, so can courses in statistical method, experimental method, field methods, and computer programming.

In effect, this is arguing for a rapprochement between logic and psychology, in particular that branch of the latter that studies problem solving.[15] The intervening link is, I think, through the notion of "representation." Voss (Chapter 4) demonstrates the central role of representation in problem solving, and I am arguing here that teaching techniques of logic, particularly diagrammatic techniques, constitutes training in modes of representation that can be taken far beyond the logic classroom, and even beyond the focus on argumentation itself. Virtually all methodologies of problem solving (see Neimark, Chapter 3) recommend diagrammatic representation as an important and useful heuristic, and many concerned particularly with creative thinking recommend that we should transform our beginning representation of the problem into some other form: from verbal to symbolic, from physical to graphic, and so on (Anderson 131). Note that through this essay I have made use of trees, intersecting circles, and flow charts, three of the most basic of diagrammatic representational devices— and one could easily extend it to matrices. The lengthy discussion above of the difference between Euler and Venn diagrams, although earlier couched simply in terms of their differences as validity-checkers, is really a discussion of the characteristics of different representational systems and can be so treated in a logic classroom.

On this proposal, the contribution of logic courses to logical thinking is by way of consolidating (Hayes; Neimark, Chapter 3) at some higher level what students learn from the practice of logical techniques. In other words, logic can also be made practical by connecting it to psychology, or, as Mill says, to the philosophy of mind:

In the department of pure intellect, the highest place will belong to logic and the philosophy of mind: the one, the instrument for the cultivation of all sciences; the other, the root from which they all grow. It scarcely needs to be said that the former ought not to be taught as a mere system of technical rules, nor the latter as a set of concatenated abstract propositions. The tendency, so strong everywhere, is strongest of all here, to receive opinions into the mind without any real understanding of them, merely because they seem to follow from certain admitted premises, and to let them lie there as forms of words, lifeless and void of meaning. The pupil must be led to interrogate his own consciousness, to observe and experiment upon himself: of the mind, by any other process, little will he ever know.[16] (1836, 181)

NOTES

1. In the medieval university, by contrast, the paradigmatic teaching method, the "disputatio," *legislated* that arguments must be in syllogistic form. In that context, the "real life" arguments would be easily analyzable. Since the number of syllogistic patterns is limited, and the smaller number that were valid could be worked out, the utility of syllogistic argument was clear. Modern logicians are powerless to effect such legislation, and in any case, we now believe that the number of even valid structures is infinite.

2. There is also a theoretical difficulty in determining what *the* structure of a given argument is. *Every* valid argument with two premises is also an instance of the invalid structure, "P, Q, therefore, R." Hence, the fact that an argument has *some* invalid structure does not conclusively establish that the argument itself is invalid. What matters is whether there is *any* structure that is valid and that is also the structure of the argument under consideration. This removes validity assessment even farther from the level of ordinary language arguments.

3. See Maimon, Belcher, Hearn, Nodine, and O'Connor, where we attempt to present Toulmin's logic in a way that would be practical for the writing classroom.

4. For example, the famous "hobbits and orcs" or "missionary and cannibals" problem (Newell and Simon). What could be more artificial and removed from a "real life" example than the Tower of Hanoi?

5. Emphasis added. The reference to "the skill...which he has in himself" should not be taken as an innate or unteachable capacity; he has in mind that the skill should be "internalized."

6. The "principle of charity" comes into operation here. See Blair and Johnson, Chapter 5 this volume.

7. Definitions are given more conventionally like this: A and B are *contradictory* if, and only if, they must have opposite truth values. (If A is true, B must be false; if A is false, B must be true; if B is true, A must be false, and if B is false, A must be true.) A and B are *contraries* if, and only if, they can both be false but cannot both be true. (If A is true, then B must be false; if B is true, A must be

false; but if you know A is false, nothing follows for B, and if you know B is false, nothing follows for A.) A and B are *subcontraries* if, and only if, they can both be true but cannot both be false.

8. I cannot resist giving my favorite example, from Beardsley: "What is the relationship between (a) Pileggi, the plumber, is the strongest man in town, and (b) Pileggi is the strongest plumber in town?" (60). Virtually every student answers that (a) implies (b)!

9. The Venn diagram is also superior because it, unlike the Euler diagram, is a special case of a matrix diagram, which then makes possible (in principle) the representation of an unlimited number of terms or classes. Schwartz provides the best account of how Venn diagrams can be extended beyond the classic three circles to multitermed arguments, and indeed to arguments in propositional logic.

10. Compare the argument relating elephants, dogs, and mice given by Moshman and Franks, Chapter 1 this volume, illustrating the same point in terms of formal operations.

11. This raises the sticky point that sometimes the best decision strategy is decidedly noncomplete—for example, Newell and Simon's "satisficing." I certainly do not intend to suggest that only algorithmic methods count as "logical" ones; but at what point a method ceases to be logical, I am unsure.

12. The method involves listing in separate columns possibilities in the categories: character, setting, goal, obstacle, means of overcoming obstacle, and ending. Then one slides the columns up and down against one another looking for novel combinations.

13. A very complete catalogue of such methods (70 in all) is given by Van Gundy. Also see Rickards and Whiting.

14. The categories of the short list, which is intended to suggest ideas for inventions, are: (how can I) put to other uses, adapt, modify, magnify, minify, substitute, rearrange, reverse, combine?

15. The linkage between logic and problem solving is most clearly seen in the work of Dewey, although I think his view of *inquiry* is broader than the notion of problem solving found in modern literature (see O'Connor).

16. It may be observed that what Mill has in mind here is what we have come to call metacognition.

WORKS CITED

Anderson, Barry F. *The Complete Thinker*. Englewood Cliffs, NJ: Prentice-Hall, 1980.

Aristotle. *Nicomachean Ethics*. Trans. Martin Ostwald. Library of Liberal Arts. Indianapolis: Bobbs-Merrill, 1962.

Beardsley, Monroe. *Thinking Straight*. 4th ed. Englewood Cliffs, NJ: Prentice-Hall, 1950.

Cederblom, Jerry C., and David W. Paulsen. *Critical Reasoning*. 2nd. ed. Belmont, CA: Wadsworth, 1986.

Ennis, Robert H. "Rational Thinking and Educational Practice." *Philosophy and Education, Eightieth Yearbook of the National Society for the Study of Education.* Part I. Ed. Jonas F. Soltis. Chicago: University of Chicago Press, 1981. 143–183.

Hayes, John R. *The Complete Problem Solver.* Philadelphia: The Franklin Institute Press, 1981.

Johnson, Ralph H., and J. Anthony Blair. *Logical Self-Defense.* 2nd. ed. Toronto: McGraw-Hill Ryerson, 1983.

Maimon, Elaine P., Gerald L. Belcher, Gail W. Hearn, Barbara F. Nodine, and Finbarr W. O'Connor. *Writing in the Arts and Sciences.* Cambridge, MA: Winthrop, 1981; Boston: Little, Brown, 1982.

Mill, John Stuart. "Civilization." 1836. *Mill's Essays on Literature and Society.* Ed. J. B. Schneewind. New York: Collier, 1965. 148–182.

———. "Inaugural Address." 1867. *Mill's Essays on Literature and Society.* Ed. J. B. Schneewind. New York: Collier, 1965. 353–410.

Newell, Allen, and Herbert A. Simon. *Human Problem Solving.* Englewood Cliffs, NJ: Prentice-Hall, 1972.

O'Connor, Finbarr W. "Dewey, Inquiry, and Problem Solving." *Values and Value Theory in Twentieth-Century America.* Ed. Ivar Berg and Murray G. Murphey. Philadelphia: Temple University Press, 1988. 82–100.

Osborn, Alex F. *Applied Imagination.* 3d rev. ed. New York: Scribner's, 1963.

Reichenbach, Hans. *Experience and Prediction.* Chicago: University of Chicago Press, 1938.

Rickards, T. *Problem Solving Through Creative Analysis.* Essex: Gower Press, 1974.

Schwartz, Thomas. *The Art of Logical Reasoning.* New York: Random House, 1980.

Scriven, Michael. *Reasoning.* New York: McGraw-Hill, 1976.

Thomas, Stephen N. *Practical Reasoning in Natural Language.* 2d ed. Englewood Cliffs, NJ: Prentice-Hall, 1973.

Toulmin, Steven, Richard Rieke, and Allan Janik. *An Introduction to Reasoning.* New York: Macmillan, 1979.

Van Gundy, A. B. *Techniques of Structured Problem Solving.* New York: Van Nostrand Reinhold, 1981.

Whiting, C. S. *Creative Thinking.* New York: Reinhold, 1958.

Young, Richard E., Alton L. Becker, and Kenneth L. Pike. *Rhetoric: Discovery and Change.* New York: Harcourt Brace Jovanovich, 1970.

CHAPTER 8

Willingness to Reason and the Identification of the Self

Jerry Cederblom

"I'VE BEEN RIGHT ALL ALONG"

The wish to *already* be right—not to have to change one's beliefs or learn from someone else—is a wish we all share. This is understandable. I tend to associate my set of beliefs with what I am. If I find that I was mistaken about something, then I must admit that until now I have had a certain defect. If my set of beliefs has been closer to the truth than yours, then I have some grounds for thinking myself better than you. It is natural, then, to resist admitting that beliefs I once held seem now to be mistaken.

The attitude just described, although a natural one to take, has obvious drawbacks. The most serious is that it stands in the way of improving my set of beliefs. Still, this attitude seems preferable to the alternative of keeping in mind at all times that this set of beliefs I associate so closely with myself is largely defective. That much humility is difficult to maintain. Perhaps it is because this self-effacing attitude seems to be the only alternative that the attitude of wanting to have been right all along is so common.

There is, however, a third alternative, a different attitude that can be cultivated regarding myself and my beliefs. That is, I can identify myself not with the set of beliefs I hold, or have held, but rather as a belief-forming process. In the course of this essay, I will argue that this attitude is closely connected with willingness to reason and is reflected in the best and most productive critical dialogues. I will suggest that it is also reflected in a kind of writing that is highly effective in leading both the reader and the writer from a less to a more adequate set of beliefs. Finally, I will explore the idea that acquiring the ability to take this attitude might be likened to a developmental stage.

Before proceeding, I should say more about what I mean by such phrases as "identifying myself with a set of beliefs," or "identifying myself as a belief-forming process." Several questions come immediately to mind. Do I mean to suggest that I can take any attitude I wish toward myself? Shouldn't my choice of which attitude to take be based on an investigation of what my self really is?

Let me admit at the outset that I am not attempting to say anything deeply philosophical about the self. I am not claiming that the self is best defined as a belief-forming process rather than as, say, the mind, or the brain, or as a self-conscious entity that is the subject of experience. What I am concerned with is the much more pedestrian sense in which an athlete, for example, might identify herself with her body, or a singer might identify himself with his voice and his ability to control it.[1] What is central to this sense of identification of self is its connection with taking pride or credit, or feeling ashamed and inadequate. I believe that, taken in this sense, the way in which I identify myself *is* largely a matter of choice. But, as I shall argue, reasons can be given for choosing to take one attitude rather than another.

Furthermore, I am not suggesting that self-identification always has to do with beliefs. You might identify yourself as a parent, as an artist, as a golfer, and as a gambler. And these identifications might not be affected by whether you also identify yourself as a set of beliefs or as a belief-forming process. I am certainly not suggesting that you identify yourself in this latter way as opposed to, say, identifying yourself as certain kind of parent or artist.

My basic idea about identifying myself as a belief-forming process is that we sometimes identify ourselves in terms of particular static features but at other times in terms of activities we carry out or abilities we have. The body builder, for example, takes pride in what his body is—what it looks like, how it is shaped, the size and definition of the muscles. By contrast, the athlete takes pride in the ability of his body to function well in a sport.

The person who identifies with his set of beliefs takes pride in thinking that these beliefs are true and important. This is similar to the attitude of the body builder. What I am referring to as identification of the self as a belief-forming process is more like the attitude of the athlete. A sense of pride would stem from an ability to function well.

THE CASE FOR IDENTIFYING MYSELF
AS A BELIEF-FORMING PROCESS

There is a tradition in American philosophy that conceives of epistemology as a part of ethical theory.[2] The argument has been made by Roderick Chisholm, building on the ideas of Charles Peirce and C.I. Lewis, that acts of deciding what to believe are not unlike overt social acts in being under our control and having consequences for others. Chisholm acknowledges that there are good reasons for not punishing people who don't fulfill their "epistemic obligations," reasons such as the preservation of freedom of thought (227). But both Chisholm and Lewis see beliefs as being appropriately subjected to normative judgments. Furthermore, both see the rightness of overt physical action as being dependent on the justifiability of beliefs concerning the consequences of these actions. Epistemology, then, becomes that part of ethics which has to do with the critique of acts of belief.

This analysis can be carried further. It is not only particular acts that are subject to a moral critique. Questions concerning which attitudes, habits, or traits of character should be cultivated are also ones that ethical theory attempts to address, because particular acts flow from attitudes, habits, and traits. Now suppose that it is true (as I will argue) that the attitude I cultivate toward myself in relation to my beliefs (e.g., viewing my self as a collection of beliefs or as a belief-forming process) has broad consequences for particular actions of believing. Then the question of which attitude to cultivate becomes an overarching epistemological/ethical question.

As I claimed earlier, the chief drawback of identifying myself with my set of beliefs is that this view leads me to see a mistaken belief as a defect in myself. This inclines me to reject a belief that conflicts with my own, even when I have good reason to accept it. I say "inclines" rather than "compels" because in many cases the desire to already be right will be outweighed by the force of reason in favor of the conflicting belief. But the identification of myself with my past beliefs is an obstacle to improvement.

Consider the dynamics of a disagreement in which each party wants to show that he has been right all along. Such an exchange becomes a kind of contest.[3] If I admit that your position is more reasonable, then I have lost the contest and you have won. There is some degree of humiliation in losing, and I will do my best to avoid defeat. Because of this, it is unlikely that I will seriously consider the reasons you give for your point of view. I don't *want* your reasons to be compelling because I don't want to lose.

And yet it is ironic that we speak of a "loss" in this situation. What has actually taken place when an argument has been "lost"? I have been given reasons that I now see as adequate for adopting a belief that I previously lacked, of which I can now make use of in my dealings in the world. And I have weeded out a belief that I now see as inadequate. Considering myself as a belief-forming process, I have functioned well and am now in an improved position. It is only if I identified myself with my past beliefs that I would have grounds for dismay.

This, then, is the main argument I see against cultivating an attitude toward myself as my past set of beliefs and in favor of viewing myself as a belief-forming process. For each of us individually, the former attitude stands in the way of improving beliefs. For all of us collectively, the unwillingness to admit past mistakes stands in the way of fruitful dialogue by making us view disagreements as contests to be won or lost. For our young students, the wish to already be right works counter to their disposition to become educated. If these considerations are compelling, it will be important to investigate how the attitude of seeing oneself as a belief-forming process can be cultivated.

There are, however, several possible objections to the argument I have made. First, it is not entirely clear that thinking of my self as my past set of beliefs would be discouragement from admitting that some of these beliefs are mistaken. Why wouldn't I be eager to admit mistakes so that I can improve myself? Second, all I have argued so far is that thinking of myself as a belief-forming process has certain important advantages. I haven't considered whether there are overriding advantages to thinking of myself as a set of beliefs or in some other way. I will consider these objections in turn.

To restate the first objection, if I identify myself with my set of beliefs, why couldn't I see it as a victory, or at least a pleasing outcome, to have improved myself (my set of beliefs) by replacing an inadequate belief with a more adequate one? Admittedly, I must see myself as *having been* inferior, but I should still be happy that my self is now improved.

Compare this situation with that of a person who has been in terrible physical shape but sees that she needs to improve and begins exercising and dieting. She could identify herself with her body as it has been and see herself as defective. Or she could adopt a "new image" of somebody whose body is improving. But she could still identify herself with her body. She needn't identify herself as some kind of "body-conditioning process" (comparable to a "belief-forming process") in order to want to exercise and at the same time salvage some self-respect.

Similarly, then, why isn't it possible to identify myself with my set of beliefs and to see that self—that set of beliefs—as improving? This attitude could then lead me to welcome the arguments of those who disagree with me, to listen to them eagerly. Let's explore this further.

One difference between the out-of-shape person and the person with inadequate beliefs is that the person who is out of shape can see that her body will be in much better shape, if she exercises, in the not-too-distant future. But the person who identifies with his past set of beliefs can't realistically think that as soon as he welcomes a few corrections of his past beliefs he will then be pretty much correct about everything. Considering all there is to be known and the way in which theories are continually developed, refined, and replaced, it is surely unrealistic for any of us to take pride in having a set of beliefs that needs little improvement. A more appropriate comparison might be to someone who has a glandular condition that will prevent her from ever getting her body in very good shape but who is nevertheless skilled at certain athletic games. To the extent that this person identifies herself with her body at all, she might well wish to identify with the operations of her body as it performs in athletic activities—that is, as a process—rather than as a fixed object. And similar reasoning would lead us all to cultivate our ability to reform and replace inadequate beliefs and to identify ourselves in terms of this kind of ability.

But I need also to consider the objection that there are advantages to thinking of myself as a set of beliefs rather than as a belief-forming process. Isn't it important and admirable to stand firmly on certain principles? A dedicated pacifist might see her beliefs about the wrongfulness of war to be an essential part of what she *is*, a part of her that she should not give up. An egalitarian, a devout religious believer, an atheist who takes pride in having stood against conventional beliefs, would all hold these particular beliefs as important in their self-identification. They might be willing to leave beliefs concerning less important issues as incidental to their self-concepts, but not these. It could even be claimed that the argument I have been making in this essay shows that I hold a certain belief firmly—the belief that it is important to be willing to reason. Wouldn't it be a self-contradiction to detach myself from that belief, on the grounds that I should just think of myself as a belief-forming process?

I believe this objection has some merit. Perhaps it is unreasonable to expect myself to never identify with any of the beliefs I have developed carefully and consider important. But it might be possible to develop a willingness to subject any and all beliefs to critical scrutiny (by myself and others) on occasion. It might actually be best to identify myself with certain beliefs when it is necessary to maintain strong resolve and to carry out important action. A character from fiction comes to mind here: John Le Carré's intelligence agent, George Smiley. Smiley realizes as he acts that it is quite possible that his whole system of political beliefs is wrong. He has thought carefully in the past about these beliefs, and he continually reevaluates them. His self-identification seems to be that of a reasoner, a ponderer. But he acts decisively when he must.

Let me emphasize, then, that I am making a considerable concession to the objection that has just been raised. It would be a mistake to think that I must identify myself at all times either as a set of beliefs or as a belief-forming process. We might fault the former attitude as being associated with extreme rigidity of belief, but we can also fault the latter as promoting flexibility to an unjustifiable extreme. Still, whenever the opportunity for critical dialogue is at hand, and doesn't conflict with the necessity for action, there is good reason to cultivate the identification of my self with my reasoning abilities—that is, as a belief-forming process.

There is a related objection that could be made, but that really raises a new topic that should be discussed with some care in the following two sections. That is, just as the adversary system in a court of law might be the best way of getting at the truth, might not a society in which each individual identifies strongly with her or his beliefs and argues vigorously for them be one that is more likely to progress in its knowledge than one in which each person leaves things "open to discussion," as my position would seem to recommend?

DETACHING BELIEFS FROM ONESELF
IN CRITICAL DIALOGUES

At the beginning of this essay I suggested that identifying oneself as a belief-forming process, rather than as a particular set of beliefs, is an attitude closely connected with willingness to reason and is reflected in the best and most productive dialogues. I will begin to make a case for these claims by presenting a brief analysis of a basic kind of reasoning process. We can then look at some connections between willingness to reason in this way and the identification of oneself as a belief-forming process.

One important kind of reasoning is the presentation and evaluation of arguments. This is a procedure in which reasons (premises) are given in support of a point of view (a conclusion) and an attempt is made to determine whether the point of view being advanced really follows from the reasons given (i.e., whether the argument is valid) and whether the reasons themselves should be accepted (whether the premises are true).

This procedure probably occurs most naturally in a dialogue between two people, in which one person advances an argument in order to persuade another, who in turn evaluates the argument to determine whether she should accept it. But the procedure can also occur in a "dialogue with oneself," in which someone attempts to decide whether she is justified in holding a certain belief.

This procedure, although it sounds straightforward and simple, can be difficult to initiate and often gets sidetracked. What occurs more often in dialogues is one person asserting a point of view and the other denying it (no reasons given, none asked for), perhaps followed by apology for disagreeing (as though that were an offense), or anger and name-calling. What occurs when a single individual raises the question of whether to continue to hold a certain belief is more varied and more difficult to analyze. But oftentimes the individual gets sidetracked into assessing how he will be affected if the belief is given up rather than deciding whether adequate reasons could be given to support it.

It is not difficult to see how willingness to reason in the sense described above would be affected by the way I identify myself in relation to my beliefs. If I identify myself with my set of beliefs, then I will be resistant to entering into this procedure for fear that I will be changed or will be shown to be inadequate. If, however, I identify myself as a belief-forming process, this reasoning situation is an opportunity for me to flourish, to use my abilities. It is like a player being invited to play.

It seems an easy step to move from this analysis to the claim that this attitude toward oneself is reflected in the most productive dialogues. However, I should consider at this time the objection that was mentioned earlier: Isn't the identification of myself with my beliefs a strong motive for me to argue vigorously in favor of these beliefs? If so, wouldn't society benefit most by having these spirited contests to witness, in which each person has given the strongest arguments available in an attempt to avoid damage to herself?

This is a good question, and I am raising it seriously. It will be raised again with regard to the kind of attitude toward self that is reflected in the best writing. The question brings to mind the accounts that are given of Samuel Johnson arguing with such energy and wit in order to *win*. Would the intellectual life in London have been improved if Johnson had been less inclined to win arguments?

Perhaps Johnson's acquaintances did benefit from his desire to win arguments, but even if this is the case, it does not show that identification of self with beliefs is a more beneficial attitude. This identification was not what motivated Johnson—he often played devil's advocate, arguing for positions he didn't really hold. As I consider again the dynamics of critical dialogue, it occurs to me that it is possible, and perhaps not uncommon, for a person to enjoy engaging in reasoning with others as a kind of game or competitive enterprise, but not with a view to defending beliefs that he associates with himself. This kind of attitude might indeed motivate one to reason well without being defensive about giving up a prized belief.

Still, as long as this competitive motive drives the dialogue, it is difficult to tell when a participant is maintaining his position because the reasons given on the other side are not strong enough and when it is because he simply doesn't want to be the loser in his competitive game. This can be confusing. It is difficult to tell whether you should keep trying to see things the way he apparently does or whether there is really nothing to be seen.

To have a dialogue with this sort of person is preferable to having one with a person whose identification with his beliefs prevents him from seriously considering reasons for an opposing view. But it is not as worthwhile as a dialogue with someone who is both free of self-identification with a particular belief and is trying to determine what is reasonable to believe, not to compete.

WILLINGNESS TO REASON REFLECTED IN GOOD WRITING

There is a kind of writing often engaged in by philosophers, but also by essayists in various fields and by some more popular writers, in which the author detaches herself from the idea, claim, or argument put forward and seems to join with the reader in assessing its worth. This is particularly effective in drawing the reader into the stream of thought of the author. I believe that this kind or writing is also a reflection of the identification of the self as a belief-forming process rather than as a particular set of beliefs.

The kind of writing I have in mind is similar in its effect to dialogues such as Plato's in which the author uses various characters or voices to advance arguments and theories and to reply to them. Such a dialogue allows the author to detach himself from a particular belief by putting himself in the mind of a character who would oppose it. The reader also can identify with each character speaking rather than thinking of himself as an opponent in a contest with the author.

But a dialogue form need not be used to achieve this kind of effect. A writer such as Hume will present a theory or idea as something he sincerely wishes to investigate, to follow wherever reason leads in his investigation. It will be obvious, when he raises an objection against his own argument, that he is truly seeking to determine whether or not it should be accepted. At the beginning of the appendix to his *Treatise of Human Nature* Hume writes:

> There is nothing I wou'd more willingly lay hold of, than an opportunity of confessing my errors; and shou'd esteem such a return to truth and reason to be more honourable than the most unerring judgement. A man, who is free from mistakes, can pretend to no praises, except from the justness of his understanding: But a man, who corrects his mistakes, shews at once the justness of his understanding, and the candour and ingenuity of his temper. (623)

The connection is surely not accidental between this attitude and Hume's effectiveness in bringing his reader willingly along as he discovers where reason will lead him.

Even though writing that reflects the author's willingness to detach herself from her ideas is particularly effective in the way just described, it would surely be an overstatement to claim that good argumentative writing should always reflect this attitude. To claim this would be to ignore such obvious examples to the contrary as Thomas Hobbes, who writes with such confidence that he seems to have been born with his beliefs, or Samuel Johnson, who has such apparent disdain for his opponents. But if an attitude of detachment is *sometimes* a virtue in a writer, it is worth our deliberation to see why this is not always the case.

Consider the following passage from Johnson's *Preface to Shakespeare*, in which he defends Shakespeare's plays against the criticism that they violated the unities of time and place.

> The objection arising from the impossibility of passing the first hour at Alexandria, and the next at Rome, supposes, that when the play opens, the spectator really imagines himself at Alexandria, and believes that his walk to the theater has been a voyage to Egypt, and that he lives in the days of Antony and Cleopatra. Surely he that imagines this may imagine more. He that can take the stage at one time for the palace of the Ptolemies, may take it in half an hour for the promontory of Actium. (456)

We might object to Johnson that he is making straw men of his opponents and not really trying to discover something worthwhile in their reasoning. Surely there is a stronger case to be made for the maintenance of continuity of time and place in drama than that the audience can't imagine being first in one place and then another. Still this passage is highly entertaining and in many ways effective. Perhaps it is safer to see a position attacked in writing than to have it attacked in a face-to-face confrontation. The fun that Johnson has with his imaginary opponent makes me line up on his side, but at the same time I look carefully at the mistake he is ridiculing, so that I will be sure not to make it myself and open myself up to embarrassment.

What should probably be conceded is that there are many qualities that can make writing good, and some of them will not always be compatible with a tone of detachment on the part of the author. The kind of humor Johnson achieves in this passage, and the particular way in which he gets the reader to see the error in question, would have been lost if he had adopted a detached tone.

The case of a writer such as Thomas Hobbes, who is not so much combative in his tone but simply confident of his every assertion, is also worth exploring. *Leviathan* has been praised as a literary masterpiece, and I find it hard to disagree. And yet here seems to be a case in which the attitude toward self that I have been criticizing—the identification of oneself with one's beliefs—seems strongly present. Would Hobbes have been more effective in leading his readers to see the worth of his ideas if he had raised possible objections to them as though he really might change his mind?

It is worth noting that when one uses a book like *Leviathan* in the classroom, it is necessary to point out to students that some thinkers have seriously held positions contrary to the ones Hobbes advances. Some have held, with supporting reasons, that life in a state of nature would not be all that bad, or that there might be obligations that are not based on agreements. Once students see reasons for taking these positions seriously, they see Hobbes's arguments (opposing these positions) as more important to assess. If Hobbes himself had presented opposing positions more sympathetically, then it wouldn't be necessary to supplement his writing in this way.

Furthermore, even though Hobbes appears in his writings to be the sort of person who would identify himself with his firmly held beliefs, it doesn't follow that he arrived at his positions by taking this attitude. It seems more likely that he ended up writing with such a tone of conviction because he had already gone through the process of taking very seriously the objections to his views that he convincingly rejects in his writings.

If it had been Hobbes's object, then, to proceed still further with the development of his views and to guide his readers through a consideration of what is reasonable to believe, then he might have done best to take the attitude I have been discussing—that is, identifying oneself as a belief-forming process. As it is, we have in his writings something that is perhaps more like a retrospective report of someone who had taken this attitude previously in dialogues with himself (and perhaps with others).

WILLINGNESS TO REASON AS A DEVELOPMENTAL STAGE

I would like to explore now the possibility that willingness to reason in a way that detaches oneself from one's past beliefs can be likened to a stage of cognitive development. My suspicion is based on observation of and discussion with my students in critical reasoning classes through the last 10 years. Admittedly, this investigation has been less than systematic. But let me describe what I have observed.

I used to give my students an assignment in which they were to write a short essay, advancing an argument in favor of some point of view. Then, they were to raise objections to their own argument— objections that they thought would be made by a competent critic, and reply to these objections. This seemed simple enough to me and to many of my students, but for a certain number in each class, the assignment was virtually impossible to understand and carry out. They would say things like, "We're supposed to argue for something and then against it?" "What if I'm really for it?" "Won't I be contradicting myself?"

Explaining the assignment again and constructing a sample essay would help some of these students, but not all. A few would bring themselves to raise the most ludicrous "straw man" objections to their own arguments, and then hastily reply to them, as though they were stepping close to the edge of a roof and then stepping back. But for a significant number of students in each class, the assignment remained impossible to carry out.

There have been occasions when, in frustration, I ended up dictating the last part of the essay to the student in my office. He would copy down the words as though he were writing in a foreign language: "Against my first premise, someone might raise the objection that..." If an objection to the student's argument sounded convincing, the student would ask if he shouldn't change the first part of the essay, where he stated his argument, so that it would get around the objection.

What was going on in these cases? Several of the students who could-not complete the assignment had done an adequate job of criticizing arguments in other assignments and tests. So it wasn't that they didn't know how to criticize. And it wasn't that their own arguments were such good ones that it would have been difficult to think of criticisms. The only explanation I can see is that they couldn't criticize these arguments because they were their own.

What I am suggesting, then, is that this task of bringing up hypothetical objections to one's own argument requires a kind of complete willingness to reason—that is, a willingness to consider objections to the argument as though it were not one's own. This kind of willingness to reason, I have claimed, is associated with freeing one's identification of self from one's set of past beliefs. I would like to suggest now that this kind of attitude might represent a kind of developmental leap forward. My suspicion that this is so is based on the inability of some people to carry out certain tasks of self-criticism.

It will probably be replied that discovering a kind of task that some people can't carry out isn't discovering a stage of development. What is it that constitutes a developmental stage?

One feature that psychologists seem to look for in identifying a developmental stage is a qualitative change. I am assuming that since some students can carry out the assignment described above but others can't, the ones who can would have once been unable, but became able. I admit that this assumption could be incorrect. It could be that the students who have the ability in question had it (or some form of it) all along. In other words, instead of looking at students who are at different stages, I could be looking at different kinds of students.

Psychologists also seek to locate a supposed stage in a sequence with other stages, and they look for a constancy in sequence from person to person. I don't know if there is a stage that might follow this one, but it is interesting to speculate whether a stage can be described that would constantly precede it. For example, would people regularly progress from being unable to seriously consider reasons in favor of a view that contradicts their own, to being able to seriously entertain such reasons, to then being able to raise hypothetical objections to their own views?

Questions such as this last one seem worth pursuing, not only in order to learn more about the way in which willingness to reason develops but also in order to employ ways of teaching critical reasoning that would be in step with this development.

At the beginning of this essay, I suggested that the way in which I identify myself is largely a matter of choice, and I gave reasons for identifying myself as a belief-forming process rather than as a set of beliefs. Now I am entertaining the possibility that the ability to take this attitude occurs as a developmental stage. It might be claimed that there is an inconsistency here. If the ability to take this attitude occurs as a developmental stage, doesn't this mean that before this stage occurs I couldn't take this attitude even if I tried?

This question leads naturally to another one: When a person fails to detach himself from his set of beliefs, is it because he is *unwilling* to do so, or is it because he is *unable* to do so?

If I had to guess, I would say that the ability to identify oneself as a belief-forming process, rather than as a set of beliefs, does occur as a stage of development. But after this stage occurs, we have a choice of whether or not to cultivate this attitude. It is then a matter of whether we are willing to take this attitude, not whether we are able.

Perhaps the educator has two different tasks regarding this attitude toward the self. The first, as I suggested above, would be to adopt ways of teaching reasoning skills that are in step with the student's development of her ability to detach herself from her particular set of beliefs. The second would be to help her explore the reasons for identifying herself as a belief-forming process, rather than as a set of beliefs, once she has the ability to make a choice.

NOTES

1. In this sense of identification of self, I can identify myself in more than one way (i.e., I can associate what I am both with my voice and my body), and I can assign relative strengths to these identifications (i.e., I can associate what I am more strongly with my mind than my body).
2. The development of this idea is discussed by Chisholm.

3. The contrast between disagreements as contests and reasoned criticism in developed in Cederblom and Paulsen, chapter 1.

WORKS CITED

Cederblom, Jerry, and David W. Paulsen. *Critical Reasoning: Understanding and Criticizing Arguments and Theories*. 2nd ed. Belmont, CA: Wadsworth, 1986.

Chisholm, Roderick M. "Lewis' Ethics of Belief." *The Philosophy of C.I. Lewis*. Ed. Paul Arthur Schilpp. La Salle, IL: Open Court, 1968. 223–242.

Hobbes, Thomas. *Leviathan*. 1651. Ed. C.B. Macpherson. Baltimore, MD: Penguin, 1968.

Johnson, Samuel. *Preface to Shakespeare*. 1781. *The Great Critics*. Ed. James Harry Smith and Edd Winfield Parks. New York: Norton, 1960. 443–460.

Hume, David. *A Treatise of Human Nature*. 1739–1740. Ed. L.A. Selby-Bigge. New York: Oxford University Press, 1967.

PART 3
Writing

FROM THE PERSPECTIVE
OF COMPOSITION SCHOLARS

Writing is thinking made visible. Yet, for much of this century teachers of writing ignored the vital connection between writing and thinking and focused instead on writing as the transcription of letters and punctuation marks rather than on writing as the composition of ideas. A study of transcription, while highlighting differences between the grapholect and various spoken dialects, kept the field confined, for the most part, to matters of grammar and usage. Although writing teachers never really believed that surface features defined writing, textbooks and syllabuses nonetheless reflected that belief. Assuming that matters beyond the surface were under the aegis of the Muse and therefore unteachable by ordinary mortals, writing teachers avoided making connections between writing and thinking. In the last 25 years teachers and scholars have shifted attention back to composition, the creative act of forming and arranging linguistic elements that generate and express thought.

When, as teachers of writing, we decide that we are not teaching transcribing, we are thrust willy-nilly into the teaching of thinking. A preoccupation with the written code in and of itself had been an escape from bewilderment about where to find teachable and testable connections between writing and thinking. When scholars and teachers made up their minds to find these connections, they explored four major areas: the history of rhetoric, cognitive psychology, philosophy, and semiotics.

Some teachers of writing, those schooled as rhetoricians, had never followed the retreat of the majority of English teachers to the surface of the text. As James Kinneavy's bibliographic essay suggests, the revived interest in composing involved quite literally a renaissance of classical approaches to rhetoric and dialectic as integrally connected to fundamental actions of mind. Such connections are complex and multidimensional. Classical writers assume interrelationships between forms of expression—for example, poetry and science—and modes of thinking. They may have discussed knowledge and wisdom but not what Linda Flower calls "conscious, reflective thought." Nonetheless, Kinneavy's essay exemplifies the history and reestablished centrality of internal intellectual processes in the field of rhetoric. (In Kinneavy's discussion of rhetoric in the 19th century we can also see in the work of Bain and Genung roots of the polarization between writing and thinking.)

Rather than exploring the history of rhetoric, Linda Flower looks to cognitive psychology for the means of plumbing the depths of written composition. She does so both in methods and in models. Her method is empirical. She performs a series of systematic observations under carefully controlled conditions, and in that way she functions as a social scientist. Her model for thinking is connected with "consciousness," a concept not probed by classical rhetoricians. Flower focuses on "conscious thought" and asks what it's good for. Conscious thought, she answers in a way the rhetoricians would have approved, is good for dealing with complexity, because it involves the generation of meaning, not merely transcription. Flower emphasizes the conscious, reflective crafting of meaning through writing. Making meaning involves taking thought.

Kenneth Bruffee challenges the fundamental metaphors and vocabulary that both Kinneavy and Flower employ. While Kinneavy and Flower assume the existence of a human mind that can be educated for the purpose of generating and expressing ideas, Bruffee, drawing on the work of social constructionist philosophers (Kuhn, Rorty), suggests that what we call mind is really the internalization of the way that particular human communities use symbols. Making meaning, in Bruffee's terms, involves not taking thought, as Flower would say, but making conversation among people who speak the same language. Mind is not "interior" but "internalized." Thinking, according to Bruffee, is preeminently a process of making judgments—"knowledgeable, discerning, reliable decisions." And the way to make good decisions in this social constructivist view is to practice making judgments cooperatively with other people. Writing provides the occasion for making a complex set of judgments with language and about language. In that sense, writing and thinking exist in pragmatic relationship.

Sharing Bruffee's skepticism about the metaphor of the mind as an interior entity as well as his conception of thinking as a discursive process, Haney-Peritz also searches for a pragmatic relationship between writing and thinking. She is committed to the idea that teachers can make a difference in communicating both substance ("what we know") and process ("know-how"). But her philosophic position, derived from Saussure, Peirce, and other semioticians, compels her to deal head on with the interdependency of thought and language as well as with the problem this interdependency presents. Assuming that we cannot think or know without signs, Haney-Peritz describes the cognitive subject as running a never-ending race from one sign post to another, a race in which thought, knowledge, and meaning are elusive goals—ones that would put an end to thinking. As a matter of course, Haney-Peritz represents thinking as discursive—as a process of deferral and displacement. How then can teachers productively intervene in this slippery process?

If thinking is ever-changing—a work-in-progress—then we can best teach thinking by teaching revision. Instruction in writing provides an appropriate occasion for revision, since the writer, reader, and text exist in dynamic relationship, with the text in constant flux, as the reader and writer change in their relationship to each other. The student in the composition classroom can quite literally revise a text in the sense of looking at it again. Haney-Peritz would, like Bruffee, endorse conversation about work-in-progress, since such activity would help students to imagine an unfamiliar reader, someone who might by his or her response both transform the writer and be transformed by reading the writer's message. But Haney-Peritz rejects Bruffee's rationale for the teaching of signs. "Community" in Haney-Peritz's terms is nothing more than an idea that is itself subject to the commutability of signs.

Although each composition scholar defines thinking and writing in different ways, all of them would agree that we teach self-awareness by teaching writing. Classical rhetoricians, cognitive psychologists, social constructionist philosophers, and semioticians all see the teaching of writing as an occasion to imagine self-transforming encounters with a stranger. Through a discursive encounter between the writer, the text, and an imagined reader, students have opportunities to contemplate the responses of others to their thinking, to plan systematically for ways to achieve goals, to find viable means for joining new communities, and to develop self-analytic habits. Such teaching is bound to make a difference.

FROM THE PERSPECTIVE OF PSYCHOLOGISTS

Yet the cognitive psychologists as empiricists would ask us to identify and quantify this difference. Of the four composition scholars only Linda

Flower, who draws her own perspective from social science, would be prepared to give attention to such empirical matters. Kinneavy, in contrast, approaches the connection between writing and thinking, not as a scientist, but as a historian of rhetoric. His evidence, consequently, is an accumulation of historical references to work that served as a basis for educational practices from antiquity through the 19th century. We see in this essay evidence of over 2,000 years of concern about the connections between kinds of writing and kinds of thinking. Are these so intertwined that neither can be defined independently of the other? Can we find empirical evidence to support Kinneavy's claim that those who cannot write persuasively themselves will be vulnerable to the persuasion of others? Will those who do not read or write poems lack aesthetic sensibilities? Psychologists *qua* psychologists would require different sorts of data to support or refute Kinneavy's claims.

Just so, they would test Bruffee's concepts against their own empirical definition of evidence. Might we select subjects from one community who, as students, are moving toward membership in an educated community? How do we deal with individual differences in the student community? After opportunities for participating in a classroom organized according to Bruffee's philosophy, what differences should we look for in students' conversation and writing?

But, perhaps more importantly, the psychologists would find disturbing differences between Bruffee's constructionism and the constructivism of Piaget and other developmental and cognitive psychologists. Voss's essay (Chapter 4) provides the nearest analogue to Bruffee's ideas. Even if Bruffee were to accept Voss's vocabulary of experts and novices, Bruffee would deny that cognitive structures change. The very notion of cognitive structures *inside* the individual is, in Bruffee's terms, a metaphoric fallacy. The mind, in his lexicon, does not have structures, and nothing changes "inside" the individual. Any changes occurs instead within the functional relationship between the individual and the group. Since Voss identifies the move from novice to expert as progress, his view is not in accord with Bruffee's relativist position that calls into question the developmental, well-nigh deterministic, construct of Piaget, Voss, Basseches, and, in fact, all the psychologists in this volume.

The cognitive psychologists would agree with Haney-Peritz's positive regard for the teaching of revision as a way of teaching thinking, although they would take a different route to the same conclusion. More convinced by the systematic observations made by Flower and other researchers than by semiotic analysis, cognitive psychologists would endorse the teaching of revision because experienced writers engage in such activity. Psychologists' understanding of the human memory would also justify the teaching of revision. Writing allows individuals to manipulate many items in addition to the seven stored in short-term memory. When writers write and then read the texts they have generated, their reading stimulates memories of other related material, which, in turn, leads to further reconsideration and revision of the texts. Since each new version of text will evoke new memories and new revisions, the writer will be caught in an unending loop—not dissimilar from Haney-Peritz's race between signs in an unattainable pursuit of meaning. In both the semiotic and the psychological constructs, the individual makes a difference by asserting an arbitrary stopping point (or resting place).

FROM THE PERSPECTIVE OF LOGICIANS

It is a commonplace of intellectual history that logic and rhetoric have viewed one another with suspicion, if not downright hostility. Yet to philosophers reading Kinneavy's essay what stands out is the extent to which we share common literary roots. As Kinneavy begins his survey of rhetoric with Plato and Aristotle, so would we a survey of logic, although we might focus on different works. Ramus, too, has a role in both histories. In the 17th and 18th centuries we might have looked to Galileo, Descartes, Bacon, and Newton as important characters in Kinneavy's story. Their debates over "scientific method"—what it is, and whether it exists—provides a significant departure from the classical paradigm. Interestingly, it is in the 19th century that our bibliographies begin to diverge: Bain and Genung are unlikely candidates for a history of logic.

In trying to find a "fit" between informal logic and the concerns of rhetoric, the distinction Blair and Johnson (Chapter 5) make between informal logic and critical thinking seems most pertinent. As they observe, critical thinking is, or should be, the province of Everyone, whereas informal logic is a field of study. As the notion of critical thinking seems ever to expand, so Kinneavy sweeps into the jurisdiction of rhetoric dialectical thinking, aesthetic thinking, rhetorical thinking, and expressive thinking. Informal logic lays claim to a more modest territory—certainly, rhetorical thinking, and perhaps dialectical thinking. As informal logic has developed, however, it is now possible for logicians and rhetoricians to converse in a way that would not have been possible some years ago. For formal logic, context and audience play no role in argument evaluation. For rhetoricians, they are crucial factors; so they are for informal logicians.

Of the three remaining essays in this section Linda Flower's is most readily assimilated to the conventional logic classroom. Certainly the need to teach skills in a context that makes clear their "real life" goals is all too familiar to teachers of logic. Further, the conceptual apparatus informing her essay—awareness, reflective awareness, representations—is easily assimilable. To the extent that the content of a logic classroom is supposed to be everyday reasoning, the teacher of logic sets out not so much to teach reasoning itself—presumed already an ability of the student—but techniques that promote awareness of the nature of the reasoning and which may promote reflective awareness in addition. Thus, if analogical reasoning is the topic at hand, the object of the teaching is to increase awareness of what makes a piece of reasoning analogical and what makes it weak or strong. It is a further step, but one quite compatible with the goals of a logic course, to teach how the choice of analogical reasoning may further the student's objectives; this is reflective awareness.

Thus, to the degree that the teacher of logic and the teacher of composition are both intent on teaching cognitive skills, Flower's analysis has a familiar ring to the former. In another sense, however, there is a deep disparity between Flower and modern logic. The concepts of cognitive science from which she draws has antecedents in John Dewey's *How We Think* (1910) and *Logic: The Theory of Inquiry* (1938). Dewey argued that there were not different "kinds" of thinking or reasoning; rather, the way in which a person goes about dealing with the most mundane of everyday problems is just how a scientist deals with the most sophisticated of problems. They differ in the degree of reflective control and objectivity with which they apply the same method. Significantly, Dewey proposed the theory of inquiry as a logic, but in this he was by and large ignored, and it had little effect in logic textbooks. Some sympathetic critics viewed him as having made a contribution to methodology, or perhaps to philosophy of science, but not to logic as such.

The implications for the logic classroom of Bruffee's and Haney-Peritz's essays are more difficult to tease out. They both raise the question of the relationship between a theory and its practical consequences—or in this case, pedagogical recommendations. On the one hand, their pedagogical recommendations are easily transferable. Collaborative learning, as a technique, is justifiable in the logic classroom as in any. And in a classroom where arguments are to be analyzed and evaluated in terms of credibility of premises, as in Johnson and Blair's approach, group assessment of premises is a nice pedagogical fit. It is noteworthy that Haney-Peritz identifies as a significant problem in the composition classroom the same phenomenon Cederblom (Chapter 8) finds in the logic classroom—an inability, or unreadiness, on the part of some students to review their views. And Haney-Peritz's discussion of the Achilles paradox, although she applies it to the problem of how thought is related to signs, draws our attention to the problem of how thought is related to signs, draws our attention to problems of recursion that are also encountered in logic. Thus, for example, Johnson and Blair analyze an argument by asking about three features of it—relevance, sufficiency, and credibility. But they point out that none of the three can be settled finally until the whole analysis has been completed. The process of analysis involves a constant cycle of revision and return. Haney-Peritz might see in this the paradox—if we cannot settle any one without settling all, how can we settle any of it? Yet, of course, we do.

The more profound puzzle involves the philosophical commitments Bruffee and Haney-Peritz have—social constructionism in the one case, and deconstruction in the other. These are intensely controversial views in the philosophical community, and this is not the place to debate their philosophical merits. But it is worth asking whether adopting such philosophical positions requires a revision in one's views of logic.

Historically logic has been remarkably immune to philosophical differences. Disagreements as wide as those that divide empiricists and rationalists, idealists and realists, nominalists and conceptualists, have led to differences over what logic is about, or its source of certainty—in other words, differences in the philosophy of logic. The philosophical divide does not necessarily lead to differences on what inferences are good ones, or what standards of reasoning we should defend. People with very deep philosophical differences can teach the same logic course.

So social constructionism or deconstructionism might yield a distinctive position on philosophy of logic, but this does not necessarily require a different view of the content of logic. Yet this may be too sanguine a conclusion. Traditionally philosophical schools have agreed to take logic as having some kind of privileged status. They have also agreed in associating logic with objectivity and in valuing objectivity. The privilege claimed by logic need not be that it yields fundamental truths about the nature of the universe. The privilege can be that of elucidating the meaning of some fundamental words in our language (such as "not," "if," "and"), or that of expressing the basic lessons of the past in understanding experience, or even that of conventional rules of human intercourse. But it does seem to demand some privileged status. To the extent that to a deconstructionist all claims to cognitive privilege are questionable, it is unclear whether any logic is admissible.

CHAPTER 9

Thinkings and Writings: The Classical Tradition

James L. Kinneavy

In a sense the title of this book has to be rewritten for this chapter: *thinking, reasoning,* and *writing* all have to be put into the plural to reflect the essence of the classical tradition. And it was precisely the movement from the plural to the singular that signaled the partial eclipse of the strong classical tradition. This paper will attempt to discuss the formation of the classical tradition in Plato and Aristotle, its spread and historical diffusion in the Middle Ages both in the Christian West and the Islamic East, its partial decline in the period from the Renaissance through the 19th century, and its resurgence at the present time in the field of composition and rhetoric and in other fields.

To put the classical theory in a nutshell, it could be said that the major classicists concerned with the relation of thought to writing felt it necessary to recognize three to five different kinds of thinking, each specific to a particular kind of writing.

THE FORMATION OF THE CLASSICAL
MODEL: PLATO AND ARISTOTLE

Plato, in the *Ion*, one of his earliest dialogues, occupied himself with the problem of the kind of knowledge a poet had as distinct from that of an expert in the field of a subject a poet might write about, such as a general or a physician or a pilot of a ship. Socrates has Ion admit that, in these subject matter fields, the expert's knowledge is superior to that of the poet (538B, 540A, 541B). In the *Gorgias*, also an early work, Plato makes a similar distinction between the knowledge of the rhetor and the knowledge of experts in various subject matters (449B–454B) and indeed concludes that rhetoric in the courts and other assemblies creates "the sort of persuasion which gives belief without knowledge" (454B). In the *Phaedrus*, a later work, Plato does concede that there might be a valid rhetoric, which would take the truths delivered to it by dialectic and would add to these truths the techniques and emotion of the art of persuasion in order to create a true rhetoric (259D–260A). In any case, it seems clear that, for Plato, there was a different kind of knowledge (thinking) practiced by the poet, the rhetorician, and the dialectician.

Aristotle followed Plato in these directions, but he placed such distinctions in the framework of an elaborate mental physiognomy, a framework that was rather generally adopted by Western civilization for the next 3,000 years and that is still being disputed today. This intellectual profile is carefully drawn in Book VI of the *Ethics*, in which Aristotle describes the intellectual virtues. The virtues are partitioned in three areas, the area of theory *(theoria)* in knowing, the area of practical wisdom in acting *(praxis)*, and the area of art *(techne)* in making things. The hardiness of this tradition can be seen by examining Aquinas in the 13th century, Hobbes in the 17th, Kant in the 18th century, Marx and left Hegelians in the 19th, and contemporary Marxists in the 20th.

Aristotle's speculative virtues of knowing are wisdom, science, and understanding (there are other translations of the Greek); they operate in certain sciences of philosophy, mathematics, physics, astronomy, and so on. The virtues operating in the probability areas of action *(praxis)* are the moral virtues, political wisdom, and economic wisdom (having to do with house management). The virtue of art operates in the fields of poetics (*poein*, meaning to make, includes sculpture, poetry, music, etc.) and the field of rhetoric. Aquinas had no trouble incorporating this entire schema into his treatment of virtue in the *Summa Theologica*; the tripartite structure is the same, and all of the intellectual virtues, including art, are incorporated by him and most of the scholastics into medieval thought (I–II, Q. 57, art. 1–5). Hobbes's schematic outline "Of the Virtues commonly called Intellectual; and their contrary Defects" is presented in Part I, Chapters 8–10, of *Leviathan*, and the structural similarity of his system to Aristotle's is obvious if one examines the schematic presentation in Chapter 10 (72). Kant's three *Critiques* reflect the same tripartite structure in the 18th century. The left Hegelians in the 1840s and the young Marx turned their attention to the critical distinction between *theoria* and *praxis*, insisting on the importance of political action, as distinct from the merely speculative intellection of *theoria*. This distinction is critical to the contemporary treatments of Jürgen Habermas, Richard Bernstein, N. Lobkowicz, Jean-Paul Sartre, and many Marxists.

Not all these thinkings, these intellectual virtues, issue in discourse. But Aristotle, Aquinas, Hobbes, and many others closely relate these intellectual virtues to matters of writing.

Aristotle, in effect, took the general statements of Plato in the *Phaedrus* about persuasion and created the first full-blown rhetorical theory in his *Rhetoric*. His rhetorical theory is, despite some major differences, a construct built upon the specifications of the theory of rhetoric outlined in the *Phaedrus*. Further, he articulated much more carefully the Platonic distinctions among different levels of certainty as they related to different kinds of discourse. To do so, he distinguished among scientific writing, dialectical writing, rhetorical writing, poetic writing, and sophistic writing— the five major purposes writers have, in a general way. By and large these distinctions followed the structure of the intellectual virtues. Writing in the "knowing" area was certain and included writing about metaphysics, about physics, about mathematics, and about astronomy. Writings in the "probable" areas of ethics and politics involved decisions in the field of action. The "art" areas of rhetoric and poetic operated at a lower level of certainty: rhetorical writings were in the area of the plausible, and poetic writings were in the area of the internally probable (the plot and characters had to be internally consistent in the art work). Finally, sophistic writings were in the area of zero or negative probability, the area of the fallacious. But these distinctions were not based only on degrees of probability; they were also based upon different kinds of audiences, different kinds of appeal, different kinds of arrangement, and different styles.

This framework of different kinds of thinking dictating different kinds of audience, appeal, arrangement, and style became the foundation of the liberal arts tradition in Western civilization. The liberal arts were a tradition of thinkings and writings: logic issued in scientific writing, exploration in dialectical writing, persuasion in rhetorical writing, delight in poetic writing, and fallacy in the heterodoxy of the objections of the scholastic method and, later, the antithesis in Hegel's dialectic.

It might be worthwhile to attempt a thumbnail sketch, by means of illustrative examples of each of these kinds of thinking and writing, even at the obvious risk of oversimplification. The risk is even more dangerous because different periods added on, deleted, and interpreted differently some of the basic models.

Scientific Thinking and Writing

Scientific thinking relied heavily on the rules of deduction as outlined in Aristotle's *Prior Analytics* and as practiced by Aristotle in his logical and philosophical treatises, by Euclid, by Archimedes, and by others. It also relied on the validity of inductive generalizations, discussed in the *Poster-*

ior Analytics and practiced by Aristotle in his biological treatises, by Hippocrates, by Galen, and by others.

The "scientific" way of writing was, in Aristotle's case, consciously not stylized with rhetorical or literary ornamentation. It was often esoteric—intended for an elite audience. It was frequently amended, by master or student. It was generally monologual—Aristotle gave up the dialogue as a serious scientific genre. The object of the scientific treatise was to demonstrate something as true.

Dialectical Thinking and Writing

Plato's dialogues were nearly always held up as models of dialectical thinking and writing, and his dialectical progressions from wonder and awe, often of a wrong ideal, through a series of definitions, rejected by counter examples in an elenctic climb from unexamined opinion, through examined opinion, hopefully on to truth, were partially incorporated into future dialectical thinking. Aristotle retained the antagonistic technique of the dialogue in his codification of the rules of dialectic in Book VIII of the *Topics*—the single most important influence on medieval dialectic. The *Topics* also established the many topics or ways of arguing from accident, genus, property, definition, and sameness. The careful logic of scientific deduction and induction were softened into the dialectical enthymeme and example—both operating only at the level of probability.

To these the medieval dialectician added the effective use of the fallacies in rejecting the opponent. The last book of Aristotle's *Organon, On Sophistical Refutations*, was one of the cornerstones of medieval dialectic and the scholastic method.

The usual genre of dialectical thinking in antiquity was the eristic dialogue, both in the Academy and in the Lyceum. This easily passed on into the medieval disputation. But the scholastic method, a dialectical instructment, became the established written genre in later scholasticism—and Aquinas uses it nearly all the time, even in his "scientific" writings. Both in antiquity and in the Middle Ages there was also a persistent genre called problems, or disputed questions. The purpose of the dialectical genres was, theoretically, to explore for the truth. But, both in antiquity and in the Middle Ages, the defeat of the opponent often became as important as or more so than the search for truth. Thus, the element of gamesmanship is always a danger in dialectic.

Rhetorical Thinking and Writing

In one sense it is easier to generalize about rhetorical thinking and writing because of the dominating influence in this tradition of Aristotle's *Rhetoric*—often even for people who disagreed with him.

Rhetorical thinking further diluted deduction and induction into the rhetorical enthymeme and example, and the dialectical topics into the rhetorical topics. But, much more importantly, rhetorical thinking added two critical new dimensions of thought: establishing the credibility of the speaker, and the appeal to the interests and emotions of the audience. Thus the weakened logical proof was buttressed by the ethical and pathetic proofs—as they were called.

To these three types of arguments was added the critically important stylistic dimension in rhetorical thinking and writing. Figures of speech and figures of sound were as important in classical rhetoric as the three proofs. Rhetorical thinking was obviously quite different from both scientific and dialectical.

There are many rhetorical genres, but in antiquity the most studied and practiced were the legal speech, the political speech, and the display speech. To these Christianity added the sermon. In all of these the purpose was to persuade the audience by probable arguments, emotionally and stylistically expressed.

Poetic Thinking and Writing

Throughout the classical period two texts dominate the theory of poetic thinking: Aristotle's *Poetics* and Horace's *Ars Poetica*. Aristotle—and Greek aesthetics generally—emphasized the internal structural consistency of the work of art. The governing rule is a rule of internal probability. "There should be nothing irrational *[alogon]* in the incidents [of the plot] themselves, and if there is an irrationality, it must be outside the tragedy, as in the *Oedipus* of Sophocles," Aristotle says in the *Poetics* (1454b6). Again, he says, "the poet should choose probable impossibilities rather than incredible impossibilities" (1460a26), and, in the same vein, "it is less serious for a painter not to know that a female deer has no horns than to represent one inartistically" (1460b30).

This kind of logic dominates the plot, the treatment of characters, of theme, of scenery, and of style. The artist, then, thinks aesthetically, not scientifically or dialectically or even rhetorically, though the artist may incorporate any of these other kinds of writing into his artistic purpose. The reader of the poem is primarily delighted by the work, though he will also usually be persuaded by its theme.

Horace's *Ars Poetica* fused these two purposes more consciously: "The poet's aim is either to profit or to please, or to blend in one the delightful and the useful" (1.333). But Horace also consistently emphasized the structural unity and formality of the work, although his criteria of formality were undoubtedly more conventional than those of Aristotle.

The prototype of all poetic thinking was, both for Greeks and Romans, Homer. Although Aristotle might prefer the tragedy to the epic, the epic was the dominant genre, followed by the drama in both cultures, with the lyric a clear third.

Sophistic Thinking

Sophistic thinking, as exemplified by Plato in nearly all of his dialogues, and as codified by Aristotle in *On Sophistical Refutations*, was usually incorporated into the dialectical thinking insofar as it became a heuristic for a type of writing. As Grabmann has brilliantly shown, it was the cornerstone of the scholastic method, Anselm of Canterbury's contribution, which, along with the *Sic et Non* oppositions of Abelard and the dialecticians, flowered into the fully developed method as seen in Aquinas (II: 258–340). It involved the invoking of authorities on each side of an issue and then proving one side either fallacious or misinterpreted.

These are the four (or five) kinds of thinking that make up the classical tradition of thinkings and writings that lie behind the liberal arts tradition. Although I have occasionally jumped ahead historically in this sketch, let me now briefly outline the subsequent history of the tradition.

THE MEDIEVAL PERIOD: CHRISTIANITY AND ISLAM

This tradition has been carefully traced by La Drière, McKeon, and Ong. La Drière is particularly interested in the placement of literacy thinking (poetics) in this tradition; McKeon is interested in the medieval treatment of the liberal arts as ways of thinking; and Ong is interested in what was happening to the liberal arts as ways of thinking and writing in the Renaissance and after, especially as they were affected by the new technology of print.

La Drière traces the tradition in the Islamic world, looking at Avicenna and Averröes. Speaking of the latter he says,

> He distinguishes three ranges of probability, and to each assigns a science or art: for the highest, dialectic; for the middle range, rhetoric; for the lowest, not poetic, but "ars augurandi et ars excantandi," the arts of augury and incantation. *Poetica* has somehow got lost in this improbable region, perhaps absorbed by rhetoric, possibly encompassed by enchantments. (146–147)

The vagaries the tradition took in the different authorities of the Middle Ages have been carefully chronicled by McKeon in his important articles, "Rhetoric in the Middle Ages" (1942, esp. 4–21) and "Poetry and

Philosophy in the Middle Ages" (1946, 230 ff.). The distinctions among the various arts are usually maintained, though with quite different meanings often assigned to logic, rhetoric, poetry, and especially dialectic. In careful thinkers like Aquinas and Albert the Great, the Aristotelian distinctions are preserved (see Aquinas, *Summa Theologica*, II–II, Q. 48, c, and his commentary on Aristotle's *Posterior Analytics*, In I Post. Anal. 1).

But, especially in the later Middle Ages, the simplifications of Peter of Spain, a contemporary of Aquinas, paved the way for the partial eclipse of the classical tradition effected by Rudolf Agricola and especially Peter Ramus in the 16th and 17th centuries.

THE RENAISSANCE THROUGH THE 19TH CENTURY

For the continuation of the tradition in the Renaissance La Drière considers Casaubon (1559–1614) because he represents a somewhat unconscious movement in the direction of Ramus, although he still distinguishes the faculty of disputation from grammar, rhetoric, and poetic. But he does not emphasize any separate invention (thinking process) of any of these arts (148–150).

The Ramist Revolution

The revolution of Ramus has been carefully chronicled by many scholars, among them Norman Nelson, Walter J. Ong, and Wilbur Samuel Howell. Ong's *Ramus, Method, and the Decay of Dialogue* bears the following epigraph from Justus Lipsius: "Young man, listen to me: You will never be a great man if you think that Ramus was a great man." Nelson calls him a "bold and clever ignoramus" (1).

But Ramus did effect the basic dislodgement of the long classical tradition I have been detailing. Peter of Spain in the 13th century and Rudolf Agricola in the 16th had prepared the way for Ramus. Ong has documented the massive influence of Peter of Spain on the late medieval period and of both of these authors on the 16th century (57–59, 123–126). Peter of Spain had reduced all argument to dialectic, continually blurring the distinction between certainty and probabilities and the distinctions between different kinds of purposes in discourse (60–62). Agricola continued and acerbated the conflations. As Ong says, speaking of Agricola's *Dialectical Invention*,

> ...dialectic is here taken in a large, loose, and practically undefinable sense to cover the whole field of discourse, in its rational, emotional, and

other elements; it is practically everything that has to do with discourse short of grammatical structure and actual delivery. Indeed, today Agricola's book might well be headed, "What Boys Should Know About Discourse," or better, since it is addressed to teachers rather than to pupils, "Thoughts on Discourse and How to Teach It." (100)

Ramus, following the leads of these two predecessors, cuts the Gordian knot neatly. He is concerned about the repetition he sees in a special invention, arrangement, and style for each of the separate arts (science, dialectic, rhetoric, and poetry). Why not farm out these problems once and for all? Secondly, he is not pleased with Aristotle's distinctions between certainty and different levels of probability. He solves both problems with a master stroke of simplifying:

> But because of these two species, Aristotle wished to make two logics, one for science, and the other for opinion; in which (saving the honor of so great a master) he has very greatly erred. For although articles of knowledge are on the one hand necessary and scientific, and on the other contingent and matters of opinion, so it is nevertheless that as sight is common in viewing all colors, whether permanent or changeable, so the art of knowing, that is to say, dialectic or logic, is one and the same doctrine in respect to perceiving all things, as will be seen by its very parts, as the *Aristotelian Animadversions* explain more fully. (Peter Ramus, *La Dialectique de M. Pierre de La Ramée*, cited in Howell, 154–155).

Talon, Ramus's collaborator in this revolution, explains the other dimension of the coin, the repetition of a special invention, arrangement, and style for each art.

> Peter Ramus cleaned up the theory of invention, arrangement, and memory, and returned these subjects to logic, where they properly belong. Then, assisted indeed by his lectures and opinions, I recalled rhetoric to style and delivery (since these are the only parts proper to it); and I explained it by genus and species, (which method was previously allowed to me); and I illustrated it with examples drawn both from oratory and poetry. (Talon, cited in Howell, 148–149.)

Thus Ramus wrote the logic and Talon the rhetoric for the project. There were effectively one invention system (thought), one arrangement (Ramus's method), and one style for all discourse. Ramus took care of the first two and Talon handled the third.

The influence of Ramus and Talon has been documented by Ong in *Ramus, Method, and the Decay of Dialogue* and in a book published conjointly with it, *Ramus and Talon Inventory*. The combined total of the editions of the *Dialectic* of Ramus and the *Rhetoric* of Talon is 405 between 1543 and 1700 in Europe (Ong, 296). In effect, Ramus and Talon turned the entire classical tradition in a different direction, that of a unitary logic, a unitary arrangement, and a unitary ideal style for all discourse.

Such a program denied the essence of the classical tradition, the pluralism of aims, of audiences, of logics, of arrangements, and of styles. It was attacked on the one side by scientists and philosophers, who showed that the system could not apply to science or philosophy, and on the other by poets and orators, who showed that it did not apply to their work either. Ong devotes a chapter to these attacks and the revisions by which Ramus attempted to patch up his system (214–224). Nevertheless, it had a tremendous influence in northern Europe and England, particularly in the writing of textbooks for adolescents (295–318).

Kant and the Classical Tradition

In contrast to Ramus, Kant kept the basic notion of the classical tradition alive, though with some adjustments. Like Aristotle, he restricted scientific writing to analytic; he analyzed this in his *Critique of Pure Reason*. He used dialectic as the basis for his moral, religious, and psychological thinking in the *Critique of Practical Reason*. And imagination interacting with understanding is the basis for his aesthetic in the *Critique of Judgment*, the intention of which is to "show, for the purposes of his general philosophy, that aesthetic judgments are essentially different from moral judgments on the one hand and scientific judgments on the other" (Walsh, 319). One major difference in this mental profile as compared to Aristotle's, for example, is the comparative neglect of rhetoric.

The neglect of rhetoric as a specific aim of discourse parallel to literature, science, and dialectic was an increasingly common phenomenon in the 17th, 18th, and 19th centuries because of the conflict of rhetoric with science in these centuries.

But rhetoric was not forgotten in the textbooks of the period. The Ramist influence and the decline of the classical tradition can be seen in several tendencies of the popular texts of the 19th century. Alexander Bain's texts were influential both in the British Isles and in America. In Bain, the classical tradition was melded with another facet of the classical tradition that paralleled the liberal arts, the concern over the issue or the stand to take in a given case. The stands were matters of fact, of definition, and of value, and they had been taught as a part of rhetoric in antiquity, in the Middle Ages, and in the Renaissance. In Bain, they emerge as matters of description, narration, exposition, and argumentation. They are conjoined to persuasion and poetry to make what Bain called the forms of discourse. These are an uneasy combination of residues of the classical liberal arts tradition and the status tradition.

Most of the American texts after Bain drop out either persuasion or poetry or both, and eventually the forms of discourse, as they appear in textbooks all through the 20th century, are nearly always the remaining four: narration, description, exposition, and argumentation. The under-lying assumption behind the texts of this tradition—which dominated the teaching of writing in this country and South America for almost a century—is that there is a unitary purpose for writing common to all of these forms. The examples used for imitation in these texts were fairly uniformly drawn from a literary or paraliterary tradition. Thus, there is in John F. Genung's *Outlines of Rhetoric* no hint that there were different aims in writing and therefore different logics. Comparing writing an essay or any formal type of composition to speaking, he says, "The purpose too is the same, namely, to make others see a subject must as the author sees it. . . . If we could always bear this obvious truth in mind. . .composition would cease to be the bugbear that it now too often is" (1).

THE TWENTIETH CENTURY: THE REASSERTION OF DIFFERENT THINKINGS

It was a reaction to the simplistic position of writers like Genung and others of the traditional paradigm, as it has come to be called, that has prompted several vigorous moves since the 1960's to reconsider the clas-sical position. In England, James Britton and his associates consciously discredited the prestige of the forms or modes of discourse and affirmed the primacy of the functions of language: to be expressive, poetic, persua-sive, or informative. The theoretical model they followed was that of Roman Jakobson's functions of language, outlined in an important article, "Linguistics and Poetics," in 1967.

In research going on during this same time period, I had used substan-tially the same model in my attempt to reassert the primacy of aims in studying discourse. In "The Aims of Discourse," I had attempted to show the prevalence of this model in various fields of language study: geneticists, sign theorists, logical positivists, semanticists, the liberal arts tradition, comparative philologists, and structuralists (1971, 51–60). I also devoted considerable space to the specific logic of each aim in four chapters of the book (for reference discourse, 106–150; for persuasive discourse, 236–263; for literary discourse, 343–348; for expressive discourse, 418–423).

Other movements have given more momentum to this current re-affirmation of the different kinds of thinking as they related to writing. Modern hermeneutics has given careful attention to Heidegger's funda-mental distinction between primary "hermeneutic" thinking and language and the secondary derivative "apophantic" thinking and language (Heideg-ger 156–158). Heidegger considers poetry and rhetoric as hermeneutic and science as apophantic.

This hermeneutic distinction is paralleled by a significant movement in modern thinking that could be characterized by the term *informal logic.* Rhetoricians like Chaim Perelman and L. Olbrechts-Tyteca; philosophers like Stephen Toulmin interested in legal reasoning or like Kurt Baier, analyzing ethical reasoning; anthropologists in ethnomethodology like Roy Turner; Marxists like Frederick Pollock, Theodor W. Adorno, and Max Horkheimer, rebelling against the quantification of some political and sociological concepts, as well as those Marxists mentioned earlier in this essay; psychologists like Richard Nisbett and Lee Ross, analyzing social judgments—all these scholars are differentiating between strict scientific deductive or statistical thinking and the informal thinking in different areas of human endeavor.[1]

These contemporary movements are a fresh affirmation of some of the major tenets of the liberal arts tradition in Western thought. Critical thinking is complex and many-sided. It is not enough for us, if we wish to be critical thinkers, to be trained in statistical methodology and axiomatic logic. We must also learn to think dialectically in exploring many topics and in making political and ethical decisions. We must also learn to think aesthetically, both in making our own creations and in appreciating those of others—and statistical or axiomatic models are not of primary importance here. We must also learn to think rhetorically, sometimes to persuade others, sometimes to allow us to be or not be persuaded by others. Finally—and this is the great contribution of 19th-century thought to the liberal arts tradition—each of us has to learn to think expressively; both as individuals and as members of groups we should be able to articulate our aspirations, values, and desires in emotional and intense credos and testimonials and be willing to listen to and appreciate similar expressions from other individuals or groups.

A person who does not have at least a minimal competence in any of these areas is lacking a critical dimension of thought. Such a person is mentally maimed. Let me justify this statement with some example. All of us have undoubtedly met persons who have an acute sense of proof and evidence, who can persuade effectively, and who seem able to articulate their emotions and aspirations maturely when the situation calls for it, but who have almost a childish or adolescent sensitivity to the aesthetic, in almost any medium: language, dance, sculpture, painting, architecture, and so on. Certainly such people have a stunted aesthetic sense, and their mental life is the worse for it, and their whole life the poorer for it. Those of us who are in the field of English or art have strong opinions about aesthetics and can readily recognize this type of impotence. Further, there are many others who have a sense of the aesthetic but whose sense of tragedy is limited to the soap opera, whose sense of humor is satisfied by the television sit-com, and whose sense of music is circumscribed by rock and roll and church hymns.

But consider a different sort of vulnerability. One of the educational conundrums of the 20th century has been the acceptance of Hitler by a German electorate that had been trained in one of the best educational programs on the Continent. Lest we Americans feel superior in this matter, it might be pointed out that careful research shows that Americans today make voting decisions based on brief television newscasts and advertising rather than on meticulous and accurate written or oral presentations. In fact, the very superiority of our technology may be making us persuasively vulnerable. In any case, a society that votes based on 30-second commercials and 5-minute newscasts is, for all practical purposes, politically illiterate, even though its members can read in technical areas, in sports, in hobbies, and so on. By this criterion, many modern societies, including America, may be rhetorically impaired. And such an inaptitude makes a society singularly vulnerable, whether to a persuasive politician like Hitler, or Roosevelt, or Khomeini, or Stalin, or to commercial advertising or to religious propaganda. This type of weakness or inadequacy is probably more important than aesthetic insensitivity. But we don't think much of it.

The third type of insufficiency is the inability to prove or explain a position or the inability to assess intelligently the proofs or explanations of others. This is the usual issue about which conferences on critical thinking concern themselves. Again, modern research (e.g., by Nisbett and Ross) tends to make us cautious in assessing the average citizen's ability to muster or assess valid proof or explanation for an issue, despite the heavy emphasis on such processes in the high school and college curriculum. College graduates, however, seem to have a good evaluative sense in assessing material in their specialty. But there is not evidence that this ability transfers to political or ethical decisions.

In one sense, the final area of impairment may be the most readily recognizable, due to the advances of modern psychoanalysis. People who cannot articulate their own emotions or aspirations, at least to a minimal degree, are identified by modern psychology as pathological. Yet, pedagogically, we have been slow to concede the necessity for such a mental ability—we even hesitate to call it mental. And our liberal arts tradition did not have a provision for this kind of thinking—grammar, rhetoric, and either logic or dialectic meant literature, persuasion, and either science or exploration. There was no provision for self-expression as such. This is the big addition that the Renaissance, with its emphasis on individualism (political, religious, and economic) made to the classical tradition. And it was reinforced by the 18th and 19th centuries from many different perspectives.

Nonetheless, many cultures and subcultures have not accepted this component of liberal arts, which may, ultimately, be the most fundamental of the liberal arts. The liberal arts—if the words mean anything—must

connote the preeminence of the freedom of the individual. And this freedom begins with the freedom of the individual to express his or her emotional and aspirational goals. Thus self-expression undergirds the freedom
implicit in scientific, dialectical, rhetorical, and literary freedom.

Yet our curriculum does not make explicit provision for self-
expression. Self-expression in high schools and colleges occurs indirectly in
free choices of courses and careers, in extracurriculars of all sorts, in clubs
and groups. In one sense, the American student is quite self-expressive.
But, even conceding this comparative judgment, in our own society particularly the male is still often inhibited by an Anglo-Saxon tradition of
emotional restraint that suppresses the outward expression and sometimes
even the inward experience of feelings. For many Americans, our heroes
are the cowboy, the athlete, the soldier, and similar stoic types, exemplified by such actors or characters as John Wayne, Jake Barnes in *The Sun
Also Rises*, or Humphrey Bogart in *Casablanca*. The classical tradition of
scientific, dialectical, rhetorical, and aesthetic thinkings, to which the 19th
and 20th centuries have added self-expression, is a multifaceted and complex system that attempts to meet different mental and emotional needs of
the psyche. Critical thinkings cannot be reduced to just solving problems
in a scientific way, or just analyzing an object or a process. Critical thinkings gear differently for different situations. Critical thinkings embrace the
whole person.

I am not pretending that this amended classical tradition is an exhaustive list of kinds of thought. For example, it does not address the kind of
thinking that makes for an expert mechanic or an expert athlete, to name
just two other kinds of thinkings. But the tradition does refuse to be reduced to a simple monolithic formula.

NOTE

1. Full bibliographic reference for these authors can be obtained in Kinneavy, 1983
(177–178, 202–203).

WORKS CITED

Aquinas, Thomas. *Summa Theologica*. Trans. Fathers of the English Dominican
Province; rev. Rev. Daniel J. Sullivan. Vols. 19–20 of *Great Books of the Wes-
tern World*. Ed. R.M. Hutchins and Mortimer J. Adler. Chicago: Encyclopaedia
Britannica, 1952.
———. *In Libros Posteriorum Analyticorum*. From the Leonine ed., vol. 1, Rome:
1882. Trans. Pierre Conway. Quebec: 1956.

Aristotle. *Nicomachean Ethics.* Trans. W.D. Ross. Vol. 9 of *Great Books of the Western World.* Ed. R.M. Hutchins and Mortimer J. Adler. Chicago: Encyclopaedia Britannica, 1952.

———. *The Works of Aristotle.* Ed. W.D. Ross. *Poetics,* trans. I. Bywater, 1924. *Rhetoric,* trans. W.R. Roberts, 1924. *Topics,* trans. W.A. Pickard-Cambridge, 1928. Oxford: Clarendon Press, 1908–1952.

Bain, Alexander. *English Rhetoric and Composition.* American rev. ed. Boston: D. Appleton, 1867.

Bernstein, Richard J. *Praxis and Action.* Philadelphia: University of Pennsylvania Press, 1971.

Britton, James, et al. *The Development of Writing Abilities.* London: Macmillan Education, 1977.

Genung, John F. *Outlines of Rhetoric.* Boston: Ginn, 1893.

Grabmann, M. *Geschichte der Scholastichen Methode.* Vol 1, 1909; Vol 2, 1911. Darmstadt: Wissenschaftliche Buchgesellschaft, 1957.

Habermas, Jürgen. *Theory and Practice.* Trans. John Viertel. Boston: Beacon Press, 1973.

Heidegger, Martin. *Being and Time.* Trans. John Macquarrie and Edward Robinson. New York: Harper & Row, 1962.

Hobbes, Thomas. *Leviathan: Or, Matter, Form, and Power of a Commonwealth, Ecclesiastical or Civil.* Vol. 23 of *Great Books of the Western World.* Ed. R.M. Hutchins and Mortimer J. Adler. Chicago: Encyclopaedia Britannica, 1952.

Horace. *Satires, Epistles and Ars Poetica.* Trans. H. Rushton Fairclough. Loeb Classical Library. New York: Putnam's, 1932.

Howell, Wilbur Samuel. *Logic and Rhetoric in England, 1500–1700.* New York: Russell & Russell, 1961.

Jakobson, Roman. "Linguistics and Poetics." *Essays on the Language of Literature.* Ed. Seymour Chatman and Samuel R. Levin. Boston: Houghton Mifflin, 1967. 296–322.

Kant, Immanuel. *The Critique of Pure Reason.* Trans. J.M.D. Meiklejohn. *The Critique of Practical Reason.* Trans. Thomas Kingsmill Abbott. *The Critique of Judgment.* Trans. James Creed Meredith. Vol. 42 of *Great Books of the Western World.* Ed. R.M. Hutchins and Mortimer J. Adler. Chicago: Encyclopaedia Britannica, 1952.

Kinneavy, James L. *A Theory of Discourse.* Englewood Cliffs, NJ: Prentice-Hall, 1971.

———. "Contemporary Rhetoric." *The Present State of Scholarship in Historical and Contemporary Rhetoric.* Ed. Winifred Bryan Horner. Columbia: University of Missouri Press, 1983. 167–213.

La Drière, J. Craig. "Rhetoric and 'Merely Verbal' Art." *English Institute Essays, 1948.* Ed. D.A. Robertson, Jr. New York: Columbia University Press, 1949. 134–152.

Lobkowicz N., ed. *Theory and Practice: History of a Concept from Aristotle to Marx.* South Bend, IN: University of Notre Dame Press, 1967.

McKeon, Richard. "Rhetoric in the Middle Ages." *Speculum* 17 (1942): 1–32.

———. "Poetry and Philosophy in the Twelfth Century: The Renassance of Rhetoric." *Modern Philology* 43 (1946): 217–234.

Nelson, Norman. *Peter Ramus and the Confusion of Logic, Rhetoric, and Poetry.* Ann Arbor: University of Michigan Press, 1947.

Nisbett, Richard E. and Lee Ross. *Human Inference, Strategies and Shortcomings of Social Judgment.* Englewood Cliffs, NJ: Prentice-Hall, 1980.

Ong, Walter J. *Ramus and Talon Inventory.* Cambridge: Harvard University Press, 1958.

———. *Ramus, Method, and the Decay of Dialogue.* New York: Farrar, Strauss, and Giroux, 1974.

Plato. *Gorgias. Ion. Phaedrus.* Trans. Benjamin Jowett. Vol. 7 of *Great Books of the Western World.* Ed. R.M. Hutchins and Mortimer J. Adler. Chicago Encyclopaedia Britannica, 1952.

Ramus, Peter. *La dialectique de M. Pierre de La Ramée.* Paris: Andre Wechel, 1955.

Sartre, Jean-Paul. *La critique de la raison dialectique.* Paris: Gallimard, 1960.

Talon, Omer, *Petri Rami Professoris Regii, & Audomari Talaei Collectaneae Praefationes, Epistolae, Orationes.* Marburg, 1599.

Walsh, W.H. "Kant, Immanuel." *The Encyclopedia of Philosophy.* Ed. Paul Edwards. New York: Macmillan, 1967. 4: 305–324.

CHAPTER 10

Taking Thought: The Role of Conscious Processing in the Making of Meaning

Linda Flower

> *Why take ye thought for raiment? Consider*
> *the lilies of the field, how they grow;*
> *they toil not, neither do they spin.*
> *Matthew 6.28*

It may seem ironic that anyone in higher education would bother to question the usefulness of conscious, reflective thought. Yet there is a strong tradition in philosophy, in romantic literary theory, and in modern psychology that does just that. If, as this tradition suggests, the wellsprings of insight, creativity, and mental energy lie in nonrational and unconscious processes, where is the necessity, or even the value, of conscious thought? This question seems especially relevant to the study of writing since writing is both a creative, expressive act and the output of an individual's highly automated skills of language production. After all, the writers we study, who are college age and beyond, have been speaking with language for at least 16 years and writing for 10. Furthermore, composing goes on all the time without the necessity of "taking thought"—that is, without recourse to explicit knowledge, without conscious control of the processes, without a reflective awareness of one's own thought.

In one sense, consciousness is an optional feature of thinking, a level of heightened awareness at which writers can choose to operate. Writing can be conducted, it seems, at many levels of awareness, including the shadowy, opium trance in which Coleridge said he wrote "Kubla Khan" and in the deep immersion in the topic that characterizes children's knowledge telling—in which all attention is riveted to the production of language and content. In adult writers, we begin to see an increasing awareness of plans, goals, and criteria, a conscious sense of options and alternatives, and, at times, a reflective awareness of the thinking process itself.

However, writers must pay a price for taking thought. As the level of conscious awareness increases, the writer's limited attention is diverted from the production of content and is increasingly devoted to the creation of these goals, plans, and criteria and to the acts of monitoring, evaluation, or reflection. Writing is a social, expressive, language-making act. What role does the act of "taking thought" play in this process? Put pragmatically, what is conscious thought good for?

THE ROLE OF CONSCIOUS PROCESSING

For Learners Only

One response to this question is that attention-grabbing conscious processes are inefficient processes, suitable for learners only. As William James put it, "The more of the details of our daily life we can hand over to the effortless custody of automatism, the more our higher powers of mind will be set free for their own proper work" (140–141).

The automated processes we develop with experience are fast, they operate in parallel with one another, they are not limited by short-term memory, and they demand little effort or control. They account for the difference between simply *knowing* how to spell a word and having to sound it out or to remember the rule "i" before "e" except after "c".

Monitor theory in second language learning (Krashen) levels a stronger criticism against conscious knowledge, arguing for the value of naturally "acquired" linguistic competence over "learned" knowledge on the grounds that such learned knowledge can only function as a conscious Monitor. Such knowledge interrupts production to monitor correctness, to test, and to apply rules. Monitor overusers are unlikely to achieve fluency in a second language. We should note, however, that the data that support Monitor theory are limited to showing how the conscious application of grammatical rules can inhibit fluent language production in students learning a second language. As we will discuss later, this criticism of conscious processing must be highly qualified when we turn to the more complex process of composing, where language production is only one thread on the loom.

For the Skilled

From another perspective, conscious processing is the special prerogative of the skilled. In the development of knowledge, cognitive action based on automatic, unconscious acquisition gradually yields to conscious control

(Vygotsky). Metacognition—awareness of and conscious control of one's own cognitive processes—is a late developing and slowly won power that is related to skill in reading and problem solving (Brown). In our example of the speller, conscious awareness is what allows the writer to know she doesn't in fact know the correct spelling, to deliberately consider alternatives, or to try to remember a rule or a Latin root that might help.

For Decoration

The Freudian tradition offers a third perspecitve. Just as the reasons offered by patients may be only tangential to their real emotional drives, conscious thought can be seen as a spurious play over the surface of deeper, unconscious processes inaccessible to the rational mind. In some ways, this perspective has muddied the issue considerably, since it often assumes that conscious thought is necessarily rational thought and tends to define inspiration and imagination as unconscious processes. This response is essentially a value judgment in the form of a definition. Unconscious thought is characterized as deep (inaccessible to reflection), profound (important and insightful), and creative. Conscious thought is shallow (a surface epiphenomenon, perhaps a rationalization of deeper unconscious processes) and limited (capable of merely rational, logical and noncreative processes).

Clearly this characterization of unconscious processes has given us insight into that strange tango in which emotion can lead our thought. But it is not adequate as a theory of creativity of meaning making. It does little to explain the moment-to-moment, effortful activity of normal thinking, reading, and writing or to account for the struggles of learners. Lowes's work on Coleridge to some extent redeems consciousness by translating the story of the genesis of "Kubla Khan" from a moment of mythic possession in a dream to an extended cognitive adventure story. In Coleridge's telling of the tale of how the poem was composed, the hero is the looming mythic figure of the unconscious, a demanding and possessing power that comes and goes at its own inscrutable will. In Lowes's account of Coleridge's extensive reading, drafts, and synthesis, the hero of the piece is Coleridge the thinker. His genius seems even more impressive when we glimpse its underlying process; nevertheless, as both clinical and cognitive psychology make clear, many important processes go on without the thinker's explicit awareness of those processes.

Consciousness Is for Managing Complex Problems

A fourth answer, which I will explore in this essay, is that consciousness is for managing complex problems. Conscious thought, I will argue, is not different in *kind* (i.e., we can't conveniently pigeonhole all thought as either conscious or unconscious). Rather, it represents a certain level of awareness at which a process can be carried out, on a spectrum that runs from immutable inaccessible processes, to automated ones, to ones that enter conscious attention, on up to those guided by meta-awareness. Moreover, the evidence suggests that experienced writers rise to the heightened awareness of conscious problem solving in interesting ways as they attempt to make meaning—and in ways that novice writers do not.

In understanding the role of consciousness in writing it is important first to acknowledge the advantage of nonconscious processes (if they can do the job) and the importance of mental activity of which we aren't aware. Conscious processes are only a part of the performance, yet they appear to play a very important role in the process of experts, for whom we might suppose they would be less necessary. We can see this role more clearly if we look at conscious thought as a level of processing in which writers can choose, at certain times, to engage, and if we ask the question, Why do they make this choice?

One approach to understanding thought, which we have already seen, is to categorize the knowledge itself as tacit or explicit, learned or acquired, conscious or unconscious, and then—in some cases—to argue for the value of one kind of knowledge over the other. Mandel for instance, locates creativity in unconscious knowing: "Writing is occurring, there is no one at home thinking about it—at least not during the process itself" (372). Krashen argues for the virtues of naturally "acquired" language skills and the limited utility of "learned" rules. And yet can knowledge be so easily pigeonholed as one kind or another? Experience shows us that the conscious knowledge novices struggle to learn and labor to use (e.g., how to spell hard words or write a newspaper lead) can later become so well learned that its use is automated. They are able to use this automated knowledge without conscious attention to it. How they acquired the knowledge becomes immaterial in comparison to how they use it. Research has also shown that the efficient, tacit knowledge of experienced business writers can be brought back to awareness and made explicit if they are asked to make choices or decisions about features of their text (Odell and Goswami). Even the profession of psychotherapy is based, finally, on the premise that unconscious motivations can with effort be made conscious.

In understanding writers, we think it will be more fruitful to concentrate not on knowledge as an artifact packaged in one form or another but on the act of thinking. From this perspective, consciousness becomes an optional action, rather than a kind of knowledge. Conscious awareness is a feature of a thinker's processing system, not of the knowledge itself. It is a mode of thought or a level of awareness at which information can be considered, worked over, altered, and/or applied to the task at hand.

Thinkers, it follows, can work at various levels of awareness—each of which has unique advantages and limitations. Let us consider some of these.

Tacit Processes. Some processes, including memory search, perception, complexly coordinated motor processes such as a tennis swing, and even some value judgments appear to be largely or completely tacit: The process of judgment, search, and so on is unavailable to introspection (Nisbett and Wilson) and resistant to conscious control. Much of the writer's language production process—Krashen's "acquired" knowledge of grammar, vocabulary, and acceptable locution—operates in this blessedly tacit manner. Native speakers, like the lilies of the field, can do many things for which they are required to take no thought.

Automated Processes. Some processes start life as conscious, attention-grabbing processes, but with experience they slowly drop out of awareness, and we say they have become automated. "Practice makes perfect" because it gradually transfers much of the task over to highly efficient, automated procedures. As the writer learns to "sound like Samuel Johnson," the process of writing long parallel constructions or maintaining a formal style consumes less and less of the limited space available in short-term memory (or conscious attention). However, if a sentence becomes too long, this automated "parellelism producer" may hit its limits and force this task to be shifted up to conscious attention or to be ignored. We would expect to see this sort of fluent production and limited conscious attention in the performance of anyone doing an easy or a well-learned task. Ironically it may also characterize the level of awareness some inexperienced writers maintain even when the task is beyond their current well-learned skills.

When writers work at this level of awareness, their attention can be concentrated almost entirely on maintaining the flow of content. The simple knowledge-telling strategy of young writers allows them to maintain both flow and topical coherence with only minimal demands on their attention and in turn to devote all of their resources to the problems of finding and expressing new content (Scardamalia and Bereiter 1986).

Evidence of automated processes is usually indirect: one observes experienced writers doing difficult things with apparent speed and ease. On questioning or cued recall, one finds that even simple decisions, such as the form of personal address in a business letter, are made on the basis of a rich knowledge of the situation (Odell and Goswami). However, it seems likely that the more well-learned these procedures are, the harder they will be to recall. Inexperienced writers with partially automated skills may often be better informants about some complex processes.

In general, automated processes are the rewards of learning—they let the writer learn to do more with less effort and less attention. However, most complex writing tasks cannot be managed at this level of attention, except by the easy but inefficient process of generate and test.

Active Awareness/Rhetorical Problem Solving. When a writer is engaged in fast, fluent production, her active awareness is occupied with content information and the language of her discourse. The act of composing is guided by automated processes. But if a problem arises or automated processes are unavailable, the work of writing is shifted to conscious attention. As the writer enters into active rhetorical problem solving her attention is no longer devoted solely to the generation of content, but becomes engaged in the process of drawing inferences, setting goals, making plans, analyzing the reader, simulating a reader's response, evaluating not only the text produced so far, but also the plans and goals that are in place, and diagnosing problems. And to complete the circle, the writer may go from the detection and diagnosis of a problem back to fresh planning. All this complex activity can go on with vigor and rapidity—as thinking-aloud protocols show—even though the writer may only dimly recollect all these decisions after the fact.

This shift to active awareness is itself a decision. For example, when the automated attempt to produce a complex parallel structure runs amuck, the writer can either ignore the problem and accept whatever comes, initiate a series of generate and test efforts, or rise to active awareness. At this level she might notice that the text isn't working, maybe diagnose the problem as parallelism and isolate the offending words, or perhaps step back even further and wonder if the ideas themselves were logically parallel. If this were a major introductory sentence, this diagnosis might lead to a whole new episode of text-level planning.

One test for conscious awareness is how much interference the thinker can brook and still do the task. We can carry on two highly automated procedures, such as walking and talking, at the same time, but listening to two conversations, which requires more conscious attention, is hard. Most writing tasks seem to involve both kinds of processing simultaneously—I am not suggesting people operate at one level or the other. In fact, many writing decisions seem to be made in that twilight zone of marginal active awareness. However, experienced writers are far more likely to shift up to and to manage their composing process at the higher levels of active awareness than are novices (Flower and Hayes 1981).

The most direct evidence for such active conscious processing comes from thinking-aloud protocols of the sort discussed later in Box 10.1. Thinking-aloud protocols are a widely used tool in process-tracing research in cognitive psychology. Subjects who are thinking through a problem—such as planning a chess move, doing a decision-making task, or writing an essay—are asked to think aloud *as they work*. They are *not* asked to *comment on* the process, but to simply verbalize the content of their conscious thought as they work. Transcripts of these thinking-aloud protocols have given us a new, if naturally incomplete, window on the rich activity of the writing process. They show writers to be actively engaged not only in generating ideas and text but in goal setting, planning, evaluating and in monitoring and guiding their own process. However, protocols also show that much of this active awareness is suprisingly fleeting. People appear to do a good deal more conscious consideration than they remember having done after the fact.

There are a number of possible explanations for the fragility of this recollection. Such thinking may require only an instant or two of attention; the thinker may be only *marginally* aware, devoting but limited resources to a decision, and finally, once a goal has been acted upon, the thinker may simply clear the slate, so to speak, and forget both the intention and the action that got him there. (This latter phenomenon is known as the Zeigarnik effect.) Whatever the reason, it is important to distinguish the rich array of thinking processes that go on in writers' active awareness during composing, from the far more limited and synthesized accounts found in people's retrospective reports.

Reflective Awareness. This fleeting awareness is, of course, not always the case. Writers can also choose to rise to what we might call a reflective awareness or meta-knowledge of their own process. Even greater conscious attention is demanded as the writer tries to consider not only the task but herself performing the task.

Although active problem solving and reflective awareness of that problem solving are often discussed within the general notion of meta-cognition (Brown), I am drawing a distinction here in order to highlight the *thinker's own level of active awareness*, since heightened awareness appears to be the fast lane to learning from experience. When writers take a reflective, "rise above it strategy" (Scardamalia and Bereiter, 1985), they may choose to categorize and evaluate the approach they are taking, or to evaluate and reflect upon their own behavior. Evidence for this level of awareness appears in thinking-aloud protocols. It also appears in more elaborated form in interviews and retrospective accounts, although in such cases it is often hard to distinguish an after-the-fact interpretation from awareness that actually guided the process as it occurred.

This level of knowing has an interesting status. Researchers such as Brown and Scardamalia and Bereiter (1986) have made a strong case for meta-knowledge as a skilled processing strategy, one that offers writers far more control and more options. Composition theorists associated with the "new rhetoric" and textbooks that reflect this perspective (Young; Young,

Becker, and Pike; Hairston; Lauer, Montague, Lunsford, and Emig; Flower 1985) emphasize teaching not only heuristics for managing the writing process but a new degree of self-consciousness about using those methods. On the other hand, meta-knowledge and introspection have had an interestingly checkered career as research tools. As Nisbett and Wilson have shown, subjects are easily led into "Telling More than We Can Know," giving rationalizations in their effort to account for their own behavior and decisions, many of which were carried out by tacit processes or based on cues of which the subject was not aware. The most unreliable reports are in fact those reports which interviews typically elicit—people's accounts of "why" they acted in the way they did. Thinking-aloud protocols (when correctly collected) tap a different body of knowledge (Ericsson and Simon; Hayes and Flower). They are a detailed (and unsifted) record of concurrent processes; they capture that information which is continually shifting in and out of the writer's focal attention (which can be quite different from a digested, after-the-fact interpretation). They record the writer's reflections and meta-comments only when, in the process of composing, the writer shifts attention from managing the task at hand to reflecting on his or her own process. As a research tool, then, this meta-knowledge seems most reliable when it is combined with process evidence for what the writer actually did.

The limitations of working at the higher levels of active awareness are obvious: the writer's limited attention is momentarily diverted from the ultimate goal of generating content and is channeled into the less immediately "productive" process of thinking *about* the task and about the process of doing the task. On the other hand, taking thought may in the long run be the best or even the only way to solve some problems. Writers, we would argue, work at all of these levels of awareness, from fully tacit to highly reflective thought, and they do so because each level serves special purposes. Working at the lower levels of awareness is more efficient (when it is possible) and more productive in terms of generating topical content and language. Shifting to active awareness is a problem-solving procedure in which the difficulty of the problem seems to justify the use of this more expensive level of operation.

Active Awareness and the Skilled Writer

If rising to active rhetorical problem solving is an expensive but powerful option, how do expert writers use it? Research that traces cognitive processes in writing points to some distinctive features of the expert process.

1. Experts shift into sustained, active awareness when the problem demands it. The expert writer appears to spend no more time working at the level of reflective awareness or problem solving than necessary. On

familiar or easy tasks we can expect to see high fluency, little planning, and less evaluation—just the sort of streamlined process Janet Emig saw her skilled high school student use to whip out a five-paragraph theme. However, the mark of an expert writer skilled across domains is the habit of shifting levels from text generation to problem solving as the task demands it. The skilled writer shifts to active awareness to examine problems, to plan around them, and to control, monitor, and even learn from his or her own process in doing so.

The writing college students and other adults do appear to present such complex problems with great regularity. Experts, unlike novices, rise to extended problem solving as they explore a new rhetorical problem and develop their representation of the task. The social science experts studied by Voss, Greene, Post, and Penner built complex task representations by actively searching for constraints on the task and by testing potential solutions against new constraints. Likewise, the expert writers in Flower, Schriver, Carey, Haas, and Hayes built integrated networks of goals, plans, and criteria as they worked through the task. In revision, we see the same difference: when experts encounter global problems in the text, they attempt to diagnose the problem and often turn to extended periods of problem solving that involve categorizing the problem, paraphrasing, reviewing goals, stating a gist, and generating and evaluating possible solutions (Flower, Carey, Hayes).

2. A second feature of the expert process I will turn to in the second half of this essay is the way in which experts flexibly shift among various ways of representing knowledge. Unlike novice writers, who leap into text production with little planning, and unlike novice revisers, who leap from detecting a problem into deleting the offending bit or into producing new text on the spot, experts do not limit themselves to producing and altering potential text—they think and work with other representations of meaning. As experts write they generate plans, goals, subgoals, and criteria; they rise to statements of their "gist" or point, in some cases forging a gist with difficulty out of the flow of thought or the confusion of a first draft; and finally, in rising to reflective awareness they generate what we might call meta-goals and diagnoses of their own processes. In the remainder of this essay I will examine this second feature of expert thought in more detail.

WRITING, COGNITION, AND THE MAKING OF MEANING

Current work in composition and an even longer tradition in rhetoric asserts writing is a generative act—a process of not just "expressing" but "making" meaning. But it is sometimes hard to make good on our claims about invention and discovery to the skeptical student who replies, "I know what I mean; I just can't express it." How should we answer the student's rival hypothesis, which holds that writing is only a transcription of the known? Can we accurately describe just what it is that people discover or make when they turn to writing?

One answer, born of romantic theories of creativity and inspiration, is that writing leads to "eureka!" experiences—the discovery of shocking new insights or even the reversal of old ideas. Such acts of meaning making are dramatic but rather rare. They won't justify mounting 150 sections of freshman composition every term.

An answer at another extreme is that all language production is creative—every lexical decision (I could have chosen to say "word choice" or "linguistic option") reflects a change in meaning. This shades-of-meaning vision of writing is often quite persuasive when applied to literary works that achieve complexity through ambiguity and resonance. And kaleidoscopic shades of meaning can indeed be found in all expository writing, from students' papers to scientific reports. However, most of these differences are going to seem trivial to most writers and readers. Defining discovery in terms of lexical choice is unlikely to convince our skeptical student or the skeptic in ourselves that writing can be both a normal (rather than rare) process and a powerfully generative process. We need to show, in more operational detail, how composing helps writers build significant new cognitive representations of meaning.

In "Images, Plans, and Prose: The Representation of Meaning in Writing," John R. Hayes and I proposed a descriptive account of writers' knowledge and how it is altered, under the name of the "multiple representation thesis." This descriptive theory may offer a partial answer to our question. The multiple representation thesis is based on four observations drawn from our own data and from other research in rhetoric and psychology. It begins with a definition: *Planning in writing is an act of cognition in which writers create an internal, mental, representation of their meaning.* In the act of planning writers do a number of things: they generate information (either by retrieving it from long-term memory or books or by drawing inferences and generating new ideas); they organize and structure this information in meaningful ways; and they also generate goals and criteria, which form an additional part of their "meaning." Our first observation about the process of building a mental representation is as follows:

1. Writers represent their meaning (or current knowledge) in a variety of symbolic ways.

These mental representations may involve visual imagery, abstract, partly verbalized schemas, concepts, propositions (in the linguistic sense, in which arguments and predicates exist without specific lexical instantiations), metaphors, verbal fragments, and finally, fully formed prose. Our point is not to create an exhaustive taxonomy but to recognize that writers think with multiple, alternative representations of their meaning—they are not limited to the medium of prose or even of words.

2. These mental representations differ in the amount of linguistic information they contain.

From the writer's point of view this is an important observation since the writer's necessary goal is prose. However, an imagistic representation typically lacks information on matters such as syntax and spelling or even on appropriate verbal categories. Consider the brief story followed by excerpts from Robbins, Bruun, and Zim's field guide to *Birds of North America*, in Figure 10.1.

In the experience described in Figure 10.1, much of the writer/thinker's knowledge is decidedly non-verbal: the shape of the bird and its wingspan, the arc and sound of its flight, the cry described as a scream, the feeling of tension in the viewer's own muscles, the shock running down the back stimulated by feelings of both fear and elation. A writer trying to make sense of this event or even describe what she saw will find that much of what she "knows" is not verbal. Even when it has been verbalized, the simultaneous nature of the experience may resist a standard linear, linguistic expression. The writer must translate a variety of internal, mental representations into their "best analogue" in prose. (And sometimes even the "best" is approximate; there is no simple one-to-one translation for many kinds of information. The Greeks may have had a word for it, but we often find we don't.)

Writers face this problem all the time. Field guides are a particularly good example because the authors must struggle with turning perceptual, taxonomic, and statistical information into a book adapted to the needs of readers in the field. In their guide, Robbins, Bruun, and Zim used a combination of a verbal representation and two visual ones, a painting and a silhouette. Notice how each of these representations is particularly good at capturing certain features of the phenomenon. The silhouettes show comparative shape, mass, aned postures; the paintings capture color, pattern, and age, sex and seasonal differences. In fact, there is some controversy among field guides over whether one should use paintings, photographs, or drawings. The needs of the reader—who may be trying to distinguish one shape flitting through the twilight from another—impose another constraint on the representation. They dictate an emphasis on comparative information and "field marks," even though other features of the bird might be far more salient or interesting to the naturalists, Robbins, Bruun, and Zim. In other words, "knowing birds" does not mean one can *write* about birds or write a field guide with a representation *readers* can use.

Finally, as this guide makes clear, writers/thinkers use multiple repre-

The Experience

You are walking through an open pine woods in Wyoming when above and behind you, you hear a faint, high scream that turns into a distant shape with spread wings diving through the trees in your direction. As the hawk pulls up, you see a nest in a tall lodgepole pine and a second hawk coming toward you from the right with a similarly wonderful but ominous cry. You decide it would be wise to move on. Back at home, with the help of your field guide, you find a name for this apparition, so you can now talk about seeing a red-tailed hawk, and you infer that there was a pair guarding a nest and that they were, indeed, speaking to you.

Representations of Birds from a Field Guide

(a) Verbal Description: A well-known and common buteo [note the author's use of the Latin genus name for hawk]; nests in woodlands and feeds in open country. The uniformly colored tail of the adult—reddish above, light pink beneath—and the dark belly band are the best field marks. . . . Body is heavier than other buteos', plumage extremely variable. Flying head-on, light wrist area gives impression of a pair of "headlights." Often perches on poles or treetops, rarely hovers.

(b) Visual Representation: Painting

(c) Visual Representation: Silhouette

(d) Verbal Description of Sound: "Call is a high scream, often imitated by jays."

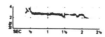

(e) Visual Representation of Sound: Sonogram of red-tailed hawk

Figure 10.1 Alternative Representations of Knowledge (From *Birds of North America* by C. Robbins, B. Bruun, and H. Zim, illustrated by A. Singer. New York: Golden Press, 1966. Reprinted by permission of Western Publishing, Inc.

sentations because different ways of "knowing" or representing meaning are best for different purposes. How does one capture a meaningful, expressive sound? The squiggles and smudges of the sonograms in *Birds of North America* (Figure 10.1e) are a heroic attempt to turn that sharp cry that cuts across the valley out of the trees into visual, conceptual, and mathematical representation. The written description (Figure 10.1d) simply puts a conventional verbal label on the sound—apparently you needed to be there.

The range of possible representations writers generate during planning varies in yet another important way.

3. Linguistic representations themselves also vary in the prose constraints they entertain.

Were we to observe a writer planning, producing text, and revising, we would see further variety within her verbal and linguistic representations. Some would display all the special constraints we associate with polished prose, such as standard spelling, correct grammar, precise diction, the felicities of usage and style, and the fine rhythms and logical crescendo that the periodic sentence can produce. Other representations would not entertain such constraints, though each would have its own power. The writer's mental representations might entail a body of written (or mental) notes, fragments, key words and/or sentences produced by the goal-directed process of brainstorming, or as a result of freewriting, they might emerge as a verbal stream of thought linked by local associations. The freewriter's representation would probably contain more of the syntactic and lexical features of prose but less information about rhetorical or logical structure than that of the brainstorming planner. We might also see our writer representing her meaning as a topic outline (a simple ordered list of topic names) or more complexly in the form of organizing concepts or gists or topic statements. (These latter representations are often more difficult to generate than an outline because they typically do the hard job of restructuring information around the writer's purpose). Finally, we might see drafts and fragments in which the writer had begun to entertain the added constraints of local logical and syntactic relations, word choice at all levels of the sentence, spelling, grammar, and so on.

With the Multiple Representation Thesis we attempted to describe some of the dramatically different representations that are the stuff of planning in the writer's mind. We did not suggest that a prose representation is necessarily "better" for all purposes (cf. Olson). However, when we look at alternative linguistic representations, we can see that as a writer moves closer to prose, new information—information that did not exist in another representation—is being added to the writer's mental representation of meaning. To write, the thinker is often transforming a body of topic knowledge into a new structure dictated by her rhetorical goals and in many cases transforming blissfully inarticulate intutions into a more precisely detailed network of information. To do this she is probably drawing inferences and creating connections that she did not before possess. The map of her knowledge, like the propositional networks drawn by linguists, is in essence taking a new shape and receiving new "named" links and conceptual nodes. Such prose representations are typically instantiations of more abstract representation, to be sure. But given the wealth of possible instantiations most rhetorical goals and complex concepts allow, two writers watching the flight of the same hawk might offer us two representations with substantial qualitative and quantitative differences in the information they contained. The fourth point of the multiple representation thesis acknowledges this reality.

4. Writers must typically translate meaning—held in various forms—into the demanding and highly constrained medium of formal prose. This necessity is both a source of difficulty in the composing process and evidence of the writer's skill.

Two common examples will illustrate. The mental representation of the student who "knows its but can't express it" may be perfectly adapted to some uses, but it lacks the information (whether that be concepts, lexical items, or precise logical or syntactic links) that prose requires. And it may not be well adapted to conducting sustained inquiry and analysis. Creating a prose representation may mean that the writer has to generate a substantial body of new information, including not just words for things, but new inferences, concepts, relations, and a meaningful structure for the lot. Ironically, experts on a topic, who have already developed a store of concepts and well-articulated ideas, may be less likely to face this daunting re-representation process than will a freshman in a typical composition class who is asked to write about a complex, previously unarticulated personal experience. Because the process of representing one's knowledge in prose can involve the quite literal creation of new information or meaning, we can see how writing is a more creative force than the shades-of-lexical-meaning argument mentioned earlier was able to support. And we can see why this creativity is far more "normal" than the eureka theories would suggest.

Signs of a writer's ability to represent and re-represent are often evident in the way the special properties of prose are exploited and adapted to the writer's rhetorical purpose or to the reader's needs. In the excerpt below, two writers are describing a windhover. One, Gerard Manley Hopkins (66), uses the resources of poetic discourse to capture both the physical sensation, the emotional resonance, and the symbolic meanings of the bird's flight.

I caught this morning morning's minion, kingdom of daylight's dauphin,
dapple-dawn-drawn Falcon, in his riding
Of the rolling level underneath him steady air

Although the other writer, Hausman (205), uses imagery and analogy too, his technique is in the service of different goals—the creation of useful and explicit field notes. Comparing these two descriptions reminds us that a writer's representation is both a highly selected, created entity and a strategic one.

Often hovers over a field some fifty feet or so high, perfectly motionless except for its beating wings—appearing to be suspended from the sky by an invisible wire.

Strategies for Making Meaning

How do writers go about the process of constructing these representations? The following excerpt from a thinking-aloud protocol illustrates some important features of the way meaning making operates and some of the strategies experienced writers use. Even though many parts of this writer's process are automated and some are inscrutable, a great deal of her process is taken up by purposeful cognitive action. The writer is a college junior, composing an application for a summer fellowship for student writers. At the point in composing at which we enter, she had just created a general plan to convince the judges that "the way to learn is doing." The episode in Box 10.1 illuminates some of the ways this process of meaning making operates. Let me note as preface that this excerpt was designed to work as an illustrative example in teaching (Flower 1985), and I present it here for the same purposes of illustration. The actual protocol data and actual process of this writer were both richer and messier and far longer. In order to illuminate certain strategies relevant to our discussion, I have chosen to eliminate other features and have made her exploratory rambles look deceptively streamlined. Although writers like Monci are constantly rising to moments of heightened awareness and problem solving, like blips on an active radar screen, such cognition often goes on against a rich background of memory searching, idea shaping, and language play.

Moving Among Representations. In the 20 lines of this protocol, the writer appears to draw on a variety of mental representations of meaning other than standard edited prose (or even proto-prose). In line 4, for instance, the writer refers wryly in passing to a schema she knows well—the starving/ deserving artist schema. The fleeting reference to this schema works as a pointer to an organized body of knowledge that she could, if she chose,

BOX 10.1
Excerpt from the Monci Thinking-Aloud Protocol

1. *Um...and so maybe as a writer I don't need* (**D1**)*...to go to classes and have to hack out stuff that won't help me in any development as a writer.* (Generating ideas)

2. *What do I need...*

3. *I'm just thinking that that's the angle that's coming out.* (Monitoring and evaluating ideas)

4. *That um...it's the same old story about I am an artist so help me, feed me, pay me money so I can create and work.* (Laughs) (Drawing an inference and evaluating)

5. *I think. Umm...*

6. *What do I need to say?...*(Sets goal). *I need to be allowed to develop on my own and to go.* (**D2**) (Writes text)

7. *For some reason, right when I started to write "develop on my own" I thought of Star Trek.*

8. *The Star Trek Convention just popped into my head.* (Making associations)

9. *And um...that reminds me that one of the things I am interested in is...finding out exactly why stuff like that pops into your head.* (Generating ideas)

10. *I'm thinking this is a good idea.* (Monitoring process)

11. *And I should get it down.* (Setting a process goal)

12. *What are the cues that stimulate a person to remember something?* (Generating ideas)

13. *How can I put this for those ladies in the pink hats?* (Setting a goal)

14. *Ladies' Club women, want to give a scholarship...*(Analyzing audience)

15. *O.K., the point is I want to learn as a writer how to go looking for those cues in the right place.* (**D3**) (Writing trial text)

16. *How does that fit in?* (Evaluating and trying to organize ideas)

17. *Let's see. Well, that's a kind of creativity.*

18. *And you sure have to create that one on your own.* (Drawing an inference; generating ideas)

19. *Maybe I should emphasize that instead.* (Diagnosing and setting a goal) *Like all writers I need to learn to find those cues on my own.* (**D4**) (Revising text)

20. *O.K., now where am I?*

"Transcript of a Writer Thinking Aloud." From *Problem-Solving Strategies for Writing*, second edition, by Linda Flower, copyright © 1985 by Harcourt Brace Jovanovich, Inc. Reprinted by permission of the publisher.

unpack and consider. That is, she might choose to open the package and devote her attention to reviewing the contents of her mental schema. Instead she uses the schema to swiftly categorize her current thinking while she maintains her focus on the task.

Line 7 lets us infer the presence of another form of representation—an episodic memory of an event, in this case of the Star Trek Convention, which the writer had recently attended. Such knowledge is typically vivid, represented by images, feelings, and remembered episodes of conversation and action. It is typically not represented in memory by nicely formed propositions and, for all its vividness, can be difficult for a writer to translate into prose. (Consider, for instance, the relative difficulty of merely recalling how you responded to a recent film, compared to the task of describing your response in an essay, compared to the task of articulating the "meaning" of the experience—even though all are representations of your "knowledge" of the event.) The Star Trek episode in our example is interesting for the different kinds of representations it appears to involve. The episode begins with a personal association (of some sort) which triggers a *memory of the event*, from which the writer pops up to *meta-awareness* of her own process in which things "pop into your head," which leads her to a *verbal proposition* about that process, which she eventually transforms into a *sentence* she can use in her draft. In following even this single train of thought, we can see the writer moving among various ways of representing her knowledge and developing meaning.

Building a Network of Meaning. In the process of planning, writers not only generate content structures (hierarchical or associative structures of topical information and actual text), they generate a body of goals, plans, and criteria—a network of Working Goals. The Working Goal Networks of experienced writers are typically more elaborated and more highly integrated structures than those of novices (Flower, Schriver, Carey, Haas, and Hayes). If we plot the writer's knowledge as a propositional network of these goals, plans, and criteria, we can see how writing adds new nodes and new connections to the writer's representation of the meaning on this unique structure. Figure 10.2 shows the Working Goal Network we can infer from the Monci protocol, in which goals, plans, and the criteria generated by acts of evaluation are treated as nodes. Draft sentences are noted within brackets on the network at the point at which they were written.

The Monci protocol illustrates at least three ways writers add information to this network: by adding superordinate categories, concepts, and gists; by adding new nodes or inferences that link ideas; and by restructuring knowledge in answer to a rhetorical purpose. When Monci evaluates draft sentence 1 [D1], she recognizes that her claim falls into a familiar category—"the old starving artist story." This recognition adds a new node

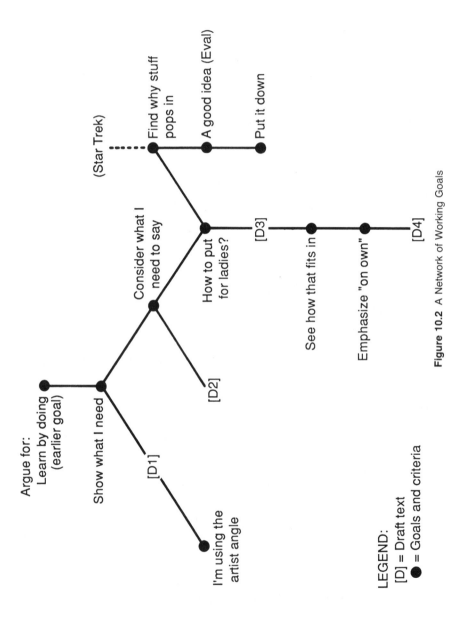

Figure 10.2 A Network of Working Goals

to her image of her own claims and becomes a part of her current ideas and goals. Recognizing that her ideas fit into the "deserving artist" category does not spawn a "new idea" in the eureka sense. However, by articulating (in line 1), then evaluating (in lines 3 and 4) a claim she wants to make, she has created a meaningful addition to her current network of ideas. Did this addition represent an epiphany for Monci—for example, a new insight into her own assumptions? We can't tell, although it seems unlikely. What we do see in her action is the process of *constructing and elaborating* a particular representation or configuration of meaning.

An instance of meaning making more uniquely attributable to writing occurs in the Star Trek episode, where even a stray thought becomes grist for the writer's mill. When that association popped into the picture (through some invisible link), it could have merely preempted the author's attention for the moment then faded out in the way unbidden thoughts about lunch and other matters frequent writers' minds. The Star Trek association could have stolen focal attention for a few seconds (just long enough to merit mention in the think-aloud protocol) and then dropped out of short-term memory, as Monci returned to the task at hand. Instead, something else happened that lets us trace the path by which an association can lead to text. Although the Star Trek association itself did not prove to be particularly relevant, our writer's meta-awareness of her own process leads her in line 9 to generate a proposition about that process. In her energetic search for topic information, she evaluates this observation as a good idea and worth noting down. Note how in the noting down she then recasts her observation about "stuff that pops" into a more elaborate proposition about "cues that stimulate." And she adds it to the network of potential topic knowledge she is building.

Our student's next move in constructing meaning demonstrates restructuring—an important expert strategy for building a new network of ideas adapted to the writer's purpose. Various studies have shown that one of the halimarks of novice writers is their failure to restructure knowledge or adapt it to a rhetorical problem. Young children depend on what Scardamalia and Bereiter (1986) describe as a "knowledge-telling" strategy that lets them focus all attention on generating content, a search constrained only by minimal tests for staying on topic and within the genre. By high school the ability to restructure becomes a more critical skill. Langer found that students whose knowledge of a topic has a loose and associative structure may succeed on essay assignments that ask them to "write about" a topic but may fail on exams and focused assignments that ask for hierarchically structured information organized around a question or problem. The students' mental structure of information is inappropriate for this special task, and they have not learned how to operate on that structure to make it fit a new purpose. The problem, however, it not simply a matter of age or experience. Even adult writers regularly end up with "writer-based" prose in which an egocentric focus and a narrative of descriptive structure reflects a writer talking to himself about his own knowledge (Flower 1979). Using the structure of information in one's own memory is, it appears, an excellent strategy for retrieving information, and a writer-based focus often shows up in the mental text and first drafts of good writers. The expert writer, however, takes one more step, revising the text as needed to produce hierarchically structured, reader-based prose.

In the Monci protocol, starting in line 13, the writer takes two steps toward a more purposeful use of her knowledge. She recalls her rhetorical goals (those ladies in pink hats she intends to convince); she reviews their goals as she imagines them; she then consolidates her observation into a gist, which she calls "the point." The new idea she drafts as D3 is a crossroad at which all of these elements of her planning and thinking meet. It reflects her observation about finding ideas, in a new form adapted to carrying out her rhetorical goals and adjusted by her sense of the reader's expectations. In line 17 Monci looks even more like an expert when she decides to test her ideas by creating yet another representation—a paraphrase. In doing so she creates another node in her representation, which specifies an optimal emphasis and which eventually results in a change in her text.

This excerpt shows us in miniature the way a writer's process of planning, evaluating, and consolidating not only alters and reorganizes old information but constructs new representations of knowledge. An important part of the new representation constructed here is Monci's final claim, that she, like all writers, needs to learn about the cues that prompt creation. A pleasing irony of this protocol is that it lets us observe the writer carrying out the very *process of constructing idea* that she claims in the text that she, the writer, needs to learn.

Purposeful Cognition. It is important to note that draft sentence 4 did not drop into this writer's lap as a fully formed and elaborated concept— Athena springing from the head of Zeus. In fact, one might even take issue with the implicit theory of creativity Monci seems to hold—a theory that emphasizes the "cues that stimulate" rather than the "processes that construct" meaning. A good deal of this writer's time and attention is devoted to acts of purposeful cognition by which she manages her composing process and constructs topic knowledge. She not only draws inferences and notes categories, she sets and reviews goals, gives herself process plans (e.g., write this down), evaluates her text and her plans, switches from goals to gists to text and back, and monitors her own process, both to observe and to guide it. Her process shows how purposeful cognition functions as a normal part of the writer's process and how a student writer like Monci regularly rises to conscious problem solving in order to make meaning within a rhetorical situation.

Let me sum up the two major sections of this essay by pointing to the parallel conclusions they reach about the nature of cognition in the writing process.

1. Writers work at various levels of awareness during the process of composing, ranging from fully tacit processes such as memory search, to well-learned automated processes, which can be promoted to consciousness, to the more demanding processes of rhetorical problem solving. In general, these processes work in close synchronization—the difficult tasks gaining the writer's focal attention and conscious processing.

On simple or highly practiced tasks experts stand out by their sheer fluency and automaticity—they can draw on stored plans and schemas to make the task easy. However, on difficult or new tasks, experts stand out by the willingness with which they abandon the more straightforward process of text generation in order to rise to rhetorical problem solving. Experts are marked by their persistence and attention to the larger problem. They spend more time planning, monitoring, and evaluating, and when they encounter problems, they turn to extended episodes of diagnosis and planning.

2. Writers also create and work among multiple representations of meaning. The very nature of writing compels writers to translate nonverbal information into language, while the standards for written text impose even further demands for specificity and coherence on verbal meaning. Rerepresentation appears to be a fact of life for writers. Ironically, it may be a particular problem for student writers, who are frequently asked to write about experiences that they may not have thought about or stored in highly verbalized ways.

One of the distinctive features of expert representations is the way writers move back and forth between potential content and more abstract representations. Experts think with goals, plans, gists, and paraphrases. These more abstract blueprints for text are easier to think with and easier to throw away. Like meta-knowledge about one's own process, they give the writer more flexibility and control.

How Might We Teach Such Cognitive Processes?

There is a long tradition in rhetoric of teaching the art of discourse by teaching students to use certain heuristics or rules of thumb. Aristotle's *topoi* worked as aids in the process of invention, by suggesting likely plans for creating an effective argument. The "new rhetoric" and other rhetorically oriented process pedagogies have extended this interest in strategies, by teaching students problem-solving strategies for writing itself. That is, one can hope to intervene in the writer's process by teaching specific rhetorical strategies for the act of composing itself. Much of this pedagogy has focused on the processes of planning and invention. For example, a "new rhetoric" such as Young, Becker, and Pike's *Rhetoric: Discovery and Change* or *The Four Worlds of Writing* by Lauer, Montague, Lunsford, and Emig, teaches the student to use systematic invention procedures for exploring one's own knowledge. Peter Elbow's *Writing Without Teachers* leads the student through a sequence of timed freewriting episodes, followed by an attempt to sum up what one has done and rewrite. In *Problem-Solving Strategies for Writing*, I emphasize the goal-directed nature of invention, which leads one to teach heuristics for analyzing one's rhetorical problem and for generating plans and goals. Each of these approaches and others within the rhetorical tradition of instruction teach specific strategies for the process of writing. This focus on thinking strategies seems to be particularly helpful not only to students who are ready and able to take more control of their own thinking but to very inexperienced writers who had been locked into a text-based theory of composing that led them straight into text production with few strategies for planning, generating ideas, revising, or getting out of dilemmas. The assumptions and limited repertoire of strategies these students bring to composing may be a major hobble on their performance.

However, the process approach has its difficulties, as does any pedagogy. One, according to a recent study by Arthur Applebee, has surfaced with what he calls the "natural process" approach in which students are not taught rhetorical strategies so much as they are immersed in the process of writing and led through a number of steps, which include prewriting, working collaboratively, reading each other's work, and revising. In the hands of some teachers, he suggests, the "process" becomes an arhetorical series of classroom activities. Students have difficulty seeing the goal of any given exercise (such as writing a journal) and are unlikely to transfer it to other writing activities outside of composition class.

One conclusion is that the writing process needs to be taught not just as a procedure or a set of "natural" activities but as purposeful cognition. Students need to be actively aware of the rhetorical goals behind a writing strategy and learn not only how to use a thinking procedure but when and why it might be worth trying.

A second problem in teaching cognitive processes is the difficulty of teaching any performance skill—especially when it is a rich and seldom-seen mental performance. As educators we are used to teaching content knowledge, to monitoring the students' understanding, and to predicting what might go wrong in that learning process. However, we are less experienced with teaching strategic or process knowledge—knowledge about how to orchestrate an intellectual process. In the Strategic Learning Project at the Center for the Study of Writing, Carnegie-Mellon we have begun to experiment with ways to demonstrate or model the strategic knowledge experienced writers bring to certain tasks. For example, reading-to-write is a standard college task, in which writers are asked not only to comprehend and interpret a text but to synthesize information under the guidance of their own writing plan and goals—goals that they are typically developing in conjunction with the act of reading. For all its familiarity, reading-to-write is an impressively complex cognitive process.

To help student writers develop some of the strategic knowledge that more experienced writers use to manage this task, we need to teach not only strategies (or procedures) for entering this process but some of the goals and tests for success that are also a part of the expert's strategic knowledge. In our research we are experimenting with thinking-aloud records, such as the Monci protocol, and other computer-aided means in an effort to demonstrate the writer's thinking process more vividly and to encourage students to experiment with new thinking strategies.

I believe there is a good deal we need to learn about teaching purposeful cognition. However, let me offer the following sequence of assignments we use in our freshman program at Carnegie-Mellon to suggest one approach to the matter. In this course, we devote the first unit to helping students learn to analyze problems while at the same time they begin to examine their own writing process. We naturally rely on both direct instruction and assignments beyond what is mentioned here. However, this sequence and its variations is one we have found useful. These ask the student to analyze a problem, then to rewrite that analysis either for a different reader or from the perspective of a different discourse community. In parallel with this sequence, the student is doing a self-analysis and using the problem analysis assignments as a window on his or her own writing process.

ASSIGNMENT #1: JOURNAL ENTRY ON A PROBLEMATIC DECISION.

Choosing to go to college, choosing a college, or choosing a major are often difficult decisions for many people. Look back on your own experience and use journal writing to explore one of these decisions. What made it a problem *for you*? What sorts of goals, assumptions, demands, or desires were in conflict in a way that made this a genuine problem?

Comment: The journal entry allows the student to explore a problematic situation freely (but still in writing), to articulate ideas that don't yet fit together, and to forestall the tendency we all have to define problems simply in order to jump to a solution.

ASSIGNMENT #2: DEFINING THE PROBLEM WITHIN THE SITUATION.

Looking back over your journal entry on a problematic decision, think about the problem some more and write a brief (1–2 sentences) analysis of this problem in which you try to define the central issue or the critical conflict that makes this a real problem—not just a choice you made. Present your definition of this problem as precisely as you can at the beginning of your analysis and use it to organize your discussion of the important aspects of the problem.

Comment: A problem analysis is a difficult thing to write. It asks writers to look at a problematic situation, to sort through the history and circumstances of a situation, and to identify for themselves the critical issues or the underlying conflicts that create a problem. The process is actually more like "forging" an issue than it is merely "identifying" or selecting one, and it is likewise difficult to move from narration and description of a *situation* to an articulate statement of the problem itself. Furthermore, as a writing task this is new to many students used to doing either personal, expressive writing or five-paragraph themes in high school. Instead of merely organizing standard knowledge on a given topic or following out their personal response, they are asked to produce a precise, direct statement of a conflict or an issue—and to do so for *significant* problems that they may not know how to resolve. In some ways this unit of the course is an initiation into academic discourse. It takes some effort to master, but it has dramatic payoffs for the students in the papers that follow and in their other courses, which typically *expect* analysis even when the assignment appears to call for knowledge-telling.

ASSIGNMENT #3: JOURNAL ENTRY ON YOUR PROCESS.

Defining a problem is a creative task. It is up to the writer and thinker to decide where the issue or the conflict really lies and to find ways to turn experience into concepts or ideas.

How did you handle this process? What writing/thinking strategies do you use? It might help to look at the part of this process that was problematic for you. What made it difficult and how did you respond?

ASSIGNMENT #4: ADAPTING TO A DIFFERENT PURPOSE (VERSION A).

In writing an analysis the way you see the problem is often affected by who your readers are and what they *need* to know or what you *want* them to think about. The Advising Program here at the university would like to send a mailing to parents to help them understand the problem students face in choosing a college or a major. Revise your original anlaysis so that it recognizes this problem from a new point of view. You wish to inform these readers of the problem as students see it, or you may want to think about how your audience would see this problem and include that perspective.

ASSIGNMENT #4: ADAPTING TO A DIFFERENT PURPOSE (VERSION B).

People do not write in a void. We all belong to some discourse community that shares certain assumptions about what is important and certain ways of using language. You probably wrote to the community of this class, which shares to some extent the language of standard academic discourse. But what would happen if you had to analyze your problem from a different perspective?

What if you were an economist looking at this situation in terms of the economic incentives and barriers, at the cost and benefits, and at the way a person's social and economic circumstances give them strong messages about who they are and what is best to do?

Or what if you were a family counselor, focusing on the family pressures, on the social background, or on the social history of a student and acutely aware of the role a person's recent or distant personal history plays in creating issues and conflicts?

[In different classes, teachers have offered a variety of thumbnail sketches of different social or intellectual roles and asked students to choose one of these perspectives to revise from.]

Take one of these new perspectives and think about the questions it would lead you to ask, the issues it would make you see, and the language people within that special discourse community would use. Revise your analysis for that community. Don't be surprised if you see the problem quite differently and come up with new ideas.

ASSIGNMENT #5: UNDERSTANDING YOUR OWN WRITING PROCESS.

What happens when you revise or rethink a first draft? This assignment will give you a new window on your own thinking and ask you to write a short analysis of your own process.

When you sit down to do assignment #4, be prepared to do a thinking aloud protocol of the sort we discussed in class. Look back over your first paper and think (aloud) about how you are going to revise it. Think aloud as you make your plan and generate ideas for the new version. Then, instead of doing a complete protocol, turn your taperecorder off and work silently. However, at regular intervals "check in" with the tape and interview yourself. Talk to the tape about what you are doing, about your plans, problems, and current decisions. Check in frequently, since these verbal notes will be your "window" when you go back to look at your own process. Good times to do this are when you get a plan, start a new unit, change your mind, lose your concentration, or take a break. At the end of writing have one final interview with your yourself and try to describe the key points in your process as you remember it, the problems you encountered, and the writing strategies you used. These check-in interviews are very important because you will be surprised to discover how much writers—absorbed in the act of writing—forget about their own process even minutes later. In the next day or so, go back to the tape and take notes on what you said and did. You may want to listen to the tape a couple of times. You now have some fresh information on which to base this next assignment.

One of the best ways to understand a process is to compare it to a different one. In this paper, we would like you to explore your own process and describe some of the thinking/writing strategies you used in these papers—look at the ones that work well for you as well as the ones that don't. Use the comparison between how you wrote your first version of the problem analysis and how you did the second one to help you describe your own strategies. Don't simply rely on your memory. You will find that looking closely at the various traces of your process will help you discover interesting features of your own process. These traces include: Journal Entry #3, which compared an earlier set of papers, the texts you wrote for Assignment #2 and Assignment #4 (how do they differ?), and finally, your notes from your thinkingaloud and self-interviews. There is a lot to discover about how you work as a writer, and this evidence will help you.

Comment: This set of assignments obviously depends upon other instruction that is going on in the class—we are trying to teach students how to do problem analysis, to teach them about the influence of "discourse communities," to preview the role of revision, and to help them gain insight into their own writing process. Perhaps the most unconventional part of this assignment is asking students to collect actual information on their own process, rather than simply rely on introspections. We do this because such introspections tend to turn up what people already assume rather than surprise them with new visions.

In other ways we are simply combining our regular instruction with a parallel set of assignments that both "invite" and help the student reflect upon his or her own thinking and learning. This parallel clearly takes real time and teaching; it is a significant part of the "content" of the course, not an afterthought. However, we feel it not only fosters meta-knowledge but helps students grapple with the intellectual skill of problem analysis more effectively.

As a rhetorician I am committed to teaching specific strategies—problem-solving processes that are more efficient, more powerful, or potentially more creative than other ways of doing things. If there is an expert strategy that I as a writer could try, I would want to know about it. However, as a teacher, I am also convinced that much of what makes us successful in teaching cognitive processes, and makes students enthusiastic about their new-found powers, lies not only in the specific strategies we teach but in the new perspective on writing and their own cognition that students develop. When students become aware of composing as a dynamic process, of their own acts of cognition, and of the choices they are making, they gain the inestimable power of having options and the power to learn from their own experience.

WORKS CITED

Applebee, Arthur. "Toward a Post-Process Paradigm: Notes on the Failure of Process Approaches to Writing Instruction." *National Society for the Study of Writing Yearbook*, 1986.

Brown, Ann L. "Metacognitive Development and Reading." *Theoretical Issues in Reading Comprehension*. Ed. Bertram Bruce, Rand Spiro and William Brewer. Hillsdale, NJ: Erlbaum, 1980.

Elbow, Peter. *Writing Without Teachers*. London: Oxford, 1973.

Emig, Janet. *The Composing Process of Twelfth Graders*. Urbana, IL: NCTE, 1971.

Ericsson, K. Anders, and Herbert Simon. "Verbal Reports as Data." *Psychological Review* 87 (1980): 215–251.

Flower, Linda. "Writer-based Prose: A Cognitive Basis for Problems in Writing." *College English* 41 (1979): 19–37.

———. *Problem-Solving Strategies in Writing*. 2nd ed. San Diego: Harcourt Brace Jovanovich, 1985.

———. "The Construction of Purpose in Writing and Reading." *College English*, forthcoming.

Flower, Linda, Linda Carey, and John R. Hayes. "Diagnosis in Revision: The Expert's Option." *Communication Design Center Technical Report* #27. Pittsburgh, PA: Carnegie Mellon, November 1985.

Flower, Linda, and John R. Hayes. "A Cognitive Process Theory of Writing." *College Composition and Communication* 32 (1981): 365–387.

———. "Images, Plans, and Prose: The Representation of Meaning in Writing." *Written Communication* 1 (1984): 120–160.

Flower, Linda, Karen Schriver, Linda Carey, Christine Haas, and John Hayes. "Planning in Writing: A Theory of the Cognitive Process." Technical Report. Berkeley, CA: Center for the Study of Writing at Berkeley and Carnegie Mellon, 1988.

Hairston, Maxine. *A Contemporary Rhetoric*. Boston: Houghton Mifflin, 1978.

Hausman, Leon. *Field Book of Eastern Birds*. New York: Putnam, 1946.

Hayes, John R., and Linda Flower. "Uncovering Cognitive Processes in Writing: An Introduction to Protocol Analysis." *Research in Writing: Principles and Methods*. Ed. Peter Mosenthal, Lynne Tamor, and Sean Walmsley. New York: Longman, 1983. 206–219.

Hopkins, Gerard Manley. *The Poems of Gerard Manley Hopkins*. London: Oxford University Press, 1967.

James, William. *Psychology*. 1892. Greenwich, CT: Fawcett, 1963.

Krashen, Stephen. "The Monitor Model for Second-Language Acquisition." *Second Language Acquisition and Foreign Language Learning.* Ed. Rosario Gingram. Washington, DC: Center for Applied Linguistics, 1981. 1–26.

Langer, Judith A. "Effects of Topic Knowledge on the Quality and Coherence of Informational Writing." *Research in the Teaching of English* 18.1 (1984): 27–44.

Lauer, Janice, Gene Montague, Andrea Lunsford, and Janet Emig. *Four Worlds of Writing.* New York: Harper & Row, 1985.

Lowes, John Livingston. *The Road to Xanadu: A Study in the Ways of Imagination.* Boston: Houghton Mifflin, 1955.

Mandel, Barrett. "The Writer Is Not at Home." *College Composition and Communication* 31 (1980): 370–377.

Nisbett, Richard, and Timothy Wilson. "Telling More Than We Can Know: Verbal Reports on Mental Processes." *Psychological Review* 84 (1977): 231–259.

Odell, Lee, and Dixi Goswami. "Writing in a Non–Academic Setting." *New Directions in Composition Research.* Ed. Richard Beach and Lillian Bridwell. New York: Guilford, 1984. 233–258.

Olson, David R. "The Languages of Instruction: On the Literate Bias of Schooling." *Schooling and the Acquisition of Knowledge.* Ed. Richard C. Anderson, Rand J. Spiro, and William E. Montague. Hillsdale, NJ: Erlbaum, 1977. 65–90.

Robbins, Chandler, Bertel Bruun, and Herbert Zim. *Birds of North America.* New York: Golden Press, 1966.

Scardamalia, Marlene, and Carl Bereiter. "Development of Dialectical Processes in Composition." *Literacy, Language, and Learning: The Nature and Consequences of Reading and Writing.* Ed. David Olson, Nancy Torrance, and Angela Hildyard. Cambridge: Cambridge University Press, 1985. 307–329.

———. "Composition." *Handbook of Research on Teaching.* Ed. M. Wittrock. New York: Macmillan, 1986.

Voss, James F., Terry R. Greene, Timothy A. Post, and B.C. Penner. "Problem Solving Skills in the Social Sciences." *The Psychology of Learning and Motivation: Advances in Research and Theory.* Ed. Gordon Bower. New York: Academic Press, 1983.

Vygotsky, Lev. *Thought and Language.* Cambridge, MA: MIT Press, 1962.

Young, Richard, Alton Becker, and Kenneth Pike. *Rhetoric: Discovery and Change.* New York: Harcourt Brace Jovanovich, 1970.

Young, Richard E. "Arts, Crafts, Gifts, and Knacks: Some Disharmonies in the New Rhetoric." *Reinventing the Rhetorical Tradition.* Ed. Aviva Freedman and Ian Pringle. Conway, AR: L & S Books, 1980. 53–60.

CHAPTER 11

Thinking and Writing as Social Acts

Kenneth A. Bruffee

Most cognitive and development discussions of thinking, reasoning, and writing, including most of those in this book, make what are called mentalistic and universalist assumptions. These assumptions are familiar to all of us, so familiar that we may not be aware that we hold them or that there are in fact any alternative assumptions available to us to hold. "Mentalistic" and "universalist" assumptions are based on the belief that all the creatures we regard as human have a "human mind," an item that is endowed with an inherent, universal, internal structure of its own. This structure implies or is consonant with universal laws of conceptual thought, reason, and critical inquiry. It implies that not all human minds work according to these laws, of course, but all of them can, and all "well-developed" or "mature" ones do. The ability to work according to these laws is regarded as a "higher order" reasoning ability.

To teach people this higher order reasoning ability and to think and write in ways appropriate to it, the argument goes, we have to inquire into the nature of that universal mental structure and bring out people's ability to apply those universal mental laws. Language, according to this view, is a medium of exchange or a technique of communication by which intercourse between minds may be carried on. To teach people to write, we have to show them how to express in language the universal laws

Portions of this essay have been adapted from the introduction to Kenneth A. Bruffee, *A Short Course in Writing*, 3rd ed. (Boston: Little Brown, 1985). Copyright (c) 1985 by Kenneth A. Bruffee. Used by permission of Little, Brown and Company.

of thought or higher reasoning as they are typically discovered in or impressed upon the universal mental structure.

The alternative to this set of assumptions offered in this essay is neither mentalist nor universalist. It is "social constructionist." This essay assumes that there is no inherent, internal, universal mental structure that can work according to "the universals of sound reasoning." It assumes instead that what we call the universals of sound reasoning or a higher order reasoning ability is an internalization of the language use, or more broadly speaking the symbol use, of certain human communities, in particular our own literate Western European-American culture.

A SOCIAL CONSTRUCTIONIST VIEW OF WRITING

To base our talk about thinking and writing on these assumptions leads us to take the position that what appear to be inherent structure and laws of thought originate, generally speaking, in social processes and arrangements of the sort that we often call conversation, among people who "speak the same language." People who speak the same language are members of the same community and are committed to the community's conventions, values, traditions, interests, and goals. In the case of the community of literate Western European-American culture, these conventions and so forth include the universals of sound reasoning.

A social constructionist way of talking about thinking and writing does of course assume that thought obeys rules. But these rules are not universals. They are the rules or conventions of the grammar, syntax, rhetorical behavior, and social relations of the communities to which we thinking and writing persons of Western European-American literate culture belong. That is to say, "good grammar" and "effective rhetoric" are certain kinds of social behavior that help cement a community and, not at all incidentally, that help distinguish members of the community from nonmembers. To learn the usage of standard written English, for example, is to learn the language behavior of a particular community. That community is, granted, a very large, prosperous, and influential one. Furthermore, it is the community to which I and all my readers belong. It is certainly the community all of our students want to join or (we feel) should want to join if they know what's good for them.

Not only does a social constructionist way of talking about the issues raised in this book assume that thought obeys rules, it also distinguishes between what goes on inside the mind and what goes on outside it. But it does not say that what goes on in the mind is some kind of isolable interior process or entity—the structure of the mind. It says that what goes on in the mind, to borrow a distinction from Steven Toulmin, is not an "interior" thing but an "internalized" one. It is a version of the social use of language: conversation.

When we talk at this level of generality about writing instead of just about thinking, of course, the case is somewhat more complicated. When we write, according to this alternative, social constructionist way of talking, we re-externalize a linguistic process that we had earlier internalized. That is, the "writing process" begins as we continually internalize the language forms given to use by our community, along with the various processes of using them approved of by that community and many of the things said ("ideas") that are approved of by that community. What we write is a version of what goes on inside our minds after it has gone on "out there" in the conversation of the community we are members of. Writing is a stage of conversation displaced from the conventions of face-to-face conversation. Writing obeys the social conventions of language that govern face-to-face conversation, modified by the limitations of one technology (language as alphabetically signed) as opposed to the limitations of another technology (language as phonetically signed).

Perhaps it would help clarify the implications of this social constructionist alternative way of talking about the issues raised in this book if we turned the process around and watched it work from another direction, starting with the act of writing and working backward toward thought. We ordinarily think of writing as a private, individual act originating inside us. And it is incontrovertible that inscribing—the act of putting alphabetical signs onto a page or microcomputer screen in conventional ways—is a private, individual act. In most cases it would be highly inefficient to try to "write" in this sense in any other way than privately and individually. But once we begin to think of writing in a broader sense as a whole process of generating and shaping language for the purpose of technologically displacing conversation, then the social nature of writing asserts itself in startling ways.

It is simply the case that we absolutely must write as a cooperative or collaborative social activity within a conversational community, because we must write to people who already "speak our language." If we write to people who don't speak our language, nobody can understand us. Nobody hears us, because nobody listens. What we write and how we write it is governed by the language of the community of people within which we write, to whom we write. Writing—a form of conversation— begins in conversation and remains within that conversational community. "Good writing" requires us also , furthermore, to learn to use language *about* writing itself, writing as a continual process of making decisions or exercising judgment, as those decisions and that judgment are applied to our community. That is, good writing requires us to be able to talk about writing in a way agreed upon by the conversational community we are members of, talk that ranges from the correct spelling of "there" to the nuances of constructing reliable enthymemes.

Implications for Teaching Writing

The social constructionist way of talking about writing and thinking that I have sketched briefly here has, inevitably, some implications for teaching writing. These implications differ in certain ways from what is implied about teaching writing by mentalistic, universalistic ways of talking. In the latter case, the questions that teachers ordinarily ask are questions that the essays in this book typically address. They are questions like, What's going on inside my students' heads? and How can I get in there and change what's going on? These are the questions implied when we wonder how to "reach" students and how to implant in their heads what we believe is going on in our own. Teaching writing and thinking by this token is thus a little like trying to repair a pump at the bottom of a muddy well. We feel around and tinker blindly with what we think might be there, in hopes that we can improve the flow.

In contrast, to think of writing and thought as versions of the conversation going on in a community of people who speak the same language brings the whole process into the open. We say then that the people we want to teach writing to already converse in languages quite adequate and appropriate to their communities' conventions, values, traditions, interests, and goals. What they don't do (naturally) is converse in a language that is adequate and appropriate to *our* community's conventions, values, traditions, interests, and goals. But that community, our community, is the community we want them to join, and that we suppose is in their best interests to join. Teachers are the members of any community whose job it is to help nonmembers become members.

Talking this way about teaching writing, then, changes the questions we ask as teachers. We no longer ask questions about getting into heads. Instead, we ask questions like, How do I get my students to want to give up the values of the communities they are now members of, or at least to soften their loyalty to and dependence upon those communities? and How do I help students join another community in ways that make that change as comfortable and fail-safe as possible?

The short answers to these questions, based on studies of people's experiences living in communities and changing from one community to another suggests that the best way to help people reacculturate themselves

KENNETH A. BRUFFEE   **217**

is to help them form a new, temporary, transitional community made up of people who want to make the change. This sort of community is often called a support community. It approximates some of the conventions, values, traditions, interests, and goals of the communities people are leaving and also some of the conventions and so forth, of the community they hope to join. But the most important conventions, values, traditions, interests, and goals of a transitional support group have to do with acknowledging the stress of change. Much of the conversation that cements the members of a transitional support community has to do with what it was like in the old community, what it may be like in the new community, and what a pain it is to change. Much of it also, of course, has to do with figuring out how one is expected to converse in the community one is joining and involves practicing that particular sort of conversation.

The teacher's job in dealing with this transitional support group, after helping form it in the first place, is to help its members gain fluency in the language (or other symbol system) of the new community they want to join. Teachers can do this in a number of ways, but mainly by helping the students translate out of the language and symbol system of their old communities into the language and symbol system of the new. Eventually, of course, the teacher's job is to help students entirely to internalize the new community's language: to help them, as we say to "think in it." Thus for writing teachers the moral of this story is relatively easy to say but (like most morals) hard to carry out. It is to set up as many occasions as possible for conversation of the sort that requires students to look for and use the kind of language we want them to use in their writing.

WRITING AS CONVERSATION

In actual classroom practice this moral comes down to helping students converse effectively about writing itself. This role is not an unfamiliar one for composition teachers. What makes it unusual and somewhat challenging when we act on the social constructionist assumptions I have sketched here is the particular nature of the conversation required. Thinking of writing as social and collaborative implies that teachers help students converse effectively, especially about writing, not with teachers but with the students' peers. Productive conversation for all of us is most likely to occur with people we regard as equals, members of our own community. Conversation with members of another community is always somewhat mannered and strained, something of a performance. Students' conversation with teachers, although obviously of value in learning to write, is conversation with a member of another community. If we regard conversation as the key to writing considered as a social, collaborative act, then student writers must learn to converse about writing in a profitable way with people who are more or less their equals with regard to learning to write.

That is what students learn to do in a course that applies the assumptions I have been discussing here. Central to such a course is students engaged in conversation with each other as peers about writing, conversation both in its face-to-face form, talking to one another, and in its displaced form, writing to each other. Instruction and direction by the teacher in such a course takes the form of tasks that the teacher asks students to undertake together, collaboratively. Students engage in conversation about writing every step of the way: finding a topic; deciding what they want to say about that topic; developing material to defend or explain what they say; reading, describing, and evaluating what they have written; and rewriting.

The long-range purpose of conversation in a writing course is to help writing students learn how to internalize their conversation about writing. When students learn to internalize conversation, they develop the ability to displace conversation—carry it away with them—whenever they have to put pen to paper. This displacement by internalization is what lets us work together, as Robert Frost said, whether we work together or apart.

Learning to internalize conversation helps students learn to write in part because writing involves judgment, and good judgment—making knowledgeable, discerning, reliable decisions—is something we learn best collaboratively. The British biologist M.L.J. Abercrombie demonstrated this principle 30 years ago. At the invitation of a University College London medical unit, she devised a way to teach medical students the hardest and yet most important thing in medical education to learn: diagnostics, medical judgment. Most medical students practice diagnostics by examining patients individually and then telling the teaching physician the diagnosis they have, individually, decided on. Abercrombie made what seemed to be a slight change in this procedure. She asked a small group of, say, five medical students to examine a patient together, and then as a group arrive at a consensus about what is wrong with the patient. Instead of five diagnoses, one from each student, she asked for one diagnosis from the five of them.

This change had significant results. Medical students learned diagnosis faster and more reliably by working collaboratively than they had by working individually. Abercrombie's experiment showed, and many composition teachers' experience with collaborative learning during the past decade seems to verify, that the best way to learn good judgment is to practice making judgments in collaboration with other people who are at about the same stage of development. If we learn in this way, it seems, when we make mistakes we make them together—we're all in the same boat. We are less afraid of risking errors that are inevitable whenever we try to learn something new. But, in fact, working together we tend to make fewer mistakes because we help each other see things we would not have seen on our own, we assert the conclusions we come to with confidence because we have talked them over and back each other up, and we are likely to learn to make judgments better later on as individuals because we have internalized this kind of conversation. We will have learned to talk with ourselves as we have learned to talk with others.

The analogy between Abercrombie's experiment and teaching composition is apt, because writing is a process of making judgments continually, every one of them having an effect on all the rest. What to write about, what to say about it, how to say it, how to begin, what word to use, how to phrase this sentence, where to put that comma: one decision after another. Learning to make judgments in speaking or writing a language is even more difficult in one respect than learning medical judgment. The "patient" we are trying to "diagnose" when we write, the bit of language we are trying to make a judgment about, is not easily distinguishable from the medium, language, in which we are trying to make the decision. Using language to decide about a sick person is one thing; using language to decide about a troubling sentence is quite another.

Using language to decide about language complicates the problem, because in order to think about the subject we are judging (the next word to use, or its proper form, or how to begin the next paragraph), we also have to think about how we are using language to make that judgment. This process can feel as awkward sometimes as trying to cut our own hair looking in a mirror. The only way we can work our way through the tangle of language used to talk about language is to try to get outside our merely personal, as yet unshared biases and preconceptions. We have to try to see the world as it seems other people see it, or more precisely, as other members of the community we are trying to join agree to see it.

What makes these decisions in writing more complicated still is that we make them to suit the tastes, interests, and knowledge of at least three communities of readers at once. We make them to suit ourselves and the communities we are accustomed to, the communities we are already a member of. We make them to suit the community of peers that we hope to join. And we make them to suit the enormous community whose "language game" is standard written English, the community that demands that writing be "correct" according to its standard, as well as "unified," "coherent," "appropriate to the subject matter," and so on.

WHAT TEACHERS AND STUDENTS DO

In practice, of course, what students do in a course that applies social constructionist assumptions and what teachers do in such a course is somewhat different. In learning writing this way, collaboratively, *students* focus primarily on what each other has say in response to tasks set by the teacher. They also examine the ways other students and they themselves make judgments and arrive at decisions. Learning occurs in large part as a result of changes in the kinds of relationships that occur among the students involved.

The *teacher's* role in a composition course (and perhaps in other courses as well) that applies social constructionist assumptions is *to create conditions in which learning can occur*. Students do the learning, for the most part, although sometimes teachers learn, too. Teachers set the stage for learning.

Teachers create the conditions for learning in most composition courses by assigning essays to write and read, by lecturing, by leading discussions, even by giving exams. Any one of these, used appropriately, can contribute to the collaborative nature of students' learning. But more typically teachers create conditions in which students engage in conversation, both face-to-face conversation and conversation displaced into writing. The quality of student conversation depends largely on what teachers do to generate it.

To generate conversation what teachers do in general is (1) choose or design tasks that involve students in conversation as they complete the task together; (2) organize the community of students so that productive conversation can occur; (3) help students negotiate among themselves to resolve differences of opinion and judgment, help them understand why such differences occur, help them find information and gain experience that will enhance the quality of judgment finally arrived at; and (4) evaluate the quality of student development during this process and each student's contribution to the learning of others by judging the quality of written (displaced) contributions to the conversation.

When teachers design or choose the tasks that students will do and in the process converse about, they must make sure that the task is clearly defined and limited and its degree of difficulty carefully judged. It cannot be so easy that almost any student in the class could do it, working as an individual alone. It cannot be so hard that even working together students cannot do it, without falling back on the teacher's expertise. Each task must be within what L.S. Vygotsky calls the students' "zone of proximal development." It has to be something they can't quite do by themselves but can do with a little help from their friends.

Such a task is hard to come by. Good ones usually result from lots of trial and error. But some fairly standard ones are obvious. When students read their essays aloud and listen to each other reading, for example, they are working collaboratively. When they discuss topics to write about in pairs or groups of three, they are working collaboratively. When they describe or outline each other's essays, they are working collaboratively, and they are also doing so, of course, when they confer with each other about these descriptions or outlines.

Perhaps the most common kind of classroom collaboration is group work, in which the teacher asks five or six students to work together on a single task. The task in this case may be a question to be answered by arriving at a consensus, or it may be a problem to be solved to the satisfaction of all members of the group. What is essential is that the task lead to an answer or solution that can represent as nearly as possible the collective judgment and conversation of the group as a whole.

CONVERSATION, WRITING, AND LIBERAL EDUCATION

This, then, is one purpose of collaborative work of the sort that applies social constructionist assumptions: to teach students how people in a particular discipline—that is, a particular knowledge community—make and express judgments that the community regards as sound. Another and equally important purpose is to teach students how knowledge is generated and arrived at through the conversation of communities. Classroom collaborative exercises can be seen as examples or models of the sort of conversation that goes on among full-fledged members of the relevant community, the community of historians, chemists, sociologists, or even the much larger and more inclusive community of "good writers." In short, a larger purpose of courses that apply the assumptions of social constructionist thinking is to help students gain authority over their knowledge and gain independence in using it.

This process of development can occur because a necessary intermediary step to independence is effective interdependence. Collaborative work provides the transitional support communities that students can rely on as they go through the risky process of taking on authority themselves as writers and as critical readers. It provides a measure of security as students substitute confidence in their own authority for dependence on the teacher's authority.

What students learn (and teachers help them learn) is that teachers and other authorities and experts are only relatively more skillful or knowledgeable than they are themselves. No one person has all the answers. No one person's answer remains "right" for long. In the long run we have only each other to turn to. In education, if interdependence is a necessary intermediary step to independence, independence itself turns out to be just another kind of interdependence. We work together, whether we work together or apart.

WORKS CITED

Abercrombie, M.L. Johnson. *The Anatomy of Judgment: An Investigation Into the Processes of Perception and Reasoning.* New York: Basic Books, 1960.

FOR FURTHER READING

Bruffee, Kenneth A. "Collaborative Learning and the 'Conversation of Mankind.'" *College English* 46 (November 1984): 635–652.
———. *A Short Course in Writing.* 3rd ed. Boston: Little, Brown, 1985.
Castelucci, Maryann, et al. *A Collaborative Learning Packet.* New York: College of Staten Island, 1985. Available from Professor Maryann Castelucci, English Department, College of Staten Island—Sunnyside Campus, 715 Ocean Terrace, Staten Island, NY 10301.
Geertz, Clifford. *Local Knowledge.* New York: Basic Books, 1983.
Toulmin, Steven. "The Inwardness of Mental Life." *Critical Inquiry* 6 (Autumn 1979): 1–16.
Vygotsky, Lev S. *Mind in Society.* Ed. Michael Cole. Cambridge: Harvard University Press, 1978.

CHAPTER 12

Making a Difference: Thought, Signs, and the Teaching of Writing

Janice Haney-Peritz

Although reports of a "literacy crisis" have been circulating for quite some time, representations of the crisis have changed since the late 1960s. At first, we were informed that the crucial problem was that Johnny couldn't read. A few years later, we got word that the problem was more complicated; even when Johnny could read, he still couldn't write well. Nowadays, the situation appears to be even more complex and critical: Johnny not only has problems with reading and writing but also with thinking.

In the past, American educators have been quick to respond to the reported problems in literacy. When it became apparent that Johnny couldn't read, elementary school teachers devoted more time to developing and teaching new reading programs. Similarly, when Johnny's problems with writing surfaced, college teachers set about devising new courses, new approaches, and new programs in composition. But what, one wonders, are we teachers to do about the "thinking problem"?

For some, the solution to the "thinking problem" seems to be both clear and distinct: since students don't know enough to think well, they must be given more knowledge—more information about nature, society, and culture. For others of us, however, the solution is neither clear nor distinct. Too often we find that even our well-informed students fail to think through what they have learned; like their less well-informed peers, they don't seem to know how to relate and organize information, how to draw inferences, how to identify, represent, and explore problems, and how to move beyond the already known. Given this situation, many of us have come to believe that we need to learn something more about the processes of knowing and thinking, something that will help us to pass on our know-how as well as what we know.

Ideally, teachers at all levels and in all fields are equally responsible for addressing the "thinking problem." But let us be realistic as well as idealistic. Since the "thinking problem" is usually represented as a symptom of the "literacy crisis" and since making students literate is too often presumed to be the English teacher's job, it is likely that those of us who teach composition will be expected to assume a disproportionate share of the communal responsibility. In consequence, we have a special problem as well as a special opportunity. Like our colleagues, we must learn something more about the processes of knowing and thinking; however, our special problem is to articulate a pragmatic relation among knowing, thinking, and writing. If we don't address this special problem, then not only do we risk assuming that teaching thinking is a new task—something we must do in addition to teaching reading and writing—but we also risk missing an important opportunity: the chance to convince our colleagues that writing across the curriculum can be an effective way of responding to the "thinking problem."

But how can the relation among knowing, thinking, and writing be articulated? Since semiotics is based on a critique of the notion that thought exists prior to and independently of signification, I believe that it may help us to answer this question. Stated more positively, semiotics is founded on the principle that signs are all we know on earth. However, as important as this principle is to those of us who teach writing, it is by no means all we need to know. We also need to know how and why writing can make a real difference in how and what our students think. In short, it is simply not enough for us to assert the interdependency of thinking and writing; our problem is to figure out a way of making that relation a pragmatic one for the student—for the subject of cognition.

REPRESENTING THE PROBLEM

In an essay published in 1868, Charles Sanders Peirce broached the subject of cognition in a way that seems especially relevant to those of us interested in articulating a pragmatic relation between thinking and writing. To begin with, Peirce considered the possibility of "intuitive cognition"—the possibility that thinking is based on the immediate grasp of either an external or internal object. In exploring this possibility, Peirce found that in actuality, the "intuitive cognition" of common sense depends upon a knowledge of prior testimony. This finding not only prompted Peirce to conclude that "testimony is even a stronger mark of fact than *the facts themselves*, or rather than what must now be thought of as the *appearances* themselves" (5:233) but also led him to pose the question of "whether we can think without signs" (5:250).

At least two of the contributors to this volume imply that the answer to Peirce's question is no. While recounting the rise of the informal logic movement, Anthony Blair and Ralph Johnson (Chapter 5) link both formal and informal logic to the nature and functioning of language; whereas "the patterns or forms of entailment" at issue in formal logic would seem to depend on the hypothetical existence of a universal grammar (p. 94), the reasoning at work in informal logic would appear to rely on the existence of "natural language logic intuitions" (p. 96). Although her context is different, Edith Neimark (Chapter 3) also suggests that reasoned thinking depends on a sign system; in passing, she declares that "thought is by its very nature symbolic" (p. 49).

Even though Blair and Johnson, and Neimark, imply that some kind of dependency relationship exists between thought and signs, neither represents that relationship as especially problematic. Peirce, however, does just that; having posed the question of "whether we can think without signs," he responds as follows:

> This is a familiar question, but there is, to this day, no better argument in the affirmative than that thought must precede every sign. This assumes the impossibility of an infinite series. But Achilles, as a fact, will overtake the tortoise. *How* this happens, is a question not necessary to be answered at present, as long as it certainly does happen. (5:250)

As the references to "Achilles," "the tortoise," and "an infinite series" indicate, Peirce is drawing on one of Zeno's paradoxes to represent the problematic relation between thought and signs. In the Achilles argument, Zeno stages a race between the Greek hero and a slow-moving tortoise. Having been granted a head start, the tortoise reaches point A at the same moment that Achilles begins his run from point S. According to Zeno, even though the tortoise moves much more slowly than Achilles, it will have reached point B by the time Achilles gets to point A. Similarly, by the time Achilles reaches point B, the tortoise will have crawled on to point C. Since Zeno assumes that Achilles can catch up with the tortoise only when and if the two reach the same point at the same time, he concludes that the Greek hero will never overtake the other; Achilles is lost in an infinite series, a never-ending repetition of the same.[1]

To avoid Achilles' fate, people often argue that "thought must precede every sign." However, as Peirce represents it, this commonplace argument is really no reasonable argument at all, for it works by means of a threat: either affirm the priority of thought or lose the race with the tortoise by losing yourself in an infinite series of signs. Refusing to be intimidated by such a power play, Peirce responds with one of his own: while assuming the reality of an infinite series, he nevertheless asserts that Achilles does indeed overtake the tortoise. In effect, then, Peirce affirms two seemingly contradictory ideas: that thought is always caught up in an infinite series of signs and that thinking through signs can indeed make a real difference in the subject of cognition.[2]

But how does this happen? How does Achilles overtake the tortoise? How, in actuality, does thinking through signs make a difference? If Peirce's work is exemplary, it is not only because it provides us with some interesting answers to such questions but also because it offers us an unusually productive way of exploring the "thinking problem." That way begins with a displacement; instead of positing some metaphysical origin of cognition, Peirce assumes that "cognition arises by a *process* of beginning, [just] as any change comes to pass" (5:263). Since this process of beginning "must necessarily be in signs" (5:251), Peirce then embarks upon an investigation of signs and signification, an investigation that has led many to proclaim him our first American semiotician. And last but not least, Peirce draws on his semiotic research to develop a pragmatism that is both meaningful and logical. Unlike the "anti-intellectual" pragmatism that "flourished early in this century," Peirce's pragmatism is not based upon either "volition or sensation."[3] Rather, it is based upon a realization that if "every thought is a sign, it follows that every thought must address itself to some other, must determine some other, since that is the essence of the sign" (5:253).

In the remainder of this essay, I will follow Peirce's way, albeit in an abbreviated form. Based on the assumption that cognition is a process of beginning—a process that is necessarily caught up in an infinite series of signs—I will review some key semiotic principles and then suggest how those principles can help us to articulate the relation between thinking and writing in a pragmatic way—in a way that may indeed make a real difference to our students.

EXPLORING THE PROBLEM

Although contemporary semioticians have begun to assimilate some of Peirce's ideas, they still owe their greatest debt to the work of the Swiss linguist Ferdinand de Saussure. In the *Course in General Linguistics*, Saussure anticipated the emergence of a new science, the science of semiology:

> *A science that studies the life of signs within society* is conceivable; it would be a part of social psychology and consequently of general

psychology; I shall call it *semiology* (from Greek *sēmeîon* "sign"). Semiology would show what constitutes signs, what laws govern them. Since the science does not yet exist, no one can say what it would be; but it has a right to existence, a place staked out in advance. Linguistics is only a part of the general science of semiology; the laws discovered by semiology will be applicable to linguistics, and the latter will circumscribe a well-defined area within the mass of anthropological facts. (16)

Although the *Course* was published in 1916, semiotics did not become central to an understanding of the human sciences until Saussure's linguistic principles were taken up and revised by such contemporary writers as the anthropologist Levi-Strauss, the cultural critic Roland Barthes, the psychoanalyst Jacques Lacan, the philosopher Jacques Derrida, and the historian Michel Foucault.

One of Saussure's basic principles is that the value of a sign is determined by its diacritical relation to other linguistic signs. So, for example, the sign *girl* owes its capacity for signification not to a world of things but rather to its difference from other signs in our signifying system—signs like *curl, whirl, girt, child, boy,* and *woman.* More generally, Saussure's point is that language is neither primordially nor essentially a naming of things. If language were such a naming, then translation between languages would pose no problem; exact equivalences in meaning would always exist. But translation does pose problems; equivalences between signs are never exact, if only because different languages articulate the world differently (116). This being the case, it not only makes sense to say that language is a system of "differences without positive terms" (120) but also to claim that signs are arbitrary; that is, linguistic signs enjoy no positive, direct, or natural relation to things (67–74).

However, Saussure also insists that it is both possible and necessary to distinguish between two aspects of the sign: on the one hand, there is a sound image or signifier (*girl*) and on the other, a concept or signified ("girl"). Although each aspect of the sign is differential and arbitrary, Saussure argues that within a given language, their combination is neither purely differential nor arbitrary:

Although both signified and the signifier are purely differential and negative when considered separately, their combination is a positive fact; it is even the sole type of facts that language has, for maintaining the parallelism between two classes of differences is the distinctive function of the linguistic institution. (120–121)

According to this argument, the English signifier *girl* is inseparably bound to the English concept "girl" and not, let us say, to the English concept "curl." More generally, however, what is at issue in Saussure's argument is the existence of an institutionalized and communicable set of stable meanings, a set founded on the systematic distinction between and combination of signifiers and signifieds (71).

With so much at issue, one might expect that Saussure would investigate the way linguistic institutions are produced and reproduced. But this is precisely what he doesn't do. Instead, Saussre presents linguistic institutions as a given and then, in passing, refers them to a nonlinguistic ground—to an "identical collective consciousness" that perceives "the logical and psychological relations that bind together coexisting terms" in the "system."[4] Assuming that this collective consciousness is "the true and only reality to the community of speakers," Saussure concludes that language as a synchronic system of signification (*langue*) "predominates" over the diachronic production of discourse (*parole*) (90).

Since this conclusion implies that discourse is nothing more than the realization of an institutionalized language system or code, it not only led Saussure to exclude discourse from the science of semiology (16) but also encouraged later semiotic structuralists like Jonathan Culler (1975) to make assertions of the following type:

> If speakers of different ages, sexes and regions utter the sentence *The cat is on the mat*, the actual physical sounds produced will vary considerably, but those variations will be nonfunctional within the linguistic system of English in that they do not alter the sentence. The utterances, however different in sound, are free variations of a single English sentence. If, however, one speaker alters the sound in a particular way and says *The hat is on the mat*, the difference between /k/ and /h/ is functional in that it produces a different sentence with a different meaning. (10)

In accordance with Saussurean principles, Culler ignores the fact that, in actuality, dialect, tone, and situation do make a difference in the "meaning" of *The cat is on the mat*. Suppose, for example, that my husband and I had recently acquired a rare and valuable mat; given this situation, my statement to him that *The cat is on the mat* would mean something quite different than it would if the situation were otherwise. As this example suggests, the problem with Saussure's conception of meaning is that it is too ideal to account for the way signification actually works.

But even though meaning is neither as ideal nor as stable as Saussure claims, his argument does alert us to the institutional, ideological, and conventional dimensions of both signification and communication. So, for example, if we feel as though *girl* were the sign of something that is ultimately and unquestionably real—something that objectively exists both apart from and prior to testimony—then it is probably because there is a conventional link between the English signifier *girl* and the English concept "girl." On a more general level, Saussure's argument implies that common sense is nothing more than an ideology, a set of concepts that emerge from an institutionalized distinction between and combination of signifiers and signifieds.

Although Saussure alerts us to the ideological dimensions of common sense, his limited account of meaning should also make us doubt his conclusion that as a synchronic system, language determines the diachronic production of discourse. In order to reach this conclusion, Saussure excludes a consideration of the processes by means of which institutionalized ideologies and conventions are (re)produced. Furthermore, he puts aside the problem of how an individual becomes a member of a linguistic institution. And finally, by referring linguistic institutions to the "perception" of an "identical collective consciousness," he not only represents community as a unity founded on the idea of sameness (i.e., "identical") but also projects a knowing yet unthinking and undifferentiated "mass" (71) as linguistically, if not socially, ideal.

On the one hand, such an ideal makes individuals supererogatory; on the other hand, it makes it possible for a person to become someone when, by means of a repetition of the same, that person is at one with that "identical collective consciousness." In short, a person only becomes someone by being a nobody—by having the same signature on her jeans that everyone else has. Although this contradictory situation is bound to produce problems, it is unlikely that people will recognize those problems as socially significant if they are repeatedly taught that the existence of community requires being identical or the same. Indeed, such a teaching will tend to (re)produce an institutionalized subject, someone who has little or no sense that signs can and should make a difference.

In part, it is a concern for this subject that differentiates contemporary semiotics from Saussurean linguistics.[5] Take, for example, the work of Emile Benveniste. Whereas Saussure sought to exclude discursive production from the study of language as a system, Benveniste argues that, in actuality, such an exclusion is impossible to uphold. As Benveniste notes, language includes a number of signifying forms whose meaning cannot be explained in Saussurean terms. In English, the most important of these forms are the personal pronouns *I* and *you*. Although there may be a concept "tree" to which all individual uses of *tree* refer, Benveniste points out that "there is no concept "I" that incorporates all the *I*'s that are uttered at every moment in the mouths of all speakers" (226). Nevertheless, *I* is not without meaning; when it is used in a discourse, it designates the speaker and refers to "the reality of the discourse" (226). The case is much the same for other words such as *here* and *there* as well as for verb forms that signify time; like personal pronouns, these signs mean, but they do so only in relation to the discursive subject (220). Assuming that a language without such signifying forms is inconceivable, Benveniste not only concludes that it is impossible to separate language from discourse and discourse from the subject but also insists that it is the acquisition of language that makes the subject possible (227).

As Jacques Lacan has gone to great lengths to demonstrate, the subject that language makes possible is neither a simple nor a unified subject. To begin with, the acquisition of language enforces a split between being and meaning. Since language is a system of differences without positive terms, Lacan argues that entry into this system irretrievably cuts the person off from any unmediated relationship with the real, including of course the reality of needs or drives (1977, 34–107). In exchange for this loss of being, the person receives the possibility of meaning; however, that possibility is infinitely complicated by yet another splitting: the splitting of the subject into conscious and unconscious signifying processes (146–175). According to Lacan, entry into language as a system requires the repression of prelinguistic and therefore meaningless signifiers; these repressed signifiers mark the lack of being in language and in so doing initiate an unconscious signifying process. Having given up being for meaning, the subject will attempt to locate its identity in discourse; however both the fullness of meaning and a stable identity elude the subject, not only because conscious discourse always refers in one way or another to the discourse of the unconscious ("the discourse of the Other") but also because the unconscious is founded on a signifier rather than a signified (1978, 203–229). In consequence, the most that a subject can do is to assume a cultural position, a position from which the subject may speak but one that can never truly *be* the subject's, since it exists only within a symbolic order.

Like Lacan, Benveniste also represents the subject as split. In any discursive instance, there is not only a producing subject, an "I" who speaks, but also a discursive subject, an *I* designated within the discourse. Although these subjects are related, they are never one and the same; while the discursive subject functions as a signifier, the producing subject stands as a referent. Furthermore, since the signifier *I* only has meaning and value because it is differentially related to the signifier *you*, Benveniste, like Lacan, makes the subject of discourse dependent on an other: "In some way language puts forth "empty" forms which each speaker, in the exercise of discourse, appropriates to his "person," at the same time defining himself as *I* and a partner as you" (45). However, Benveniste goes beyond Lacan when he argues that, in actuality, the split subject is a plural subject. Whereas Lacan grants the discourse of the family the privilege of determining the subject's cultural and symbolic position, Benveniste claims that the subject is produced across a range of discourses, none of which enjoys an unquestioned cultural or symbolic privilege. In consequence, the discursive positions the subject assumes will often be quite different, if not explicitly contradictory.

However, it is always possible to cover up such discursive differences and contradictions, not to mention the gap between the speaking subject and the subject of discourse. This being the case, Jacques Derrida has devoted much of his writing to an exposition of the way such cover ups are effected within the Western metaphysical tradition. According to Derrida, our metaphysical tradition has always posited some transcendent signified as both the origin and end of a meaningful human existence (1978, 279). Ideas of Reason, God, Consciousness, and Community are central to the workings of our signifying institutions; however, they are usually understood to exist apart from the discursive practices in and through which they emerge. By demonstrating that such terms are historically changeable, structurally interchangeable, and discursively (re)produced, Derrida exposes transcendent signifieds to be nothing more nor less than peculiarly powerful signifiers. In practice, these powerful signifiers cover up the fact that no signified is ever present outside a play of differences and, in so doing, work to maintain the stability of the very signifying system they have a role in instituting. Although Derrida's exposition does not deny the discursive functioning of such transcendent signifieds, it does deny that this functioning rests on anything more than a power play: an attempt to stabilize meaning by instituting a systematic distinction between signifieds and signifiers. Since such a distinction can only be maintained if some term in the system is considered to be outside the play of signi-fication, when Derrida demonstrates that the transcendent signified is in actuality a signifier, he effectively undercuts both the Saussurean distinc-tion between signified and signifier and the stability of meaning that distinction was designed to uphold.

Saussure's distinction between signifier and signified rests on an implicit metaphysics. So too do his remarks on writing. According to Saussure, the written sign is nothing more than the signifier of the spoken word (23). Furthermore, since the spoken word is in turn the signifier of a psychological entity, the materiality of writing appears to be at least two steps removed from what Saussure considers truly significant: the real yet "incorporeal" idea (117–122). As Derrida reads it, this line of reasoning about signs betrays a desire for unmediated presence, a desire that is both provoked and maintained by a metaphysical tradition that institutes an hierarchical distinction between matter and spirit, image and idea, and speech and writing (1976, 30–73). Since Saussure relies on such distinc-tions throughout his work, it is not surprising that he represents writing as a secondary and therefore relatively insignificant phenomenon.

Derrida, however, sees things otherwise. Having noted the discre-pancy between Saussure's implicit desire for unmediated presence and his explicit postulate that language is a system of differences without positive terms, Derrida opts for the latter at the expense of the former. In so doing, he not only reinscribes the secondary as primary but also treats writing as if it were exemplary. Yet writing is exemplary only to the extent that it makes it difficult for us to ignore the fact that all signification depends on difference and deferral. In writing, signification moves along a chain; one term displaces another only to be displaced in its turn by another. Since each of the terms in this chain signifies only in relation to a term that is other than itself, meaning both defers to and is repeatedly deferred by a differential and seemingly infinite play of signification.

Although those of us who teach writing are likely to appreciate the general idea that writing is exemplary, we are less likely to appreciate Derrida's specific reasons for treating it as such. Part of the problem is that Derrida has too often been (mis)interpreted as a prophet of free play—as someone who proclaims that because there are no transcendent guarantees of meaning, anything goes. But even if we dismiss this problem on the grounds that it is based on a less than careful reading of Derrida's work, another more pragmatic problem remains. By treating writing in terms of difference and deferral, Derrida seeks to displace the subject of cognition. In consequence, his way of dealing with Zeno's paradox is not especially useful to those of us who assume that, as teachers, we must address the cognitive subject—the one who knows through thinking.[6]

Unlike Derrida, Peirce does not attempt to displace the cognitive subject; instead, he broaches that subject in an effort to figure out how meaningful thought is produced. Yet, in so doing, Peirce does not ignore the issues of difference and deferral that Derrida has done so much to bring to our attention. Indeed, much of the current interest in Peirce's work is based on a realization that it both anticipates and extends the principles of such contemporary semioticians as Benveniste, Lacan, and Derrida.

Peirce anticipates contemporary semiotics in two ways. First, he treats signification and interpretation as fundamentally inseparable; for Peirce, every sign is an interpreting thought and every interpreting thought, a sign. Second, he represents thoughtful signification as a radically diachronic and hence radically discursive process; for Peirce, thoughtful signification is the "process of beginning" and "change" by means of which "cognition arises" (5:263).

But at the same time that Peirce anticipates the principles of contemporary semiotics, he also extends them in a much-needed pragmatic direction. Unlike many post-Saussurean semioticians, Peirce is intent on articulating the missing link between signification and the "real" world. As his revision of Zeno's paradox shows, he believes that, in fact, thinking through signs really matters. His problem, however, is to figure out when and how Achilles overtakes the tortoise—when and how thinking through signs really does make a difference in the subject of cognition.

Peirce's abiding concern with the sign's referentiality is one indication of his pragmatism. As he puts it, a "sign has three references: first, it is a sign *to* some thought that interprets it; second, it is a sign *for* some object to which in that thought it is equivalent; third, it is a sign *in* some respect or quality, which brings it into connection with its object" (5:283). Although the claim that a sign has some kind of "connection with its object" sounds quite pragmatic, it also seems to contradict one of the most basic of all semiotic principles: the principle that language is a system of differences without positive terms. However, as a closer analysis of Peirce's argument reveals, this contradiction is more apparent than real.

Since Peirce claims that the *first* reference of a sign is to an interpretant and not to an object, he, like Saussure, recognizes that signs have no direct or natural relation to things. Furthermore, Peirce is careful to note that the relation of equivalence between sign and object exists only within an interpretant: "in that thought, it is equivalent." And finally, Peirce not only describes this equivalence as partial and relative (i.e., "in some respect or quality") but also insists that as an interpretant it is a sign, a sign that necessarily refers to yet another interpretant, another sign. Thus, unlike Saussure, Peirce refuses to institute a systematic distinction between signifier and signified, a distinction that would make it possible to separate signification from interpretation and expression from thought.

But even though Peirce refuses to uphold a systematic distinction between signifier and signified, he does posit a temporal difference between sign and interpretant, a difference that allows for the emergence of a temporary connection between the sign and its object. Moreover, Peirce's general conception of signifying, thinking, and knowing is radically diachronic. On the one hand, he presents these processes as retrospective; the interpretant to which a sign refers is always related to some prior "testimony" (5:233), or to some "previous thought" (5:285), or to some "immense mass of cognition already formed" (5:416). On the other hand, Peirce presents these processes as prospective; by positing some temporary equivalence, an interpreting sign necessarily anticipates another interpretant, another sign: "each former thought suggests something to the thought which follows it, i.e. is the sign of something to this latter" (5:284).

In representing signification as a radically diachronic process characterized by an endless commutability of interpretants, Peirce anticipates Derrida's claim that meaningful thought always defers to and is therefore deferred by a differential and never-ending series of signs. In part, it is this deferral and difference that Peirce is referring to when he states that if "every thought is a sign, it follows that every thought must address some other, must determine some other, since that is the essence of the sign" (5:253). However, this referential interpretation is only part of what is at issue in Peirce's statement. If it were all, then Peirce would not be able to explain why and how thinking through signs can make a real difference in the subject of cognition. In fact, how is it that Achilles overtakes the tortoise?

Drawing on the ideology of humanism, Peirce first attempts to answer this question by referring us to "man" and "community." Although the signifying process endlessly defers objective fact, the signs that constitute that deferral produce the true subject of cognition—a subject that Peirce calls "man":

> . . .the fact that every thought is a sign, taken in conjunction with the fact that life is a train of thought proves that man is a sign. . . .Thus my language is the sum total of myself; for man is the thought. (5:314)

With this answer in mind, teachers might exhort their students to think through signs on the grounds that such thinking will give them access to the self and, by way of the self, to man as a sign.

However, the problem with this answer is that access to the self is not the same thing as real knowledge. As Peirce recognized, "the real. . . is that which, sooner or later, information and reasoning would finally result in, and which is therefore independent of the vagaries of me and you" (5:311). To solve this problem, Peirce posited a second answer—"community":

> . . .the very origin of the conception of reality shows that this conception essentially involves the notion of a COMMUNITY, without definite limits, and capable of a definite increase of knowledge. (5:311)

With this answer in mind, teachers might invite their students to think through signs on the grounds that such thinking will make them members of a knowledgeable community.[7]

The problem, however, is that community is nothing more than an idea—an interpretant that is necessarily subject to a seemingly endless commutability of signs:

> Finally, as what anything really is, is what it may finally come to be known to be in the *ideal state* of complete information, so that reality depends on the *ultimate* decision of the community; so thought is what it is, only by virtue of its addressing a *future thought* which is *in its value* as thought identical with it, though more developed. In this way, the existence of thought now depends on what is to be hereafter; so that it has only *a potential existence*, dependent on the future thought of the community. (5:316, my emphasis)

By representing community as an idea of the future, Peirce acknowledges the fact that what is real is not the *existence* of community but the rhetorical appeal to some such idea. But if this is the case, then "community" cannot explain how Achilles *in fact* overtakes the tortoise—how thinking through signs does indeed make a real difference in the subject of cognition.

In an essay entitled "A Survey of Pragmatism," Peirce finally realizes when and how thinking through signs really comes to matter to the subject of cognition. Once again, he considers the meaning of signification. However, this time, Peirce considers meaning not only in relation to the reference of signs but also in relation to the "proper significate effects of signs" (5:475). Although Peirce considers these effects as interpretants, he also argues that a thought can not be "the *ultimate* logical interpretant" of thinking through signs because every thought "must itself have a logical interpretant"—and so on *ad infinitum* (5:476). So what then is the ultimate logical interpretant of thinking through signs? How in fact does Achilles overtake the tortoise?

According to Peirce, thinking through signs makes a real or pragmatic difference when—and only when—it involves a *"habit-change"* (5:476)—a "modification of consciousness" (5:485) that is also "a modification of a person's tendencies toward action" (5:476). Like habit, habit-change "excludes natural dispositions" and "includes associations"; however, unlike habit, habit-change entails "transsociations" and *"dissociations"* as well as "associations" (5:476). In short, habit-change is a process of thinking otherwise, a process of "beginning" and "change" in which "thought must address itself to some other, must determine some other, since that is the essence of the sign" (5:253).

In another essay, Peirce not only associates fact, actuality, and reality with experience but also claims that "it is the compulsion, the absolute constraint upon us *to think otherwise* than we have been thinking that constitutes experience" (1:321). Thus, the fact that Achilles overtakes the tortoise may also be understood as an experience, as an experience whose "living definition...and final logical interpretant" is a "deliberately formed self-analyzing habit"—a habit of habit-change (5:491). As long as Achilles is content with being moved, he cannot overtake the tortoise. However, if he *does* something different—something other rather than the same—then he can experience the reality of thinking through signs. Hence, for Peirce, the missing link between signification and the real is praxis—the pragmatic process of beginning and change.

Once we have reached this point—the point of a thoughtful praxis— it becomes possible to develop a pragmatic approach to the teaching of thinking through writing. However, before I suggest what such an approach entails, some summarizing remarks about thinking and writing as semiotic processes are in order.

CONSOLIDATING GAINS

Semiotically considered, thinking is essentially and primordially a discursive process. As such, thinking not only depends on signs that enjoy no direct or natural relation to things but also involves the subject of cognition in a signifying process that is both retrospective and prospective. Since signification is retrospective, thinking occurs in relation to prior testimony; that is, it is always related to the established discursive institutions, conventions, and ideologies of a speech community. However, since signification is also prospective, thought can never absolutely and fully know the objects and subjects to which it repeatedly refers. But even though thinking through signs never reaches knowledge of the real, when it involves a habit-change, it does make a real difference in the subject of cognition. Then, and only then, does it become a process of beginning and change, a process of knowing.

Since writing is a signifying process, it may be exemplary for both thinking and knowing. However, if writing is to function as an exemplary instance of thinking through signs, then it must be considered as something other than the expression or the translation or the shaping of thought. In all three of these commonplace conceptions of writing, both thought and the subject of cognition are presumed to exist before and beyond the process or writing, if not before and beyond the signifying process in general. In consequence, writing becomes the representation of thought rather than the realization of thinking.

Instead of these commonplace models, we need a way of articulating writing as an act of thinking, a way that takes the following semiotic principles into account: that thoughtful signification occurs only in and through discourse; that discourse requires a subject; that the subject of discourse is itself an effect of discourse; and that the subject, discourse, and thoughtful signification always address some other, determine some other. In short, what we need is a radically discursive conception of writing, a conception that acknowledges Zeno's paradox as well as the fact that Achilles can indeed overtake the tortoise. Perhaps the following parable will help us to conceive writing along such lines.

Etymologically, the word *discourse* derives from the Latin verb *discurrere*, "to run to and fro." Thus, discourse would seem to necessitate a displacement—a running from one place to another. Like a Greek messenger, the subject of discourse runs away from home, away from a familiar or common place inscribed in memory. His running, however, requires repetition; with each step, the messenger repeats what he knows—what he has been told. In so doing, he arrives at another place, an unfamiliar place in which he finds that a message always addresses some other, determines some other. Such a finding not only frees the messenger to return but also makes it possible for him to repeat in a different way. Having been in another place, he can now retrace his steps with respect to that other and, in so doing, experience discourse as a self-analyzing habit, a process of beginning and change, and a running to and fro.

SOME PRAGMATIC SUGGESTIONS

As I see it, a radically discursive conception of thinking through writing entails making revision central to both the teaching and practice of composition. To some teachers, the centrality of revision may seem a strange idea. However, to those who are familiar with the recent reorientation in the theory and practice of teaching writing, this idea is likely to appear rather commonplace.

Whereas in the late 1960s the most common way of teaching writing was to demand that students read, analyze, and imitate beautifully crafted works by men of letters, nowadays composition specialists are likely not only to teach students strategies for generating and organizing ideas but also to supply interim reports on each student's work in progress. Among specialists, this change is often described as a shift in focus from product to process (Hairston). Although such a description is not without merit, to the extent that it implies that the product-centered teacher had no interest in process, it is unfair. A more generous approach to the past reveals not a lack of interest in process but a conception of process that is wanting in complexity. Usually, the product-centered teacher conceived writing to be a rather simple process of representing ideas in clear, if not beautiful, prose. Today's process-centered teacher, however, tends to conceive composing as something more complicated and hence often talks about the process in terms of prewriting, writing, and revising.

Although process-oriented teachers are fond of accentuating their difference from the older product-centered teachers of writing, the popularity of the three-step paradigm of writing belies the difference. Not only does the use of the term *prewriting* link the newer paradigm with the older representational model of process, but the linearity of the new paradigm also reminds one of a completed product—in this case, a correct sentence that moves in one direction from start to finish, from subject (prewriting) to predicate (writing) to end punctuation (revising). Small wonder then that even though the demand for revision is something new, it rarely if ever makes any real difference. In response to such demands, students usually search for a synonym to replace their subject, add an adverb here and there, check their punctuation, and then make a clean copy for the teacher.

As Nancy Sommers has documented, these students are operating on the assumption that words are primordially and essentially instrumets of communication—tools to be used to translate a meaning that is conceived to be existentially prior to discursive language. In an effort to make their translations both clear and proper, these students engage in such acts as correcting and rewording—acts that betray a limited conception of both thinking and writing. As Sommers so aptly puts it, such students are working with a "thesaurus philosophy of writing" (381). As this phrase implies, the problem lies not so much in the student's recourse to a thesaurus as in their common-sense philosophy—their notion that what one finds in a thesaurus is more of the same, more words that can be used to translate some preexisting meaning, idea, or truth.

Unfortunately, our tendency to conceive and represent writing as either a linear-expressive process or a goal-directed–instrumental process serves to reinforce rather than to revise the typical student's assumptions, ideas, and actions. Indeed, if we want students to think through writing in ways that really make a difference, then another conception of writing is necessary. By bringing to bear a knowledge of semiotics, we may be able to conceive writing as a discursive process and in so doing change our teaching habits in ways that may help our students to change their writing habits.

Like good messengers, student writers usually begin by repeating what they know—what they have been told. Although this repetition will always already have brought them to another place, they won't necessarily recognize that place as different before they have been introduced to the fact that "every thought must address itself to some other, must determine some other, since that is the essence of the sign" (Peirce, 5:253). Indeed, if we insist on revision before the necessary introductions have taken place, then our insistence is most likely to be interpreted as a demand to repeat the same message—only this time more clearly and properly. How then might we encourage students to engage in revisionary thinking, the kind of thinking through signs that makes a difference?

Generally speaking, what we need to do is to introduce the other. In some instances, this might mean nothing more nor less than provoking students' awareness that they think in and through signs. So, for example, we might ask a student to list the key terms she or he has used to compose a draft and then to figure out not only the relationships among the terms but also the set of assumptions the use of such terms implies. Or, we might suggest that another student put quotation marks around his or her key terms and then consider how the quotation marks change things. For a different student, however, it might be better to try something else—say an exercise in slowing language down. If so, then we might ask the student to choose the most important word in his or her draft, to generate a list of synonyms for that word, to choose one of the synonyms, and then to engage in a dialogue about how the two terms are different (Wertime). In all these instances, we would be inviting students to think not only about the language they use but also how language uses them.

But there are still other ways of introducing the other. If it is indeed the case that knowing something about semiotics can help a teacher to think otherwise about writing, then it may also be the case that introducing the student to some other, unfamiliar discourse will make a difference. For example, a student recently shared with me a draft of an essay in which she was exploring the implications of a specific problematic event: the disruption by an outsider of an intimate gathering, a gathering that this student referred to as "the typical dorm-room cocktail party." In reading this draft, I was not only surprised to hear that there was such a thing as a "typical dorm-room cocktail party" but also intrigued by the ritualistic implications of her term. In responding to her draft, I mentioned my surprise as well as my sense that a folklorist—if not an anthropologist— might be interested in such a ritual. Although my reference to folklore and anthropology was rather offhand, it provoked this student to find out something about rituals and then, based on what she had learned, to repeat with a difference.

For the student writer, however, the most important other is likely to be the reader. Although nowadays it is something of a commonplace to say that inexperienced writers fail to take the reader into consideration, I think the problem is a bit more complex. It seems to me that students do indeed write for a reader; however, the reader they write for is someone who is too familiar. Unlike the messenger who actually finds himself in another place, addressing somebody who is different, the student writer too often fantasizes the other as the same and in so doing repeats his message either to someone like himself or to someone equally familiar: the paternalistic teacher who presumably already knows the meaning of it all.

If such is the case, then our job is not merely to stage the writer's encounter with a reader but rather to stage the messenger's encounter with somebody who's different—with someone who expects to be transformed when the messenger makes the scene. In practice, I have found that differentiating the term *aim* from *point* often helps my students to imagine the possibility of another, less familiar reader. If the point is a saying or message, then the aim would be what the writer seeks to do to and for a reader by repeating that saying. Since telling a reader something that she or he already knows and believes actually does nothing, the implication is that a "doing" is tantamount to clarifying, expanding, changing, or intensifying what the reader knows and believes (Young, Becker, and Pike). In short, a "doing" must make a real and pragmatic difference in the subject of cognition—in the reader as well as the writer.

As these suggestions for introducing the other imply, making a difference is not so much a "solution" to the "thinking problem" as it is an intervention designed to provoke the realization that there are problems and possibilities worth thinking through in writing. In short, intervention is a pragmatic process; like revision, it is a "doing" that cannot be ruled by either some universal model or some foolproof method for making a difference. Nevertheless, intervention need not be haphazard, illogical, or unprincipled; if we keep in mind the paradoxical yet pragmatic argument that since "every thought is a sign, it follows that every thought must address itself to some other, must determine some other" (Peirce 5:253), then it is likely that we will intervene in ways that encourage our students to develop the habit of revisionary thinking.

Experienced writers realize that revision involves organizing information, drawing inferences, and representing problems in ways that make a real difference in how and what they know. Student writers can also come to this realization—but only if they have experiences in thinking otherwise. Such experiences should therefore be at the center of the composition course. However, one course cannot solve the "thinking problem." Students need not only lots of experience in thinking through writing but also various contexts for those experiences. In short, they need thinking through writing across the curriculum. If we teachers work together to develop and articulate a radically discursive approach to writing, thinking, and knowing, then eventually students may indeed get what they need: an educational experience whose "living definition...and final logical interpretant" is a "deliberately formed self-analyzing habit (Peirce 5:491)—the habit of habit-change.

NOTES

1. Aristotle alludes to Zeno's paradoxes in the *Physics* (239b5–33) as well as in the *Topics* (160b7–9, 172a8–10, 179b20–21). For an accessible account of the paradoxes and their philosophical implications, see Vlastos.
2. The phrase "the subject of cognition" refers both to cognition as a subject or area of research and to the person who thinks and knows. Since I believe that the study of cognition presupposes a subject and that, in our culture, the notion of a subject presupposes cognition, the referential doubleness of my phrasing is purposeful—and therefore designed to be enlightening rather than obfuscating.
3. In his introduction to *Philosophical Writings of Peirce*, Buchler explains well why cognitive psychologists, logicians, and teachers of writing should be interested in Peirce's pragmatism:

   In the versions of James and Schiller, a huge pragmatist offspring flourished early in this century. But the seeds of confusion and superficiality caused it to die as suddenly as it had been born.... Whereas Popular pragmatism is an anti-intellectualist revolt, an embrace of the "will to believe" pathetic in its methodological feebleness, Peircian pragmatism (pragmaticism) demonstrating the fatuity of an emphasis on mere volition or sensation, is precisely intellectualistic. Popular pragmatism is an interesting manifestation of the general empirical temper; pragmaticism is a step forward in the history of empiricism. It differs from the classical British tradition, from Kant's antimetaphysical scepticism, and from nineteenth century positivism, primarily in that it introduces the concept of meaning into empiricist methodology. It is the first deliberate theory of meaning in modern times, and it offers a logical technique for the clarification of ideas. It has a potential far greater than that of similar theories current today, for it embodies an analysis of knowledge with rich implications. Peirce maintains that in so far as thought is cognitive, it must be linguistic or symbolical in character—that is, it must presuppose communication. Communication takes place by means of signs, and Peirce's theory, in its investigation of the nature and conditions of the sign-relation endows with a new and vital significance the old truth that man is a social animal. His view differs from others in stressing that pragmatic definition cannot be in terms of individual reaction or private sensation, which are incommunicable, but of that which is public and general—a habit of action. If our language is to possess cognitive meaning, it must be defined by the ways it is used communicatively. In opposition to atomistic psychology, Peirce demonstrates that no thought (in so far as it is a mental sign) is perfectly unitary or simple but is in-separable from interpretation by other thoughts. . . .

A frequently repeated assertion by Peirce that pragmaticism is not a metaphysical theory but a logical rule directs attention to another of his path-breaking contributions, the conception of logic as the philosophy of communication or theory of signs. . . . The conception of logic as semiotic opens broad, new possibilities. . . . To regard empirical science, mathematics, and the whole of human discourse as so many types of domains in which signs operate, both clarifies and fertilizes the range of logic. . . . The desideratum in logical theory at present is the unification of emphases. . . . Semiotic would appear to be the answer. It is perhaps broader and more thoroughgoing in conception than what is today called the theory of inquiry, since its analysis would penetrate not only to the standards, presuppositions, and forms of the problem-solving situation but to those implicit in the most rudimentary types of all communication. (xi–xiii)[1]

4. Saussure, *Cours de linguistique general* (Paris: Payot, 1960, p.99), as quoted and translated by Samuel Weber in "Closure and Exclusion," 38. In this instance, I have preferred Weber's translation over the standard English translation not only because I believe it a more accurate rendering but also because it makes it easier for me to make my point about Saussure's appeal to sameness.

---

[1] From Justus Buchler (ed.). *Philosophical Writings of Peirce.* New York: Dover Publications, 1955, pp. xi–xiii. Reprinted by permission of the publisher.

5. Excellent introductions to contemporary semiotics are found in: Coward and Ellis; Silverman; Belsey; De Lauretis; and Blonsky. In one way or another, all these books address the issue of the subject.
6. Two recent books do address the pedagogical implications of Derrida's work: Ulmer, and Atkins and Johnson. However, in both books, the cognitive subject is most often represented as "the one who is presumed to know"—and hence, as the one who must be displaced.
7. The appeal to community is currently in vogue. For a philosopher's use of this appeal see Richard Rorty (1982, 1979). For a composition specialist's use of this appeal, see Bizzell. In the field of cognitive psychology, the appeal to community seems to take the form of an emphasis on the sociocultural bases of cognition; see, for example, Luria.

WORKS CITED

Atkins, C. Douglas, and Michael Johnson, eds. *Writing and Reading Differently: Deconstruction and the Teaching of Composition and Literature.* Lawrence: University of Kansas Press, 1985.

Barthes, Roland. *Elements of Semiology.* Trans. Annette Lavers and Colin Smith. New York: Hill and Wang, 1968.

———. *Writing Degree Zero.* Trans. Annette Lavers and Colin Smith. New York: Hill and Wang, 1968.

———. *Critical Essays.* Trans. Richard Howard. Evanston: Northwestern University Press, 1972.

———. *Mythologies.* Trans. Annette Lavers. New York: Hill and Wang, 1972.

———. *Pleasure of the Text.* Trans. Richard Miller. New York: Hill and Wang, 1975.

———. *Image, Music, Text.* Trans. Stephen Heath. New York: Hill and Wang, 1977.

Belsey, Catherine. *Critical Practice.* London: Methuen, 1980.

Benveniste, Emile. *Problems in General Linguistics.* Trans. Mary Elizabeth Meek. Coral Gables: University of Miami Press, 1971.

Bizzell, Patricia. "Cognition, Convention, and Certainty: What We Need To Know About Writing." *Pretext* 3 (1982): 213–243.

Blonsky, Marshall, ed. *On Signs.* Baltimore: Johns Hopkins University Press, 1985.

Buchler, Justus. "Introduction." *Philosophical Writings of Peirce.* Ed. Justus Buchler. New York: Dover, 1955. ix–xvi.

Coward, Rosalind, and John Ellis. *Language and Materialism: Developments in Semiology and the Theory of the Subject.* London: Routledge & Kegan Paul, 1977.

Culler, Jonathan. *Structuralist Poetics.* Ithaca: Cornell University Press, 1975.

———. *The Pursuit of Signs.* Ithaca: Cornell University Press, 1981.

De Lauretis, Teresa. *Alice Doesn't: Feminism, Semiotics, Cinema.* Bloomington: Indiana University Press, 1984.

Derrida, Jacques. *Of Grammatology*. Trans Gayatri Spivak. Baltimore: Johns Hopkins University Press, 1976.

———. *Writing and Difference*. Trans. Alan Bass. Chicago: University of Chicago Press, 1978.

Foucault, Michel. *The Order of Things: An Archaeology of the Human Sciences*. New York: Pantheon, 1971.

———. *The Archaeology of Knowledge and The Discourse on Language*. Trans. A.M. Sheridan Smith. New York: Pantheon, 1972.

———. *Power/Knowledge*. Trans. Colin Gordon, Leo Marshall, John Mepham, and Kate Soper. Ed. Colin Gordon. New York: Pantheon, 1980.

Hairston, Maxine. "The Winds of Change: Thomas Kuhn and the Revolution in the Teaching of Writing." *College Composition and Communication* 33 (1982): 76–88.

Lacan, Jacques. *The Language of the Self*. Trans. Anthony Wilden. New York: Dell, 1968.

———. *Ecrits: A Selection*. Trans. Alan Sheridan. New York: Norton, 1977.

———. *The Four Fundamental Concepts of Psycho-Analysis*. Trans. Alan Sheridan. Ed. Jacques-Alain Miller. New York: Norton, 1978.

Levi-Strauss, Claude. *The Elementary Structures of Kinship*. Trans. James Harle Bell, John Richard von Sturmer, and Rodney Needham. Boston: Beacon Press, 1969.

Luria, A.R. *Cognitive Development: Its Cultural and Social Foundations*. Ed. Michael Cole. Trans. Martin Lopez-Morillas and Lynn Solotaroff. Cambridge: Harvard University Press, 1976.

Peirce, Charles Sanders. *Collected Papers*. Vols. 1 and 5. Ed. Charles Hartshorne and Paul Weiss. Cambridge: Harvard University Press, 1965.

Rorty, Richard. *Philosophy and the Mirror of Nature*. Princeton: Princeton University Press, 1979.

———. "Hermeneutics, General Studies, and Teaching." *Synergos* 2 (1982): 1–15.

Saussure, Ferdinand de. *Course in General Linguistics*. Trans. Wade Baskin. New York: McGraw-Hill, 1966.

Silverman, Kaja. *The Subject of Semiotics*. New York: Oxford University Press, 1983.

Sommers, Nancy. "Revision Strategies of Student Writers and Experienced Adult Writers." *College Composition and Communication* 31 (1980): 378–388.

Ulmer, Gregory. *Applied Grammatology: Post(e)—Pedagogy from Jacques Derrida to Joseph Beuys*. Baltimore: Johns Hopkins University Press, 1985.

Vlastos, Gregory. "Zeno of Elea." *The Encyclopedia of Philosophy*. Ed. Paul Edwards. New York: Macmillan, 1967. 8: 369–379.

Weber, Samuel. "Closure and Exclusion." *Diacritics* 10 (1980): 35–46.

Wertime, Richard. "Slowing Language Down: A Strategy for Systematically Getting at the Issues." *Thinking: The Second Invitational Conference*. Ed. D.N. Perkins, J. Lochhead, and J. Bishop. Hillsdale, NJ: Erlbaum, 1987. 487–506.

Young, Richard, Alton Becker, and Kenneth Pike. *Rhetoric: Discovery and Change*. New York: Harcourt, Brace and World, 1970.

Afterword: Two Ways of Thinking about Growth

The Problem of Finding the Right Metaphor

Joseph M. Williams

Most of the authors in this volume would agree on what to call the instrumental outcomes of a good education: intellectual autonomy, good critical thinking skills, the ability to go on learning, proficiency in written and oral communication, skilled problem solving, a mind flexible, open, and self-reflective. Those who have devoted their energies to matters of critical thinking in particular have formulated detailed lists of its principal features, to all of which we subscribe: ferreting out unstated assumptions, distinguishing between facts and opinion, evaluating evidence, distinguishing what is important from what is peripheral, recognizing logical fallacies, etc. Most of us also agree that if our students are to achieve any of these objectives, we have to do more than pass on to them information to memorize. We have to engage not only their memories but whatever other aspects of their intelligence that we would count as critical/logical/affective/moral/ethical/imaginative/reflective.

But in thinking about education, naming objectives is the easy part. The tougher part is achieving those objectives. Doing that depends on some hard preliminary thinking about a number of other matters. We all have some folk wisdom about how to teach those proficiencies that I will gather under the general term "cognitive skills": dialectic discussion, original research where possible, avoiding textbooks, peer learning groups, lots of writing, etc. But I grow increasingly uncertain that we have any sure sense of how we will know when our students have achieved any of those ends. What should we count as evidence that our students in fact think better as a result of our efforts, beyond the evidence of our final examinations, which are incorrigibly self-fulfilling artifacts? There are dozens of measures that claim to measure some quality of mental effort: IQ, SAT, GPA. Others characterize higher and lower "stages" by the manner in which a person attempts to solve a problem: Jean Piaget offers the categories of concrete and formal operational thinking; William Perry, dualist, multiple/relativist, relativist, and committed; Lawrence Kohlberg, preconventional, conventional, and postconventional. But while we can deploy a dozen or more systems of analysis and description, we also know that success in life is not well predicted by success in school or on tests of cognitive competence. We can do a better job of predicting success in life or school if we know the student's social and economic background. Never mind a student's SAT score; tell me her zip code.

Further complicating this question of how we measure cognitive growth are two issues that in recent times have been attracting increasing attention. First, some have suggested that mature intelligence may not consist of one holistic, indivisible competence, but of many: aesthetic, verbal, mathematical, spatial, musical, human relational, manual, etc. No one measure will capture the variety of components that define a person's cognitive maturity. While Piaget, Kohlberg, and Perry are roughly commensurable in their emphasis on development from less abstract to more abstract forms of thinking, they may be measuring not different aspects of a single cognitive competence, but of different kinds of competence, related perhaps, but which are not manifestations of the same intelligence.

More than that, if we include in "cognitive maturity" all the good critical thinking and problem-solving skills that we include among the aims of educational development, then we have to be extremely cautious not to confound holistic growth, growth "across-the-person," as it were, with the competence that comes from the acquisition of knowledge in particular communities of knowledge. In recent years, for example, researchers have been finding in very young children cognitive skills that were once thought to characterize only more mature minds. These skills were elicited by structuring the diagnostic problems in ways that reflected how much a child knew about the substance of the problem and how embedded the kind of problem was in the experience of the child. What might seem, then, as predictable cognitive growth in some biologically epistemic sense might be as deeply implicated in the sheer accumulation of a body of knowledge that is well structured, interconnected, and readily accessible.

There is also evidence that what we might otherwise characterize as "mature, highly developed thinking" is in fact much like a kind of thinking that distinguishes experts from novices. Let us define two kinds of novices. One we will call a "local" novice, a person who is largely unfamiliar with some well-defined field of study, unfamiliar with its knowledge, its conventions of argument and proof, its forms of discourse, but who is an expert in some other field, is familiar with that other field's knowledge, methods or argumentation, forms of discourse, etc. Distinguish that "local" novice from someone we will call a "generic" novice, someone who is not familiar with the knowledge, conventions of argument and proof, forms of discourse in any well-developed field of knowledge. If we ask those two novices to solve a problem in a field in which both are novices, we might expect the "local" novice to distinguish herself from the generic novice in the way she attempts to solve the problem; we might expect her to deploy and reveal some trace of the expert thinking skills she acquired in her own field of expertise.

But some credible experimental evidence suggests that she will not, that she and the generic novice will go about solving a problem strange to both of them in about the same way. And that way bears much in common with those who are placed at the lower end of the Piaget/Kohlberg/Perry scales: The novice problem solver will seem to display rather concrete thinking, thinking that begins with some concrete detail of the problem rather than with the abstract nature of the problem. In other words, expertise does not seem to travel well.

Moreover, after decades of attempting to teach students how to think well through courses in generic problem solving and critical thinking skills, those who have most earnestly pressed for such courses have failed to provide persuasive evidence that when a student leaves the course, he is able to think better, solve problems better, in specific fields of study. This is not to say that expert problem solvers do think in similar ways, only that good (i.e., expert) thinking may be so deeply implicated in a specific body of knowledge, in experience, that for all practical purposes, it is impossible in practice to disentangle thinking skills from knowledge.

The point is this: We have to think very hard about the utility of diagnosing a person's cognitive development by any scheme that assumes a holistic cognitive competence that grows in the way height, weight, or strength grow. It may be that rather than thinking just in terms of a holistic developmental model, another model of increasing competence might be found in the idea of *socialization into a community of knowledge,* with knowledge including skills of thinking, problem solving, etc.

For the last five years, these issues have constituted the central concerns of the Institutes in Critical Thinking at the University of Chicago. I think it is fair to say that the Institutes began by exploring the curricular implications of working within the holistic developmental model and then gradually shifted toward a greater emphasis on the social model. It was a shift from one metaphor for growth to another. Some of the essays in this collection clearly reflect those metaphors. I'd like to sketch these two metaphors and their implications, not to discredit one and urge its replacement with another (though it may seem for a time that I am doing that), but to suggest why the second metaphor has seemed so compelling to so many of the Institute's participants.

We all submit our thinking to the screen of metaphor. In our culture, anger is a "pressure" we "bottle up" inside the container of our bodies, a pressure that we must "release" before we "explode." Once we have "blown off some steam," we are therapeutically relieved. Were the culture and the metaphor different, we might give different advice about dealing with anger: When we become angry, we rev up our internal machinery too high, so we have to put our emotions into neutral and coast a bit. Under no circumstances, do we uncap the radiator until after we have cooled down. By one metaphor, the release of anger is therapeutic by preventing greater damage. By another metaphor, it is the release of anger that could injure us.

Let me describe a metaphor that I think many of us tacitly use to organize how we think about cognitive growth from whatever counts as uncritical thinking/ineffective problem solving to good critical thinking/effective problem solving. Because the metaphor is so powerful, as I wrote that sentence, I had to struggle to avoid using it. I found myself writing "whatever counts as *lower* order *thinking/immature* thinking..." I was drawn to the conceit of growth and development as represented by a rising left-to-right line on a graph.

We typically graph development as a movement from lower left to upper right. The line may be a smooth curve or a stairstep. Ordinarily, we do not visualize this "growth" line as a staggered series of increasingly higher peaks and less deep valleys. That is, we do not get lighter before we get heavier, shorter before we get taller, less intelligent before we become more intelligent, less competent before we become more competent. We grow steadily more competent, with perhaps some plateaus before we move on to the next higher stage.

In the form of a stairstep, it is the model we use to account for the movement of a person through Kohlberg's three stages, or Piaget's four, or Perry's five. The person begins at lower left and achieves higher stages, not steadily to be sure, but over time (measured left to right) predictably ("naturally," given normal intelligence and the right environment) the person moves upward and onward, toward a goal located somewhere in the upper right quadrant. Most developmentalists build in a period when the child/student may seem to show some retrogressive behavior as a result of conflicts between what he has assimilated and what he is experiencing, but that "backsliding" or "regression" is only a prelude to further growth. It is a metaphor that encourages other metaphors: If we "lay a solid foundation in the base[ics]," and then "reinforce" growth, then the person both "maintains" what she has learned and "builds" on it toward mastery. Each Institute has explored some aspect of this notion of development.

It is an appealing metaphor because it has been richly developed by developmentalists and because it allows us to account for so much of experience with students. It also provides us with a ready rationale for criticizing apparent failure to grow. If any of our students do not seem to have achieved the level of development we expect, then we can criticize those who should earlier have raised that student to an appropriate level of performance. Thus if we think our first year students can't think and can't write at a level we expect, then we can blame high school teachers. If we teach advanced undergraduates who can't construct an argument and write clearly, we can blame teachers of freshman composition. If we teach graduate students who can't construct a coherent argument, we can blame their undergraduate teachers. At whatever level, we can blame the failure of our students on those who did not provide them with the foundation, the base[ics] that the student needs to perform at a higher level.

It is metaphor that may also encourage us to understand ourselves and our students in ways that affect our perceptions of responsibility. When we place our students on a graph, we pigeonhole them by giving them the name of the point on the graph defined by the system of measurement—thus our students are "eighth decile IQ," or "concrete operational," or "dualist," or "conventional." We chart their growth as they "rise" through subsequent stages, as they "become" those "higher" stages. When they do not develop, we might wonder what they need to grow—perhaps a richer intellectual environment, more stimulation, etc. But however we might define our responsibility to the student on the graph, we stand in an observer's third dimension, disconnected from the metaphor that figures forth the student and his progress. We may go back to the classroom and change the ecology to encourage growth, but as we think through the problem, our students remain essentially "others." We are the "we" who measure and they are the "they" who perform. The metaphor of the graph does not encourage us to put ourselves into the figure as we consider it.

There are other consequences of this metaphor: Just as getting taller and heavier is something that just happens, intellectual growth seems inevitable; it is what all normal people do. So if a student does not grow, then something may be wrong with the student, but in any event, the student seems to have a say in the matter no more significant than the observer's. The metaphor does not encourage us to look upon retrogression as desirable. With Piaget, Perry, and Kohlberg, we may know that retrogression is predictable, but once a person has achieved a "higher" level of performance, a "lower" level of performance is something to endure. And the metaphor defines the goal of growth in achieving the upper right hand corner of the chart.

I am not asserting that we all think all these things about our students all the time, or that those who have offered us models of growth of the "upward–and–onward" type are wrong or misleading. I want only to tease out some ways of thinking that are surely not unfamiliar to most of us, to suggest that they may be consequences of one very common way of thinking about development, and why another has seemed so compelling.

The other metaphor is that of the outsider, standing outside a bounded area that defines the community of discourse, the interpretive community, consisting of us and our peers. The person may or may not be trying to join our community, and we may or may not be trying to draw him in. By this figure the student may still be an "other," but the figure encourages us to think about that student and ourselves in ways different from the figure of the graph. First, we are in the figure along with the student, and so we have to observe not only the student, but the student in relation to ourselves. Second, the metaphor does not encourage us to think about "higher" (and so "better thinking") and "lower" (and so "worse thinking"), but insider thinking (socialized/expert thinking) and outsider thinking (not yet socialized/novice thinking).

Third, the metaphor encourages us to locate motivation in two places. As I suggested earlier, the graph metaphor can suggest that the student may be expected to progress in the same way she gets taller or heavier or stronger: naturally, perhaps inevitably, barring some failure in the environment. But with the metaphor of the interpretive community, the community of discourse, with the student standing outside, we have to consider the possibility that the student, in fact, does not want to join our community. Indeed, we may not want to socialize the student into our community, but rather to socialize him into some larger community of "generally educated citizens." The movement from outside the circle to inside is not natural, inevitable, developmental, but rather a consequence of two deliberate acts, one by the student and one by us, acts that require some thought.

More to the point perhaps, the metaphor forces us to consider more carefully our responsibility in making membership possible for the student who wants to join our community. If "joining" is by this metaphor socialization, the social equivalent of "growth," then the conditions for joining have to include our telling the student what counts as behaving like a member of our community. The student who appears to be unable to join the community may in fact not be unintelligent, intellectually immature, etc., but rather a novice, unsocialized in ways that make him appear unintelligent, intellectually immature, etc. If that is so, then we have to look carefully at our own ways of evaluating what counts as appropriate behavior. Indeed, we have to become our own ethnographers, because most of us engage in intellectual customs that we are wholly incapable of articulating because we are so deeply enmeshed in the social fabric, unaware of social conventions in the same way we are are unaware of the air we breathe.

A very short example. How many among us believe that scientific writing does not allow the use of the first person pronouns, *I* or *we*? It does, of course, but ordinarily only under certain conditions. Scientific writers frequently (not always) use *we* (less often *I* because most scientific writing is more often jointly than singly authored) when they refer to their acts of proving, defining, claiming, showing, introducing, concluding, etc.— verbal actions we might call *metadiscourse,* language that refers to the act of discoursing. Rarely do scientific writers use the first person when they are referring to their primary acts of investigation; i.e., one would rarely find, "I intubated the rat," instead of "The rat was intubated." On the other hand, we frequently find, "I will show....," at least as often as "It will be shown...." It is this kind of tacitly understood local convention that, violated, makes the novice student seem less than entirely competent. There are countless others.

This metaphor also turns our attention to the knowledge one must have in order to behave in the way members of the community behave in regard to how they reason. For example, here is a typical practice problem from a course in generic "critical thinking."

> All his life, George lived next door to Luigi Giancana. He got to know Luigi very well, something he did not want to do, because as Luigi grew up, he became a small time drug dealer, then a leader in organized crime. Finally, Luigi was killed one night when some others in his organization tried to take over the drug distribution network Luigi had set up. Well, said George, I'm going to move away and when I do, you can be sure that I'll never again live next door to someone of that nationality. What mistake has George made?

Overgeneralization on the basis of a single observation, of course, a mistake we often make in our life–at–large. But in the field of composition research, reputations have been made by intensively observing the development of a single young writer. In short, what counts as adequate data in one interpretive community, one community of discourse, may count as inadequate in another. The point is that the metaphor of the community forces us to think not just about what globally counts as "correct knowledge and good thinking," but "what counts as correct values and behavior relative to the pertinent community."

But there is an even more interesting consequence of exchanging the metaphor of the graph for the metaphor of the community, one that particularly applies to the matter of writing. Consider what a student must do to become a member of an interpretive community, a particular community of discourse. First, she has to accumulate correct knowledge that the community defines as its special domain. Lawyers learn about the law and legal procedure, doctors learn about the body and medical treatment, English teachers learn about Shakespeare and how to read him. But more than that, she also has to learn about the history of the conversation that has led to the current state of the knowledge. Only then will she know why some questions are more important than others, why some answers no longer count as good answers. Second, she has to learn how to think like those in the community, how to pose and explore problems (another reason for learning the history of the conversation). As suggested above, what counts as a good argument to a Freudian literary critic interested in accounting for a character's mental state may seem to be sheer poppycock to a cognitive psychologist.

These two tasks alone—acquiring new knowledge and acquiring new habits of thought—would be challenging enough, but in addition, the outsider must also learn how to **sound** like a member of the community. A law student must learn not only what a lawyer knows and how to think the way a lawyer thinks, but also how to sound the way a lawyer sounds. But here's the problem: Sounding like someone in the community means learning not just what to say and how to say it, but also what not to say and especially when not to say it. We define those who are closest to us by what we don't have to say to them. When we say the things that need not be said, we seem to be saying the obvious, the things that are so self-evident to an insider that only someone not very knowledgeable would say them. And when we say very self-evident things, we may be judged not just unsocialized, but less than intelligent. It is true that Shakespeare is a well-known English playwright, but it is inappropriate to say so in a paper written in a graduate English class devoted to his tragedies.

All of this imposes an immense cognitive burden on any novice trying to join a community. And so it is not surprising that she may at times behave in ways that seem less than competent, particularly in regard to some of those skills that she may already have acquired, such as a command over clear and direct English. Recall that the novice/immature thinker is in the grip of concreteness: As a novice, she can "see" in this strange community only what is most concretely before her (hence the reason many students seem to become the equivalent of intellectual arrivistes in a field, using technical terms that they do not understand. But those terms may be the only visible, concrete signs of the voice appropriate to the field, so it is small wonder that a novice student will seize on those terms as signs of membership in the community). The rules of thinking, the values, the silences—they are all invisible, unstated, abstract. The novice learner has to infer them through experience, and so she may seem to be like a concrete operational thinker, a dualist, an uncritical thinker, an unskilled problem solver.

But in expressing herself in writing, she may also seem especially incompetent if the cognitive burden of learning new knowledge, new ways of thought, new ways of expression results in her losing some control over skills learned earlier. There is no shortage of evidence that many freshman students who have learned how to write coherent "narrative" and "descriptive" essays seem to suffer relapses in the fundamental matters of spelling and grammar when they try to deal with "expository" and "argumentative" writing. Why should that be? Narrative is a very concrete form of discourse; exposition relies on rules of form wholly invisible and abstract. As many students wrestle with those abstractions, they lose control over other less deeply entrenched skills of discourse. The same principle seems to hold when students enter a completely new community of discourse. Their performance in some areas degrade as they acquire new skills.

Now there is an immense irony in all this. We can predict that a student's control over his discourse will suffer when wrestling with other cognitive burdens. That loss of control may predictably be in the direction of simple degradation of sentence structure, paragraph structure, etc. But it may also take the form of seizing on a simpler solution to the rhetorical problem; i.e., finding a default form of organization that allows him to attend less to organization, more to content. And that typically takes the form of summarizing a text rather than "analyzing" it. This tendency is accentuated by the fact that the novice student ordinarily does not have the knowledge structure to incorporate new information in a new field. Because the student cannot hold the material internally as he analyzes it, he instead instantiates the knowledge, concretizes it by getting it down on paper in the form of a summary. Once he has filled up four or five pages, he may not recognize the difference between summary and analysis in a strange field (analysis is always an account of what is not visible), and so he feels the paper is finished.

There are other manifestations of this double tendency, the tendency to seek out a less demanding form of discourse in the face of cognitive overload and the paired tendency to seize on concrete features of the problem: How often have we seen a student give us back, word-for-word, the language of the assignment? Again, why be surprised when this is the typical behavior of a novice problem solver—seize on the most concrete element of the problem. How often do we get a narrative of the student's thinking rather than an exploration of the results of that thinking? Again, why be surprised when a student organizes her thinking in the most con-crete form available—the narrative. How often have we suggested five or six points for students to think about in connection with a problem, only to have them devote one paragraph to each point, in the order the points appeared in the assignment? Again, it is the move toward concreteness, both as a way to reduce the cognitive burden and as a typical novice move. So not only might she in fact lose control over some of her tentatively entrenched verbal skills; she may seem even more immature by seizing on an inappropriately concrete component of my problem.

In sum, of the two metaphors—that of the graph and that of the group—the second urges us toward ways of conceiving educational progress, cognitive development, in ways that seem more engaging, perhaps more productive than the widely and tacitly accepted graph-model of development. By the group metaphor, we are all novices in some regard. The advantage we have over our students is that we don't have to reveal it to them.

I don't want to suggest that all students behave in these ways. Some seem to master their fields with ease, writing well about whatever problem they attack. They tend to establish expectations, however, because they move up the scale, as anticipated. In fact, they may be the small miracles in education.

Nor do I want to claim that the insights of Piaget, Kohlberg, Perry and other developmentalists are not powerful, illuminating, explanatory. All of us recognize in our classes the students who precisely fit Piaget's description of a concrete operational thinker, Kohlberg's description of the conventional moral reasoner, Perry's description of the dualist and multiple-relativist. But as we plan curricula, as we make judgments about why our students behave as they do, as we measure failure and success, we might ponder this: It is true that we behave in ways which depend on cognitive growth defined in some global, holistic sense. A thirty-year old does not seem to think like a thirteen-year old. Much of that difference is due to experience, to increased knowledge, to learning how to sound like a thirty-year old. But some of it is also due to something that we all recognize as a mature quality of mind.

I am suggesting, however, that when we think about cognitive growth in the context of our teaching and curriculum planning, we might deliberately for a time turn from a model of growth that is mappable onto the door-jam that we use to measure our children's increasing height and try out the model of intellectual growth as socialization into a community of discourse. Such a model has its shortcomings. As some participants in the Chicago Institutes have suggested, it can easily degenerate into a superficial approach to social knowledge—just learn the tricks of voice, just learn how to sound like someone in the field, just learn the conventions—that's what's important. Of course, none of us subscribe to that notion, but it is a notion that a superficial grasp of this principle of socialization allows. It is also a model that seems to suggest that the end of socialization is full membership, when the end of education should be to change the community, to break mindless conventions.

In fact, the metaphor of the community invites exactly an inquiry into that objective, because the closed circle invites us to think about what happens when someone decides to leave the community. The metaphorical question is, Do we break out of it by leaving it behind or rising above it? And what kind of risk is entailed by that rejection? The risk of leaving off the voice of the community is apparent: we no longer are able to signal the authority of our insider's status, by using an insider's voice. We risk much when we seem to be too clear, too simple, to accessible to those not thoroughly socialized into our community. To achieve the respect that comes with authority, we must rely on other kinds of power that we may not have.

For many Institute participants, this more general voice is the object of liberal education. Few would disagree, but the nice problem is whether our students can in fact avoid passing through some period of socialization in which they succumb to that entirely predictable and natural need to sound like an insider. I do not know the answer to that question. I think it is probably not possible, but even if it were, I think it educationally valuable for a student to work within a well-developed field simply to understand what it means to be socialized into a community of knowledge. And if they are to be socialized, it is hard to imagine their avoiding all the characteristics of those who don't quite get the voice right at first, who try to sound too professional. Under any circumstances, however, the metaphor of the group again invites us to ask questions that the graph does not.

Will the Institute continue to emphasize this metaphor of the group over the metaphor of the graph? To the degree that it reflects what goes on in the community of those interested in critical thinking and problem solving, it probably will. But if the metaphor of the group is appropriate to the Institute itself, then it will have to question itself. At what point will it become merely a way to socialize those interested in cognitive/intellectual growth into the kinds of conventional questions it has been exploring? At some point, it will begin to question itself. Perhaps the response to this volume will begin that process.

Index

"Understanding Your Own Writing Process,"
209–210
in logic
argument identification: tree diagram, 134–136
Euler and Venn diagrams, 137–141
logical relationships, 136–137
students' difficulty in doing argumentative essays,
156
Assimilation, 10, 11, 12, 13, 38
Assimilators. *See* Styles
Atkins, C. Douglas, 242n.6
Audience, 4, 91, 132, 155, 165, 171, 172, 173, 177,
200, 209, 239
Automated processes, 186, 205
Averröes, 174
Avicenna, 174
Awareness. *See also* Consciousness
levels of, 189–192, 205
active awareness, 190–193
automated processes, 189–190
reflective awareness, 191–192
tacit processes, 189
of strategies, 89. *See also* Metacognition

Bacon, Francis, 126, 165
Baier, Kurt, 179
Bain, Alexander, 162, 165, 177. *See also* Discourse,
modes of
Baker, L., 61
Barker, Evelyn M., 104
Barry, Vincent, 100
Barthes, Roland, 227
Basseches, Michael, xx, 1, 2, 3, 5, 6, 24, 36, 37,
44, 53, 164
Bayesian model, 78
Beardsley, Monroe, 134, 144n.8
Becker, Alton, 192, 206, 239
Behaviorism, 1
Belcher, Gerald L., 143n.3
Belief-forming process, 87, 91, 147, 148, 153, 154
case for identifying myself as, 149–152
as a developmental stage, 158
Belsey, Catherine, 241n.5
Benveniste, Emile, 229, 230, 232. *See also* Semiotics
Bereiter, Carl, 61, 189, 191, 203
Bernstein, Richard, 170
Better Reasoning, 100
Beyer, Barry K., 105
Binkley, Robert W., 104
Biondi, A. M., 50
Birds of North America, 195, 197
Bizzell, Patricia, 242n.6
Blair, J. Anthony, xix, 86, 88, 90, 93, 96, 98, 99,
100, 101, 104, 107n.1, 114, 116, 127, 131, 132,
143n.6, 165, 166, 225
Blais, J., 79
Blonsky, Marshall, 241n.5
Bogart, Humphrey, 181
Braine, Martin D.S., 16
Brainstorming, 197
Bransford, John D., 50, 55
Britton, James, 178
Broughton, J., 17
Brown, Ann L., 55, 61, 65, 187, 191
Browne, M. Neil, 104

Bruffee, Kenneth A., xx, 90, 162, 163, 164, 166, 167
Bruner, Jerome S., 51
Bruun, Bertel, 195
Buchler, Justus, 240n.1

Cacioppo, John T., 78
Campione, Joseph C., 55
Cannizzo, Samuel R., 61
Carey, Linda, 193, 201
Carney, James D., 95, 107n.3
Casaubon, Isaac, 175
Cashmore, J., 47
Cederblom, Jerry, xix, 87, 88, 91, 100, 101, 104, 131,
159n.3, 166
Charity, principle of, 99, 143n.6
Chase, William G., 65
Chi, Michael T. H., 65, 76
Chicago (University of) Institutes, vii, 247, 254, 255
Chisholm, Roderick M., 149, 159n.2
Classification. *See* Representation
Closed system, 29, 37, 38, 40, 49. *See also* Open
systems
and sex-roles, 39
Cognition, xvi, 12, 38, 55, 69, 193, 240n.2. *See also*
Intuitive cognition; Peirce; Processes
sociocultural bases of, 242n.7
in the writing process, 205
Cognitive. *See also* Equilibrium; Representation;
Schema; Strategies; Subject of cognition
development, 1, 9, 16, 22, 41, 44, 47, 49, 156. *See
also* Perry
difficulty of measuring, 245
and willingness to reason, 156
processes, 192, 205, 206, 210
psychology, xv, xvi, xvii, 1, 2, 47, 53, 93, 106,
121, 132, 162, 164, 187, 190, 240n.3, 242n.7
developmental and information processing as
distinct approaches in, 1–2
as mentalistic, 213
skills, 13, 166, 245
contrasted with cognitive styles, 60–65
structure, 16
subject, the, 163, 242n.6
Cohen, Morris R., 122n.6
Coke, Edward, xxn.1
Colby, A., 58
Coleridge, Samuel Taylor, 185, 187
Collaborative learning, 166, 218–221. *See also*
Problem solving
peer learning groups, 245
Collins, Alan, 78
Commitment. *See* Perry
Community, xix, xxin.4, 163, 216, 242n.7. *See also*
Social constructionism; Peirce
of discourse, 210, 250
the interpretive, 250
of peers, 219
requirements for membership in, 252
socialization into a community of knowledge, 247
student, 164
transitional support, 221
Comparative philologists, 178
Composing, 190, 192, 198, 204–206
a draft, 238
as a dynamic process, 211

Higher education compared to psychotherapy, 43
Hippocrates, 172
Hirst, Paul H., xxn.3
Hitchcock, David, 99, 100, 101, 102
Hoaglund, John, 104
Hobbes, Thomas, 155, 156, 170–171
  and detachment in writing, 155–156
  Leviathan, 155, 156, 170
Hogarth, Robin M., 78
Holistic developmental model contrasted with social
  model, 247
Holistic growth, 246
Holther, William B., 99, 122n.3
Homer, 173
Hopkins, Gerard Manley, 198
Horace, 173
  Ars Poetica, 173
Horkheimer, Max, 30, 179
Horz, H., 30
Howell, Wilbur Samuel, 175, 176
Human Problem Solving, 70
Hume, David
  Dialogues Concerning Natural Religion, 122n.2
  effectiveness in writing, 154
  and fallacies, 122n.2
  Treatise of Human Nature, 154
Hypothetico-deductive reasoning, 14–16. *See also*
  Validity

I
  as the producing subject, the discursive subject,
    230
  use of first person in writing, 251
"I've been right all along," 147–148
Ill-structured problems. *See* Problems
Indoctrination, 23
Induction. *See also* Deduction; Mill, John Stuart
  and the rhetorical enthymeme, 173
Inductive
  generalizations, in Aristotle, 172
  logic, 100, 106
Inference, 190, 201
  conductive, 104
  criteria, 104
  deductive, 94, 102, 112
  dialectically acceptable, 104
  plausible, 104
  probabilistic, 104
Informal fallacies. *See* Fallacies
Informal Logic Newsletter, 86, 102, 107n.1
Informal logic, xv, xvi, xix, 5, 7, 88, 89, 90, 91,
  165, 178, 225
  contrasted with applied logic, 86
  definition of, 96, 107n.1, 112
  disagreements on
    whether abilities or attitudes are the aim of, 104
    deductive-inductive distinction, 102–103
    domain dependence and independence, 104
    role of fallacies in, 103–104
    role of formal logic in, 101
    over inference criteria, 104
    premise criteria, 104
    whether to teach informal or applied logic,
      101–102

history of, 93–97
influential textbooks of, 97–100
  Kahane, *Logic and Contemporary Rhetoric,* 97
  Scriven, *Reasoning,* 97
  Thomas, *Practical Reasoning in Natural
    Language,* 97
themes in
  emphasis on argument construction, 99–100
  real-life examples of arguments, 98–99
  treatment of fallacies, in, 99
and rhetoric, 179
Informal reasoning, 5, 6, 70, 77–80. *See also*
  Strategies
  in economics, 79
Informal thinking, 179
Informal processing, 1, 2
  model of problem solving, 70
Inhelder, Bärbel, 11, 13, 14, 16
Inquiry. 144n.15, 241n.3
Intellectual autonomy, 245
Intelligence, 9, 10–11
Introduction to Logic and Critical Thinking, 100
Intuitive cognition, 224
Invention, 175, 176, 194. *See also* Rhetoric
  methods of, 142, 144n.13, 206
  morphological analysis, 142
  sliding column method, 142
  tagmemic analysis, 142

Jakobson, Roman, 178
James, William, 38, 186, 240n.3
Jameson, F., 30
Janik, Allan, 104
Jay, M., 30
Jeffrey, Richard, 107n.3
Johnson, Fred, 102
Johnson, Michael, 242n.6
Johnson, Ralph H., xix, 86, 88, 90, 93, 96, 98, 99,
  100, 101, 104, 107n.1, 114, 127, 131, 132,
  143n.6, 165, 166, 225
Johnson, Samuel, 153, 155, 189
  Preface to Shakespeare, 155
Johnson-Laird, Philip N., 78
Joseph, H. W., 122n.6
Journal, use of, 65, 206–208, 210. *See also*
  Assignments
Judgment, 55

Kahane, Howard, 96, 97, 98, 99, 101, 132. *See also*
  Informal logic
Kant, Immanuel, 85, 170, 177, 241n.3
  on Aristotle's logic, 85
  Critique of Judgment, 177
  Critique of Practical Reason, 177
  Critique of Pure Reason, 177
  neglect of rhetoric, 177
Keeley, Stuart M., 104
Keeney, Terence J., 61
Kilminster, R., 30
King, Patricia M., 2, 4, 17, 19, 20, 87
Kinneavy, James L., xviii, 162, 164, 165, 181
Kitchener, Karen S., 2, 4, 17, 19, 20, 87
Knowledge. *See also* Development; Social
  Constructionism; Aristotle

Network of meaning. *See* Strategies
Newell, Allen, 70, 74, 143n.4, 144n.11
Newton, Isaac, 51, 126, 165
Nisbett, Richard E., 179, 180, 189, 192
Nodine, Barbara F., 143
Noller, R. B., 50
Nolt, John Eric, 101, 102, 104
　Informal Logic, 102
Nonformal reasoning in college students, 16
Nosich, Gerald M., 100, 104
Novice-Expert. *See* Expert-Novice

O'Brien, David P., 16
O'Connor, Finbarr W., xix, 86, 87, 89, 90, 91, 101, 143n.3, 144
Odell, Lee, 188, 189
Olbrechts-Tyteca, L., 179
Olson, David R., 197
Ong, Walter J., 174, 175, 176, 177
Ontology, 27, 41
　dialectical, 27, 29, 33
Open systems, 38. *See also* Closed systems
Opper, Sylvia, 13
Ornstein, P. A., 61
Osborn, Alex F., 142
Outlines. *See* Text-processing research

Paradigm. *See also* Kuhn
　expert-novice paradigm, 69
　of writing, 237
Paraphrase, 205
　for gist, 61
　as representation, 204
Parker, John F., 102
Parnes, S. J., 50
Paul, Richard, 104, 120
Paulsen, David W., 100, 101, 104, 159n.3
Peer review, 3, 90
Peirce, Charles Sanders, 78, 163, 224, 225, 226, 232, 233, 234, 235, 238, 240n.3–241, 78, 149. *See also* Abduction; Intuitive cognition; Pragmaticism; *Praxis*
　cognition, 224, 226, 232, 233
　community as idea of the future, 234
　community as interpretant, 233, 234
　and contemporary semiotics, 232–235
　habit of habit-change, 240
　and Saussure, 233
　signification and interpretation, 232
　signifier and signified, 233
　"A Survey of Pragmatism," 235
　thinking as habit-change, 235
　on Zeno's paradox, 224–226, 232
Penner, B. C., 73, 74, 76, 77, 193
Perelman, Chaim, 179
Perkins, David N., 78, 79
Perry, William G., Jr., 2, 4, 17, 18, 42, 58, 87, 247, 248, 249, 254
　commitment, 57, 246
　dualism, 57, 58, 246
　escape, 57
　multiplicity, 57
　relativism, 57, 58, 246
　retreat, 57

scheme of cognitive and ethical development, 56–57
　temporizing, 57
Persuasion, 170, 180
Peter of Spain, 175
Petty, Richard E., 78
Piaget, Jean, 1, 2, 4, 9, 10, 11, 12, 13, 14, 15, 16, 24, 29, 37, 38, 41, 49, 55, 87, 164, 246, 247, 248, 249, 254. *See also* Accommodation; Assimilation; Concrete operations; Equilibrium; Formal operations; Hypothetico-deductive reasoning; Preformal; Preparational; Scheme; Sensorimotor
　constructivism, 12, 49, 164
　and formal logic, 16, 39
　regulation
　　active, 55
　　autonomous, 55
　　conscious, 55, 59
　theory of intellectual development, 10–13
Pike, Kenneth, 192, 206, 239
Planning in writing, 194, 206
Plato, xviii, xxn.2, xxn.3, 4, 154, 165, 169, 170, 171, 174
　and dialogue, 154
　dialogues, dialectical thinking and writing, 172
　Gorgias, 170
　Ion, 169
　Phaedrus, 170, 171
　poetic vs. expert knowledge, 169
　Republic, xviii, 5
　rhetor's knowledge contrasted with expert's, 170
Plausible, xxi. *See also* Inference
Poetic thinking and writing, 173–174
Poetry, 175
Pollock, Frederick, 179
Polya, G., 50, 51, 52
Popper, Karl, 31
Posposel, Howard, 95, 107n.3
Post, Timothy A., 69, 71, 73, 74, 76, 77, 193
Post-formal level, 2, 40
Pound, Roscoe, xxn.1
Pragmatism, 226, 241n.3
Praxis, 170, 235
Preformal thinker, 14, 15
Preoperational stage, 13
Prewriting, 237
Principia Mathematica, 85
Probability, 174. *See also* Inference
　in Ramus, 176
Problem definition, 44n.1, 208
　accepted uncritically in higher education, 44
　and dialectical analysis, 33, 34, 35
Problem examples
　balance scale task, 61
　crypt-arithmetic problems, 50
　four-card problem, 78
　hobbits and orcs problem, 143n.4
　missionaries and cannibals problem, 70, 143n.4
　necklace problem, 49
　sample problems, 48
　Smith-Jones-Robinson problems, 140
　surgeon problem, 49
Problem finding, 51